STATEMENT CONCERNING PUBLICATIONS OF
RUSSELL SAGE FOUNDATION

Russell Sage Foundation was established in 1907 by Mrs. Russell Sage "for the improvement of social and living conditions in the United States of America." In carrying out its purpose the Foundation maintains a staff which, among other duties, conducts studies of social conditions, authorized by the General Director, where new information, its analysis and interpretation seem necessary in order to formulate and advance practicable measures aimed at improvement. From time to time the Foundation publishes the results of these studies in book or pamphlet form.

In formulating the problem for study, in mapping out a plan of work on it, in collecting facts, in drawing conclusions, and in the presentation of findings, authors of Foundation studies, who are always either members of the staff or specially commissioned research workers, have the benefit of the criticism and advice of their colleagues in the organization. Full freedom is given research workers for the final decision on all of these steps, and in presenting and interpreting both factual material and conclusions in their own way. While the general responsibility for management of the Foundation is vested in the Board of Trustees, the responsibility for facts, conclusions, and interpretations rests with the research workers alone and not upon the Foundation, its trustees, or other members of the staff. Publication under the imprint of the Foundation does not imply agreement by the organization or its members with opinions or interpretations of authors. It does imply that care has been taken that the research on which a book is based has been thoroughly done.

LAWYERS, LAW SCHOOLS
AND
THE PUBLIC SERVICE

BY

ESTHER LUCILE BROWN

Director, Department of
Studies in the Professions
RUSSELL SAGE FOUNDATION

NEW YORK
RUSSELL SAGE FOUNDATION
1948

WM. F. FELL CO., PRINTERS
PHILADELPHIA

TABLE OF CONTENTS

3

INTRODUCTION

"This country, in a relatively short time, has been transformed from an organization of society with predominantly local self-government, individual enterprise, and comparatively mild governmental regulation to a highly centralized, bureaucratic state of behemoth proportions in which practically all economic life is subject to or affected by governmental rule and regulation. This transformation poses and will continue to pose with great urgency tremendous problems upon the solution of which the preservation of a free society depends. Predominantly our policy-makers in the field of government and public administration, the men who make and carry out our decisions, who shape our way of life, and who determine this country's destiny have been, are, and in the foreseeable post-war world will continue to be lawyers. A survey of the direct role lawyers play in our federal and state governments and the powerful indirect influence they exert in their professional capacities makes this statement a simple, inescapable truth. Because of the inevitable part lawyers will play in the solution of these problems it seems obvious that one basic function of any law school in the future must be the conscious and systematic training of leaders in policy-making and policy-administration for the achievement of those values which are the goal of a good way of life in such a free society. A lawyer grounded only in the technical aspects of the law lacks the equipment to guide those destinies which his position and his activities necessarily determine. His training must include a synthesis of relevant human experience and knowledge in order to provide adequate guides for making and carrying out wise policy decisions."

The above paragraph, written by Professor George E. Osborne of Stanford University Law School as part of his contribution to the report in December, 1946, by the Committee on Aims and

Objectives of Legal Education of the Association of American Law Schools, is quoted here for two reasons. It is almost the very résumé of the thesis of this monograph which the writer might have prepared. But what is more significant, its statement of implications for legal education is testimony that law-school teachers are discussing, or at least beginning to discuss, the necessity for "the conscious and systematic training of leaders in [public] policy-making and policy-administration."

Differences of opinion—often profound—exist about the appropriate role of governmental intervention in the lives of the American people. Some persons wish government to be moved much farther in the direction of the service state and of greater social planning; others fear the encroachment of official power and wish the state to be sharply restrained. Regardless of these differences in outlook, the fact remains that government—federal, state, and local—today constitutes "America's greatest industry." And similarly, it is a statistical fact that lawyers play a dominant part in that "industry." The conclusion, therefore, appears almost inescapable that those professional schools which bear the burden of training future lawyers can scarcely fail, without being derelict to the trust society has reposed in them, to consider whether the professional education provided is adequate to serve the needs of government.

Because of the long-continued interest of Russell Sage Foundation in seeing the public service gain in efficiency and social responsibility, the Foundation has expressed its interest in the training of that profession which occupies so commanding a position in governmental affairs by approving preparation of this monograph, and also of Dr. Eric F. Schweinburg's Law Training in Continental Europe, which it published in 1945. The concern of the writer, therefore, is not here with legal education in general as was the case in her earlier monograph, Lawyers and the Promotion of Justice. Rather is she concerned with the question of how the law school may minister more effectively to the education of those many thousands of law-trained persons who will subsequently find themselves legislators, judges, and members—

on the policy-making levels—of the executive branch of government, or who, as lawyers outside the government, will nevertheless exert large influence over it.

The criticism will almost immediately be made by some, particularly by persons who fail to note the significance of the last clause in the preceding paragraph, that were professional training oriented toward the needs of the public service, it would be done at the expense of those numerically more important lawyers who enter and remain in the private practice of law. On two important counts this criticism can hardly be supported.

First, the private lawyer of the future can ill afford, as Professor Walter Gellhorn has cogently argued, to be unaware of what the government lawyer must know. "The fact that government is today a business partner or competitor or cherished customer cannot be overlooked by those who expect to serve business as legal advisers."[1] To no inconsiderable degree legislatures are hearing bodies before whom the different interests appear, each arguing its own point of view. Administrative proceedings, furthermore, and their attendant negotiations and litigations are not unilateral. When government law is in the making, private lawyers share in forming the product. So far beyond the offices of the government does the work of government now extend that even legislation, decision, and administration go forward in hundreds of non-official law offices the nation over. The enlarged participation of the private practitioner in governmental matters in the last generation leads to the supposition that prospective private lawyers, currently attending professional schools, will have practices largely colored by the same factors that will determine the activities of the government lawyer.

Second, the alterations in legal education which have been suggested in this monograph are not generally directed toward specific, highly technical training for the public service. Rather are they suggestions for enlarged and enriched ways of looking at law and its social function and at the art of the lawyer, that

[1] "The Law Schools' Responsibility for Training Public Servants," in University of Chicago Law Review, April, 1942, p. 474.

many thoughtful persons have considered potentially beneficial to the entire bar, regardless of type of specialization. Even the proposal for greatly increased attention to legislative drafting, which might be viewed as a narrowly technical subject, has been made in the belief that training in statutory draftsmanship is of exceptional value in developing ability in synthesis and in critical judgment—abilities as indispensable to the private practitioner as to the government lawyer.

If the monograph has erred, therefore, in emphasis, it is not in advocacy of preparation for public service at the expense of private practice, but in lack of greater precision about the nature of the professional education for public service that could be provided on the undergraduate level by law schools which would best serve the broad interests of government. The future may come to show how training for public service can be made at once more specific than that now visualized and simultaneously more rich in intellectual content and social outlook. As yet, however, this achievement is in an initial stage. Scores of law instructors have said, with much seeming validity, that more specific training for the public service cannot be given in the undergraduate law school for the very reason that most students do not know what type of legal work they will enter. In answer, Professor Elliott E. Cheatham has made the penetrating observation, "There is a similar uncertainty as to the field of private practice into which a student will go. The law schools have not believed that this uncertainty on the private side kept them from giving effective training to private practitioners."

Greater achievement, moreover, has been retarded by the fact that detailed knowledge is scanty about what lawyers *actually* do in the contemporary practice of law. Hence planning of law-school curricula has had to rest largely on *a priori* assumptions of the nature of law work. There has been growing recognition that the role of the lawyer as advocate is decreasing in relative importance; that his role as a counselor, draftsman, mediator, negotiator, and public policy-maker is increasing. But there is nothing of the precision of knowledge that a "job analysis" would provide, and that is indispensable if more than very general reorientation is to be made in teaching content and methods. The survey of the legal profession on which the American Bar Association is now embarking, if executed with scientific precision and considerable detail, should furnish to legal education a substantial body of factual knowledge from which decisions about more specific training might be possible.

For the purpose of attempting to discover to what degree and with what efficiency legal education was preparing men and women to serve the interests of government—legislative, judicial, and executive—the writer spent much of the time from the beginning of 1939 until Pearl Harbor in visits to twenty-three law schools that stretch from the Atlantic to the Pacific and from close to the Canadian border to the Gulf of Mexico. Thirteen of these schools are in the Middle States, if that term may be used to include the area between the Allegheny and the Rocky Mountains; three in the Northeast; three in the Southeast; and four on the Pacific Coast. Selection of schools to visit was determined, to some degree, by regional distribution. It was considered essential that all sections of the nation be represented, and that the Northeast—because of the greater age or prestige of some of its institutions and its proximity to Russell Sage Foundation—should not be overrepresented. Selection was determined, more importantly, on the basis of the ability shown or the desire expressed by a particular school to bring its curriculum into greater conformity with contemporary economic and social developments as they influenced the work of the lawyer. Although the twenty-three schools varied markedly in the size of their budgets and teaching staffs and in their library and clinical resources, they represented, with very few exceptions and perhaps with only a handful of omissions, the dynamic, on-going movement within legal education as it existed at the outbreak of World War II.

It was a period of fertility and development in the schools visited, especially in the Middle States, but also in parts of the

Southeast and along the Pacific Coast. Leadership in legal education was no longer centered primarily on the Atlantic Seaboard. "The great Eastern schools" were, in fact, momentarily weary or disorganized and were waiting to get their breath for a renewed effort. (Encouraging reports from several of them now indicate that that effort has been begun.) Their eclipse in leadership worked hardship on those institutions which had long used the experience of the eastern schools as a most persuasive argument in appealing to university administrators or even to colleagues for change. Other schools, however, gained a vitalizing sense of release from eastern influence; they felt at last free to experiment "on their own"; and their experiments carried them far toward building regional centers of leadership.

The writer's extended and sometimes repeated visits to these particular schools left her with the conviction that perhaps nothing in legal education at the turn of the decade was so heartening or so potentially valuable to our country as was this growth of regional leadership. Even certain schools, located on the geographic periphery or in the most recently developed sections of the United States, were not only moving in pace with institutions nearer the center of the federal government and of financial and industrial power, but were helping to accentuate the tempo.

In all intellectual honesty it must be said, however, that much of this newer leadership rested upon an exceedingly precarious base. Often it was buttressed neither by adequate financial resources nor by sufficient numbers of able, forward-looking, and energetic instructors to provide substantial guarantee of continuance. Let the dean and no more than two or three of his faculty leave some of these schools, and they might plunge from a position of leadership to a level where they closely resembled many other undifferentiated schools of law. Obviously, if legal education were to contribute increasingly to the national welfare, such uncertainties would have to be lessened.

The last, and longest, section of this monograph is the record of those aspects of this on-going movement throughout the

United States which seemed to the author most applicable to education for government service. Practically everything set down in these pages, except for references to a few law-review articles, rests upon what was learned from individual and group conferences with the faculty and administrative officers, and from attendance at classes in these twenty-three schools. Aside from a few figures clearly applicable to legal education in general and an occasional mention of specialized training for public service on the graduate level, the report is based exclusively upon that segment of the undergraduate law-school world which was supposedly representative of the most progressive thought of the period.

Illustrations only are given of experiments. Many of the illustrations were selected from specific courses being offered, or plans for new courses being formulated in a particular school at the time it was visited. Several of them represent especially encouraging postwar developments. No useful purpose would have been served, it seemed, by describing the entire curriculum of any one school, or by noting all the experiments being made in any one field. Some of the examples are undoubtedly less important than other similar undertakings that did not come to the writer's attention. Hence, they should be viewed as, in no sense, an inclusive count of frequency and distribution. Rather are they an attempt to designate the nature, and very roughly to estimate the degree, of movement in these representative institutions that might be put to the service of the prospective lawyer who would engage in governmental activities.

To many readers, particularly to law instructors who have worked so valiantly to enlarge the scope of the professional curriculum that they have sometimes come to confuse accomplishment with desire, the report will seem a very pessimistic one. It must be recalled, however, that its purpose is not to record the many and distinguished achievements in the history of legal education, but to consider a particular area of achievement whose cultivation, as it happened, had not yet extended far beyond introductory efforts.

The wrench from traditionalism had been perhaps even more painful for legal education than for other types of professional training. To divert some of the attention that had long been lavished upon the judicial process and private contracts and property rights to the legislative and administrative processes, to public contracts and property rights, and to civil rights was a slow and hazardous undertaking. So was the effort to view law, not as THE LAW, but as a flexible, ever-changing instrumentality created to aid in the resolution of social and economic problems. If the report, therefore, appears far less encouraging than the writer would wish, it nevertheless suggests that enough elements of reorientation, readily adaptable to general use, had been laid down to permit law schools to move rapidly ahead in the postwar period, should they so decide.

These visits revealed that law schools had considerable generic information about the nature of the work done by the judge, the legislator, and the lawyer engaged in litigation in the Department of Justice or in regulatory functions in the "old-line" administrative agencies. About the legal work done generally in the executive branch of government, however, information often seemed entirely too inadequate to provide a base for curriculum-planning. Answers were needed to numerous questions. In what specific kinds of tasks, other than litigatory and quasi-judicial, did government lawyers engage? How and to what extent did official work differ from that of private law offices? How were lawyers recruited? Were they dependent upon the training that had been provided them by the law schools, or did the government make formal efforts to supplement this earlier training?

One of the most important questions was that of whether government lawyers were policy-makers in any considerable numbers, and if so, *how* they made policy. Were only those who came to occupy the highest legal positions or those who passed into the ranks of administrators responsible for significant policy-making? Or was it made, although less conspicuously, in a diversity of ways by many lawyers on many levels? If so, were the law schools providing any substantial training for this essential task?

Answers to these questions were sought in the federal law offices in Washington. Had opportunity permitted, answers would also have been sought in the offices of some of the state capitals and large cities, and in those widely separated spots where the future of our national life is being decided through the development (or the withholding) of programs for irrigation, reclamation, electrification, and so on. The writer is cognizant of the extreme importance of governmental vitality in regional offices and below the federal level if democracy is to be maintained, if the several sections of the country are to achieve opportunity for maximum economic, social, and political development, and if the states are to be truly partners in a union of states.

At the time when the writer began her visits to Washington neither Harold D. Lasswell and Myres S. McDougal's article in the Yale Law Journal for March, 1943, entitled "Legal Education and Public Policy: Professional Training in the Public Interest," nor "The Lawyer's Role in Public Administration," by Fritz Morstein Marx, in the April, 1946, issue of the Journal, had been published and hence she was without the valuable guidance that these two penetrating articles might have given her. However, several "top-flight career men" and several law-school instructors who had come to the federal capital for the duration of the war interested themselves in exploring the subject with her. Broadly suggestive answers were found to most of the questions. They furnish part of the first, and all of the second section of this monograph.

Some of the answers were scarcely rewarding—as in the case of the programs of the Board of Legal Examiners, the In-Service Training Joint Committee, and the Yale Law School's experiment in apprenticeship training—if measured in terms either of the length of life or the size of the undertakings. When measured, however, in terms of their accomplishment in defining areas of "unfinished business" of government and legal education, and indicating ways for attending to that business, they warrant the rather full description that has been given them.

A score of attorneys, and law instructors temporarily in Washington, contributed to the answer of the policy-making function of government lawyers. Although many were able, when confronted with the question, to visualize only those forms of policy-making with which they were most intimately connected, the composite answer sharpens knowledge, it is believed, of the way and degree to which the official law office engages in that function. For the very reason that so much of the function is inextricably woven into legal, rather than more purely administrative work, it is both pervasive and continuing. As such, it offers a challenge to legal education only slightly smaller than the challenge offered to prepare future judges, legislators, and administrators for making and executing policy. "The socially important group in a law school," if Professor Cheatham may be quoted again, "is not composed of those who will represent private business. The men who will go into government service as elective or administrative officials, and next after them, those who will go into the government civil service, are of greater social importance. The law schools are in error in looking to the success of their graduates in 'Wall Street' practice as the measure of their own success."

To the deans and the many individual faculty members of those law schools spanning the United States and to several federal attorneys who provided long and invaluable assistance, the writer wishes to extend grateful appreciation.

E. L. B.

PART ONE

IMPORTANT ROLE PLAYED BY LAWYERS
IN OFFICIAL POSITIONS

PART I

IMPORTANT ROLE PLAYED BY LAWYERS IN OFFICIAL POSITIONS

EXTENT OF PARTICIPATION OF LAWYERS IN GOVERNMENT

ANYONE who has ever visited the annual convention of the American Bar Association and comparable meetings of state and local bar associations rarely forgets the introduction to most presidential addresses. It is the tale of the greatness of the American bench and bar, as measured by the number of law-trained men who have occupied commanding positions in the federal and state governments. The following paragraphs recapitulate such an introduction. Only the data relating to governors and state legislators have been interpolated by the writer for the purpose of further emphasizing essential facts.

"The achievements of our great profession and the prestige to which we have attained," begins the president, "can best be appraised by recalling the vast number of men drawn from bench and bar who have played significant roles in the government of the United States." Of the 52 signers of the Declaration of Independence, 25 were lawyers; of the 55 members of the Constitutional Convention, 31 represented the profession of law. Lawyers, moreover, dominated the ratifying conventions in the several states that gave us our federal Bill of Rights. Twenty-three of our 33 presidents have been lawyers.

A count, made in a recent year, showed that 66 per cent of the Congress—74 per cent of the Senate and 58 per cent of the House of Representatives—were members of the bar. So were 27 of the 48 governors. Six of the 27 had already served as attorneys general for their states, 11 had been county attorneys, and 6 had been city attorneys. Six had been either United States district attorneys or assistant district attorneys, and 7 had been judges.[1]

[1] News Bulletin of Public Administration Clearing House, Chicago, March 29 and 30, 1943.

In the state legislatures lawyers generally constitute between 20 and 25 per cent of the membership, but there are several states with percentages of more than 40. Although law-trained persons are nowhere in the numerical majority, they far exceed the representatives of any other vocation except the farmers of a few agrarian states. A not uncommon type of newspaper headline is "96 Lawyers, No Doctors in New Legislature." Nothing is more surprising than to examine the occupational classification of a legislative body. Of the 100 members in 1940 of the lower house of Louisiana, for example, 37 were lawyers. No other group exceeded 9 in number, and 19 occupations were listed as having only one representative each.

If the bar has played a role of major importance in giving the United States its chief executives and its law-makers, it has exercised an even more dominant role in the judicial branch of government. The entire judiciary—federal, state, and local—reposes almost exclusively in the hands of persons trained in the law.

"Such," concludes the president, "is the record of the extent to which the bench and bar have assumed positions of leadership in this country."

The facts as stated in these presidential addresses are always essentially correct. With them there can be little disagreement. Whether one or two men who participated in the signing of the Declaration and an equally small number who attended the Constitutional Convention should be classified as lawyers is debatable, but the question is of small importance.

Neither is there any serious disagreement with the purpose of these utterances. Sometimes representatives of other professions conclude that a larger degree of modesty might be more becoming to the bar whose triumphs have been so conspicuous that recapitulation is scarcely necessary. They admit, however, that had their own professions had such unparalleled good fortune they might have said as much. They recognize, too, that many a speaker has drawn from his laudatory presentation a conclusion of vital significance that would perhaps be more readily escapable were the "success story" less spectacular. He has asserted, often emphatically, that the attainment of high position carries with it a serious obligation to serve the public with intelligence and competency, as well as with integrity and unselfishness.

It is with the fulfillment of that obligation that this monograph is concerned. Unfortunately speeches setting forth the impressive numbers of law-trained men in official life, even when concluded with passionate exhortation that the bar assume greater social responsibility, seem to many both within and outside the legal profession to be peculiarly ineffective. The day of winning souls through exhortation may have passed forever. During the past quarter-century a substantial public contribution has been made in such undertakings as improvement in judicial procedure, drafting of uniform state laws, and restatement of the common law. In the recent war provision was made for legal services for persons in the armed forces and their families, many of whom would not otherwise have been able to avail themselves of such services if the need had arisen. The administration of law in general, however, remains far behind the advance in technology, science, and medicine, while efforts to achieve legal reforms receive little support even from lawyers graduated from the "best" professional schools in the country. In a letter written nearly twenty years ago to William Draper Lewis, Dean Everett Fraser of the University of Minnesota expressed surprise and dismay over his discovery of how satisfied the legal profession is with current conditions, how few understand the defects in the American system of law, how little knowledge exists of methods utilized in other jurisdictions and of contemporary thought regarding the solution of problems, how difficult it is to awaken interest in improvement. It was this discovery that caused Dean Fraser to inaugurate those changes in the curriculum of the Minnesota Law School, described later, which then seemed radical.

A second difficulty presents itself in connection with such speeches. The recounting of law-trained men in government positions, if extended beyond presidents, governors, legislators, and judges, rarely includes more than cabinet secretaries. There is almost no mention of those many lawyers who staff the cabinet departments and the great administrative agencies. The bar is gratified, to be sure, when one of its members becomes chairman of the Federal Communications Commission, the Federal Trade Commission, the Interstate Commerce Commission, the Securities and Exchange Commission, or the Tennessee Valley Authority. It knows that the administrative process has grown enormously in importance during the past few decades, and that lawyers play an important role in determining the effectiveness of that process. It witnessed the great migration of law-trained men to the federal capital during the economic depression to join the alphabetical agencies. More recently it had opportunity to see the search being made by the government to obtain sufficient competent lawyers for war-emergency bodies.

Yet the bar has been slow to realize that the executive branch of government has come to offer to the legal profession a strikingly important opportunity for public service, not less significant than that in the legislative or even the judicial branch. It rarely stops to consider that the chairman of a powerful administrative agency that broadly regulates an entire sector of industrial development, may exert a greater influence on American life than a senator or a justice of the Supreme Court. It fails to note that some relatively unknown attorney, employed by the federal government to supervise the writing of contracts for obtaining raw materials from Latin America during the recent war, might have done more to outline inter-American relations than a distinguished ambassador. Even casual visits to federal departments and administrative bodies would impress upon the legal profession the importance of the work of attorneys in the executive branch, whether they be those at the top of the salary scale who sit on important policy-forming committees, or whether they be those in the low-income brackets who, through interpretation of procedural rulings, help to keep the agency effectively functioning.

If the bar, therefore, is to state quite honestly the measure of its participation in public life, it must admit that law-trained persons maintain a complete monopoly over one branch of government, and considerable effective control over the other two. The fact of numerical ascendancy alone indicates that, to the extent to which government exercises authority over the development and well-being of this nation, the bar is responsible in no small measure for determining the future of our society and, as a consequence, its own future. From this heavy responsibility it cannot escape except by relinquishing, or being forced to relinquish, a considerable part of its intervention in public affairs.

Many persons have concluded that less participation by lawyers and more by other professions would be wholesome. They regard concentration of responsibility in the hands of any group as potentially dangerous. Therefore, they view with favor the rise of schools of public administration, and the movement into the cabinet departments and administrative agencies of increasing numbers of economists, political scientists, agricultural and business experts, engineers, public health officials, social workers, educators, and other specialists. Some believe that the utilization of persons with varied training and experience in research, policy-making, and administration will continue until the predominance of lawyers ceases to exist. The validity of this supposition time alone will reveal. Perhaps the bar *may* eventually occupy a relatively less commanding position. Such an occurrence would not necessarily result in a decrease in the number of law-trained persons serving in a public capacity. Some of those who view the ascendancy of lawyers with concern, moreover, seem to have little appreciation of the nature and multitude of legal problems faced by every federal officer who is charged with administrative responsibility. The very fact that only attorneys can solve such problems probably puts them in an indispensable category.

Because there are as yet no marked indications of a shift in balance of power, a small but growing number of lawyers and interested laity maintain that the legal profession must come more emphatically to grips with the question of its responsibility for the continued improvement of public service than it has formerly done. In spite of the phenomenal record of law-trained men in official life, the orientation of the bar has always been decisively toward the private practice of law. It is this fact which has made thoughtful consideration of the bar's relation to government so difficult to achieve, and presidential addresses so ineffectual. Lawyers have been prepared by the law schools for private practice, and the great majority of them have entered it. From it, through inclination or circumstance, a considerable number have moved into politics. The position of city or assistant district attorney, for example, has served as a lower rung from which many have climbed to judgeships, governorships, the Congress, or the federal Department of Justice. Others, particularly after the onset of the economic depression, found private practice unremunerative or not to their liking, and consequently they sought positions in the executive branch of federal and state governments. Beginning with the 1930's many young men went directly from the law school to cabinet departments and administrative agencies. Some considered such an experience valuable apprenticeship for subsequent private practice. Some thought of public law as a career.

In spite of the fact that many lawyers either relinquish private practice or, in increasing numbers, never enter it, the bar still conceives of its function as that of advocate and counselor for private interests, whether individual or corporate. So tenaciously has it adhered to this belief that lawyers can listen to the historical record of their elder statesmen with gratification, undisturbed by qualms about the adequacy of preparation offered the legal profession for participation in public affairs.

ATTITUDES OF LAW TEACHERS TOWARD TRAINING FOR PUBLIC SERVICE

That the ascendancy of lawyers in the nation's government, particularly in the executive branch which has undergone phenomenal growth, indicates the necessity for a type of preparation different from that for the private practice of law, *as traditionally conceived*, appears to be an inescapable conclusion. (So diversified has the work of the private practitioner become that he, too, would profit perhaps equally from a different type of preparation.) Yet it is a relatively new concept to the bar as a whole, and it is disturbing to many teachers of law. Anyone who has extensively visited law classes, even in professional schools that have moved farthest from the established pattern of instruction in the common law, is impressed with the degree to which training is still directed toward prosecution of private litigation through analysis of suits between individual businessmen that were decided often in the nineteenth century by appellate tribunals.[1]

Law-school bulletins do not adequately reveal this situation. They frequently list a number of courses such as constitutional law, administrative law, and legislation. The layman naïvely assumes that these courses are designed primarily to give the student an understanding of broad constitutional issues decided by the Supreme Court, of the purpose, function, and techniques of the administrative process, and of the place of statutory law, in contrast to common law, in modern society. In a few schools the courses achieve such ends. Generally, however, the visitor finds much time lavished upon examination of judicial veto of government action, upon the legal doctrine of separation of powers or the non-delegability of legislative power, upon the tortuous problem of how to interpret statutes, and upon preparing prospective attorneys to represent the interests of clients before administrative tribunals, boards, and officers. So highly technical are the questions discussed and so largely are they viewed from the angle of the private attorney that "the average student comes to think of a government agency," the writer was once told by Professor Harry W. Jones, "as something to be appealed from rather than as an organization for the discharge of significant public service. It is hard to describe adequately the real innocence of even first-rate students with respect to fundamental problems of public administration, whenever such problems arise in law courses."

[1] For a scathing criticism of the failure of law schools to train for public practice, see Frederick K. Beutel's "The Law Schools and the New Profession of Social Technician," in American Journal of Economics and Sociology, January, 1942, pp. 93–110.

Nothing surprises the visitor more, to give one example, than to discover that the major part of the course in constitutional law may not only be limited to scrutiny of judicial opinions relating to the commerce clause and to the "due process" clause of the Fourteenth Amendment, but that these clauses are not even examined in the fullness of their constitutional implications. The commerce clause was set down expressly to give the Congress the right to regulate commerce "among the several States." The Fourteenth Amendment was adopted in 1868, it will be recalled, for the specific purpose of protecting the civil rights of the emancipated Negro. It was neither foreseen nor intended that both of these clauses would be long used by the Supreme Court as a means for striking down much of the social and economic legislation of the states.[1] Certainly a professional school must give its students technical knowledge of what the Supreme Court has held. But students need equally to be helped, either by the law school or by being required to present a college course in constitutional law, to understand the evolution of broad constitutional issues and the function of the highest court.

The law-school visitor not only discovers that "public law" courses are predominantly taught from the viewpoint of the private practitioner rather than the public administrator, but he finds that, aside from constitutional law, almost all of these courses are elective and enrollments in some of them are relatively small in the majority of schools. Students have been so influenced by the general orientation toward private practice that they believe they must center attention upon the more traditional private law courses, which they speak of as "bread and butter" courses. They generally conclude that they cannot afford to graze in the field of public law, even when it sometimes appears temptingly green.

The difference in attitudes concerning training for public administration between professors of law and professors of political science sharpens the realization of how foreign is the broader

[1] Frankfurter, Felix, The Public and Its Government. Yale University Press, New Haven, 1930, pp. 43–51.

role of legal education to the average law instructor. As early as 1912 the American Political Science Association appointed a Committee on Practical Training for Public Service. Since then it has shown considerable continuing interest in the subject. It has been indirectly but ably assisted by the Committee on Public Administration of the Social Science Research Council and the Public Administration Clearing House in Chicago, whose stimulus and long list of publications have done much to emphasize the importance of training for government work. In 1939 the American Society for Public Administration was created to provide a common forum where public officials, research workers, and educators might discuss the science and art of public administration. Until the war brought national conventions temporarily to a close, the joint annual meetings of the Society and the American Political Science Association offered a wealth of programs relating to public administration in its many aspects.

Political scientists appear, therefore, to have clearly seen the trend toward public employment, and the responsibility devolving upon the university for offering preparation for such employment. They tend to accept this responsibility, and to believe that some training can be provided that is appreciably better than no training at all. Although they recognize that much of their current teaching is weak and fumbling, they are confident that, with time and effort, materials and staffs can be radically improved. Their goal is not in doubt; only the way to reach it is still uncertain.

They are frankly surprised that the bar has so long neglected an area of training that seems to them of primary importance. They believe that unless the profession of the law takes immediate and energetic steps to cultivate this field, the schools of public administration will increasingly gain strength at the expense of the law schools. So convinced are some of them of the growing strength of curricula in public administration and of the backwardness of law schools to cultivate new areas that they have maintained that it is already too late for the writer to make representation of the law school as a potentially important instrument for increasing the competency of the public service. Like other groups, however, they fail adequately to note how indispensable to the government are legal technicians.

Law-school teachers wish, as sincerely as do political scientists, to see improvement in the quality of government. Generally, however, they do not visualize clearly the relationship between such improvement and their teaching institutions. A score of doubts assail them. Some of these doubts appear to rest on very superficial reasoning, others have real validity. An occasional professor of law still maintains that persons cannot be trained for public service. The philosophy of those who are trying to professionalize public administration is either unknown or alien to him. He places great reliance on heredity, little on educational conditioning. He concludes that lawyers "have got where they are" because of their relatively greater ability and perspicacity. He views their favored position as recognition of their merit, not as entailing an obligation to society for having conferred special privileges on them. He considers all efforts, particularly by the laity, to encourage the legal profession to improve government service not only as futile, but as a nuisance if not an encroachment upon the liberty of the bar. He has even been heard to utter the enigmatical statement, long reiterated by the American Medical Association, that laymen are "out" to socialize the professions. Although his pronouncements are incisive, they are not representative of teachers of law or of the bar. They would not warrant consideration, were it not for his frequent success in obstructing action contemplated by his colleagues.

Another type of law teacher considers reorientation of the curriculum futile, because of his pessimism about existent conditions. He points to the unsavory political methods tolerated or employed by lawyers in their effort to raise themselves to powerful public positions. To him environment is of vital significance, and the environment of the political arena is one of sin. Would it not be naïve, he queries, to assume that the law school could serve as an effective instrumentality for improving public service if one looks realistically at the sordid facts of political life? He has neither faith nor hope in the future of government institutions, or in man's ability to reshape those institutions.

Many of his associates restate his argument in a less condemnatory but, nevertheless, negative fashion. They recall the long years that frequently intervene between law-school training and public life or government employment. The environmental influences of those years could readily counteract any particular benefit, so they argue, that the school might give a man. The chances that either knowledge or social attitudes gained in professional training would survive such hazards are too large to warrant extensive reshaping of curricula.

Statements such as these seem to us to be little more than rationalizations that could not withstand free and open-minded discussion. But there are problems to which law professors point that, although not insurmountable, deserve careful consideration. All planning for the future of legal education must take them into account. It is impossible, for instance, to foresee who of the law-trained men will go into public service or into what branch. The government is widely diversified in scope and function. How can the professional school give something, besides training for advocacy and restricted areas of counseling, that would be of fundamental usefulness to a person who may subsequently find himself in a state legislature *or* in the Antitrust Division of the Department of Justice? What is the common denominator in preparation that might serve counsel to the Department of Agriculture, the Tennessee Valley Authority, or the administrative head of the Federal Security Agency? If an answer could be found to these questions, would a teaching staff be obtainable, competent to assume responsibility for such training?

These are certainly difficult questions, but their difficulty does not absolve the law schools from responsibility for squarely facing them. A solution will be found only on the basis of much painstaking examination and consideration. The writer's brief attempt to view the broad outlines of the legal work done in the executive branch of the federal government, which constitutes the second section of this monograph, seems to indicate that answers *can* be found to the above questions. Prior to the war the bar and the law schools did little even to define the problems. The legal profession, skilled in the form of research involved in the preparation of briefs relating to a wide diversity of subjects, had engaged in little research pertaining to its own profession. An occasional law school, such as that of Indiana University, had taken initial steps to tabulate the types of positions held by its alumni. Most schools, however, did not know the distribution of their graduates. In spite of the successful completion and subsequent use of job analyses in large areas of business, industry, and even in some of the professions, no such analyses had ever been made by the bar of what lawyers do, whether they be engaged in private practice or in public service.[1]

In 1943, however, this discouraging situation began to change with the publication of an article by Professors Harold D. Lasswell and Myres S. McDougal on "Legal Education and Public Policy" which engaged the profound attention of much of the law-school world.[2] It not only pointed emphatically to the need for such studies, but it undertook to define seventeen types of activities whereby lawyers make policy. At present the Harvard Law School is conducting a survey of positions occupied and nature of work engaged in by its alumni, and the Section of Legal Education and Admissions to the Bar of the American Bar Association is about to embark on a large study of the role of the lawyer in a democracy, which will supposedly include a job analysis of the functions performed by law-trained persons. If this study is carried through effectively, the bar will have comprehensive data at its disposal on the basis of which constructive plans can be made.

When the Report of the President's Committee on Civil Service Improvement appeared in 1941, the legal profession learned for the first time how many lawyers were engaged in legal positions in the federal government.[3] The number set down, as of May 15,

[1] For a description of the system of definitions of classes of legal positions in the executive branch of the federal government evolved by the United States Civil Service Commission, see pp. 44–46.

[2] "Legal Education and Public Policy: Professional Training in the Public Interest," in Yale Law Journal, March, 1943, pp. 203–295.

[3] House Document No. 118. Government Printing Office, Washington, 1941.

1939, was 5,368. This figure came as a great surprise to many persons. One exceptionally thoughtful law-school dean, who had been particularly concerned with raising the standards of the bar and bench of his own state, had never encouraged his students to seek positions in the federal government. He conceived of such positions as low in salary and prestige, and uncertain in tenure. When he saw the statistical data, however, he concluded that a change in point of view was needed. Immediately after Pearl Harbor further increase in legal positions became necessary to service the new wartime agencies, and some of the expanded departments. It was thought, early in 1943, that the total number of attorneys was about 8,500. Publicity concerning the 1,800 lawyers employed by the Office of Price Administration at that time underscored the proportions to which the legal staff of one agency might attain.

As yet, there has been no count of the number of law-trained persons employed in non-legal capacities by the federal government. Neither is there a figure for the total number of lawyers occupying positions, whether of a legal or a non-legal nature, in state and local governments. If the Corporation Counsel's Office in New York City has a staff of over 550 attorneys and the Department of Law of New York State has nearly 300,[1] it can only be assumed that the total for the entire nation would be large.

CREATION OF TECHNIQUES FOR RECRUITING FEDERAL ATTORNEYS

For such knowledge as exists of the number of lawyers in federal public service, and for initial attempts to devise ways to obtain law-trained personnel of integrity and ability, the federal government is primarily responsible. Its interest began somewhat fortuitously through the recommendation in 1937 of the President's Committee on Administrative Management that those legal positions in the federal government which had been ex-

[1] Gellhorn, Walter, "The Law Schools' Responsibility for Training Public Servants," in University of Chicago Law Review, April, 1942, p. 470.

cluded from competitive civil service should be brought under an enlarged and improved merit system.[1] Agencies employing nearly three-fourths of all federal attorneys objected, however, to the inclusion of their legal positions within the competitive civil service, if then-existing methods of selection were continued. Their objection resulted in the establishment by Mr. Roosevelt of the President's Committee on Civil Service Improvement, for the purpose of making a comprehensive study of civil service methods for choosing lawyers and certain other categories of professional personnel.

This committee, popularly known as the Reed Committee because its chairman was Mr. Justice Stanley Reed, not only obtained the figure already quoted for number of persons employed in federal legal positions; it sought to devise a method that would guarantee some assurance of recruiting well-qualified persons to represent the interests of the government. It recommended, therefore, that a Committee on Government Lawyers be established, composed of high-ranking government law officers, law-school representatives, and private practitioners, which should have power, in co-operation with the Civil Service Commission, to administer the examinations for legal positions.

In response to the Reed report, an Executive Order created a Board of Legal Examiners to be set up within the Civil Service Commission, but with the Commission exercising only an advisory function. Between July, 1941, and July, 1943, when legislative controversy ended its independent existence and brought its work fully under the Commission, the Board achieved several goals of considerable importance for the furtherance of public administration and for stimulating interest in such administration among lawyers and law-school teachers. Its marked success resulted not only from the support given by the distinguished members of the Board, but more particularly from the exceptional competence brought to the executive secretaryship first

[1] The following record of developments culminating in the creation of the Board of Legal Examiners and of its subsequent program has been taken from Ralph F. Fuchs' "The Federal Civil Service for Lawyers," in Public Personnel Review, July, 1944, pp. 168–176.

by Professor Herbert Wechsler of Columbia University and subsequently by Professor Ralph F. Fuchs now of Indiana University. Through reports in legal periodicals and at meetings of the American Bar Association and the Association of American Law Schools, the profession was given repeated opportunity to learn about the purpose of and the progress made by the Board. This indirectly centered attention upon the importance of the lawyer in public service.[1]

The core of the Board's work was, of course, the formulation of a competitive examination soundly designed to test ability, and the establishment of methods for making the examination available to persons throughout the United States. Newer examining techniques had been little developed by law schools or bar examiners. A few professional schools had formulated admission tests planned to reveal the reasoning power and aptitude for law of the prospective student. The New York State Board of Legal Examiners and perhaps a few other state bodies had utilized forms of written tests that could be graded mechanically. In general, however, the legal profession had been both unaware of and uninterested in theories and techniques of education and educational psychology that should have become the common possession of all teaching institutions.[2] As a consequence, Professor Henry Weihofen of the University of Colorado, who was given responsibility for designing the examination, found himself faced with a large creative task. Help came from a subcommittee of the Board, staff colleagues, the Civil Service Commission, educators and educational literature, and individual

---

[1] See: Symposium on "Lawyers under the United States Civil Service," by Herbert Wechsler, John Q. Cannon, and James Willard Hurst, in American Law School Review, April, 1942, pp. 1307–1317; articles on "The Federal Legal Examining Work" by Charles Fahy, Philip J. Wickser, Ralph F. Fuchs, and Henry Weihofen, in the Bar Examiner, July, 1943; "Investigational Possibilities in the Area of Examination Techniques," in American Law School Review, April, 1942, pp. 1329–1333, and "The Written Federal Attorney Examination," in University of Chicago Law Review, February, 1944, pp. 154–176, both by Henry Weihofen; "The Federal Civil Service for Lawyers," by Ralph F. Fuchs, in Public Personnel Review, July, 1944, pp. 168–176.

[2] See W. Willard Wirtz's "Investigational Possibilities in the Area of Curriculum Construction," in American Law School Review, April, 1942, p. 1321, and Henry Weihofen's "Education for Law Teachers," in Columbia Law Review, May, 1943, p. 423.

law professors who were invited to submit questions. When completed, the examination was, in Professor Fuchs' estimation, unparalleled in careful workmanship, scope, and richness of content.

The examination was planned to be both written and oral. The written part was to be open to all who wished to take it. The oral part was to be held subsequently for as many of those who had passed the written test as were needed to make a register of the requisite size. Multiple choice items arranged in four sections comprised the written test. Two sections, dealing with law, were constructed to measure professional competence rather than knowledge. All the information required in the answers was set down; the applicant had to analyze, interpret, or marshal this information in arriving at an answer. Typically, the items required the application of statutory provisions or precedents to stated problems. A third section was a standard intelligence test of vocabulary and logic; the fourth was a test of history and current information relating to public affairs, such as a competent lawyer might reasonably be expected to know.

Local and state oral examining boards were set up in all sections of the country. These boards were requested to ascertain the proficiency of applicants in legal analysis, their ability in oral discourse, and their effectiveness in achieving professional objectives, rather than their acquaintance with random fields of knowledge. To the furtherance of this purpose more than 300 lawyers, judges, and law professors, comprising 98 boards, contributed their services generously when the examination was given in 1942. Never before had so large a group of representative members of bench and bar been brought into a co-operative enterprise in behalf of strengthening federal personnel. The interest exhibited was both gratifying to the Board and encouraging to all those who are especially concerned with seeing that the government is provided with persons potentially capable not only of efficient work but of strong leadership.

It should be said parenthetically that the interest in the examination by applicants far exceeded all expectations. No fewer than 26,000 registered for the written test; more than 13,000 took it. Approximately 3,000 were afforded an opportunity to compete in the oral part. The size of these numbers is particularly surprising when one recalls that the examination was applicable only to positions ranging in salary from $1,800 to a maximum of $3,800.

Prior to the completion of the first roster in February, 1943, the Board was obliged to authorize new appointments to positions in the four lowest salary brackets, as well as to higher positions for which the competitive examination was not designed. In a two-year period it authorized nearly 5,000 appointments. The Reed Committee had estimated that probably about 300 positions would be filled annually. Both because of the enormous wartime expansion of government and of the rapid turnover of federal lawyers occasioned by Selective Service, the task of passing quickly upon the qualifications of attorneys assumed stupendous proportions. Several methods were used. For 60 per cent of the appointments for the "duration of the war and six months thereafter," examination was limited to appraisal of the individual's detailed record and to a character inquiry. In other instances the Board's written examinations were used. In some 1,600 instances oral examinations were given by committees comprised of three lawyers each. Unsatisfactory as were a few of these emergency techniques, the very fact that the Board was expected to authorize every appointment brought it and its purpose and philosophy to the attention of many federal administrators as well as to prospective employes.

PLANS FOR IN-SERVICE TRAINING

The Board hoped that its work would not be limited exclusively to the selection of personnel. It was aware of the stultification that often comes even to able employes of any large organization, whether public or private, and consequently it wished to concern itself with the continued professional growth and development of lawyers once they had entered the federal service. In-service training could be provided that would be of invaluable assistance in orienting the new attorney and that, in a more specialized form, would be stimulating to the older employe. Experience could be varied by moving young lawyers frequently from one type of work to another. Incentive could be increased, recognition afforded, and personnel for the higher brackets ultimately assured by advancing fairly rapidly from level to level persons who demonstrated interest in and aptitude for their work.

Thus reasoned the Board. The abnormal situation resulting from the war that characterized nearly every federal unit, the excessively heavy examining task imposed upon the Board, and uncertainty concerning its own existence, all detracted from concentrated attention upon this second and potentially important part of its proposed program. Shortly before it became an integral part of the Civil Service Commission, however, a letter was addressed to the various governmental bodies that employed substantial numbers of lawyers, suggesting the desirability of in-service training. The suggestion was received with particular interest in the Department of the Interior where the Solicitor was a former law-school teacher, and a committee was appointed to discuss the institution of such training. Shortly afterward Dean Frederick K. Beutel, who had had long administrative and teaching experience in several law schools, was added to the staff of the Department. He presently found himself chairman of an In-Service Training Joint Committee, composed of representatives of a considerable number of federal agencies, which was to assume responsibility for devising a program that would meet the needs not only of the Department of the Interior but of other interested executive bodies.

Early discussion led the Committee to conclude that attention should be concentrated, at least for the time being, on preparation of teaching materials relating to three topics.[1] The first two would be of immediate value to lawyers entering the federal service; the

---

[1] The following statement concerning content of program has been taken from memoranda, prepared by the In-Service Training Joint Committee, and made available to the writer through the courtesy of Dr. Beutel. He is now offering a course at the University of Nebraska on government contracts, which utilizes the materials collected under his chairmanship of the Committee.

third would attract the interest of attorneys employed in a wide variety of agencies. The three initial undertakings, on which extensive research was done, are enumerated here as illustrative of types of subject matter that might profitably be utilized for in-service training.

1. Preparation of bibliographical tools for the federal lawyer, containing description of library facilities and source materials for government legal work. These data would supposedly be supplemented by lectures or discussions to help new lawyers in finding quickly the answers to substantive problems.

2. Examination of types of government agencies available to accomplish various tasks that confront federal executives, such as departments, independent commissions, corporations. These agencies could profitably be viewed from the manner in which they had been created, the nature of their legal structure, their purpose and function, their source of power, and the constitutional and statutory checks imposed upon their operation.

3. Collection of materials for a seminar on government contracts, including the nature of an agreement with the government; problems of government financing and disbursing of funds involved in such contracts, together with questions of the nature of the appropriations and accounting for expenditure; problems of contracts as they affect the purchase and sale of government property and custodianship; suits arising from claims against government contracts.

In addition to the preparation of this reference and teaching material a seminar of five sessions was conducted in the autumn of 1944 and another in the spring of 1945 for a limited number of experienced attorneys. The first, on elements of a fair hearing, included discussion of the following topics: the law and court decisions, qualifications of hearing officers, problems of delegation and independence of hearing tribunals, evidentiary problems, requirements of a fair hearing under the American Bar Association bill. The second seminar was devoted to federal administrative organization and procedures, and included consideration of methods of approaching the problems of federal administration, administrative boards of appeals, administrative functioning of cease-and-desist agencies, licensing by administrative agencies, rate-making by administrative agencies. A different speaker, who was a specialist in the subject under discussion, was provided for each of the meetings. In several instances he was assisted by a panel.

Persons unacquainted with the size and complexity of federal bodies may question the need for such an undertaking. They will argue that the brief, practical in-service instruction offered by many of the individual agencies should be adequate aid, or should be made adequate, for new employes, while experienced attorneys ought themselves to assume responsibility for obtaining necessary specialized knowledge. Any frequent visitor to the government law offices, however, is impressed by the number of attorneys—even in supervisory positions—who have little understanding of the relation of the work of their office to that of the department or commission as a whole. Fewer see the program of their agency within the framework of the executive branch, or concern themselves with the role that that great arm of government plays as a force for social welfare in, and social control over, this nation. Yet it is maintained by those who have made careful examination of the structure of the federal government that any person with administrative vision and intellectual curiosity should be able to view the entire machinery of government if he has had proper preparation.[1]

Lack of perspective would not be so serious in a group that was smaller or had less opportunity to move ahead to important administrative and policy-making positions. Because of the size of the legal fraternity employed by the federal government and the rapidity with which considerable numbers are advanced to positions of great responsibility, insufficiently wide knowledge and perspective are serious handicaps to the effective operation of the government and to the general welfare of the country.

Leadership in policy, so Macmahon and Millett declare, is at a critical juncture. "The need is pressing for a boldly innovative touch on the part of political officers; for the ability to popularize

[1] Sims, Lewis B., "Social Scientists in the Federal Service," in Public Policy, edited by C. J. Friedrich and Edward S. Mason. Harvard University Press, Cambridge, 1940, p. 290.

intricate programs; above all for the time and means to discover and take account of the interrelations of things."[1] Any effort, therefore, that results in giving early to the incoming attorney a survey of the nature, function, and purpose of the various executive units is potentially of great value. Any course of instruction that brings together attorneys from agencies with varied programs to discuss subjects of common interest is desirable. Whether plans formulated by the Committee were sufficiently broad in scope to provide the lawyer with some understanding of the dynamics of government and of the interrelationship between government and society is, however, doubtful.

The law-trained man, equally with other specialists, finds it exceedingly difficult to keep abreast of current growth in the content of his profession and simultaneously to view the place of that profession in society. What is requisite, therefore, in an in-service program such as this, is a sociological rather than a primarily legal analysis of the role that government should play in contemporary society and the part of the law and the lawyer within that role. Nothing short of sociological analysis is likely to produce attorneys whose eyes will be focused upon the larger goals of national welfare.

Apprenticeship Training in Washington Offices

Exceedingly useful as were the recent experiments of the federal government in indicating methods for the selection and further training of competent legal personnel, the great task of assuring such competence must rest primarily upon the law schools. Without continuous and concerted efforts by them, all later attempts are but palliative. An encouraging aspect of these government undertakings was the degree to which they were initiated by former law professors employed in Washington "for the duration." Through these teachers of law and through the experience in public law practice gained by a considerable num-

[1] Macmahon, Arthur W., and Millett, John D., Federal Administrators: A Bibliographical Approach to the Problem of Departmental Management. Columbia University Press, New York, 1939, Preface, pp. x–xi.

ber of other law instructors, legal education is now provided with the greatest opportunity it has ever had to discover to what extent the training formerly offered has been adequate preparation for public service; to what extent that training must be drastically altered.

Professor Walton H. Hamilton, who has had extended government experience as an assistant to the Attorney General and in placing law-school graduates in the federal service, has long been convinced that further steps for improving training for public service are urgently needed. The Yale School of Law, with which he is connected, had moved relatively far and rapidly during the decade of the 1930's in the introduction of public law and non-legal materials. In spite of this fact—or perhaps because of it—he believed it desirable that actual contact with legal operations supplement the professional courses; he thought that participation in a "going" law office would provide the educational stimulus that law schools found it difficult to give second-year students. With these ideas in mind, Professor Hamilton initiated an experiment, in 1942, designed to tie school and government more closely together through using federal agencies for the apprenticeship training of students.

Although the experiment was on a very small scale and has not yet been repeated, it is described here in some detail because it contains the germ of what may later evolve into a significant form of supplementary law training. "The venture was to be educational," Hamilton wrote. "It was, in plan and detail to be directed towards enlarging the vision, adding to the exposures, bringing out the awareness, developing the skills of the individual student."[1] Hence, six second-year Yale students who elected the plan spent the second semester of 1941–1942 in Washington. The law schools of Columbia University and of the University of Chicago were invited to participate, but largely because of dislocations resulting from the war were unable to do so.

Each student was assigned to a government official. In general these assignments were made to persons just under the "high

[1] Association of American Law Schools Handbook, 1943, p. 122.

command." It was intended "to place the student near enough to the top for contact with policy-in-the-making, yet far enough down for him to meet it on the intellectual rather than upon the administrative level."[1] Officials were selected, not on the basis of their being attached to particular departments, but because they had a broad outlook, technical competence, wide training, and an interest in the development of the students. Thus men such as the chief counsel for the Petroleum Administration for War, a special attorney to the Antitrust Division, an attorney for the then Board of Economic Warfare, and an economist for the Antitrust Division were asked if they would permit a student to work for them, and give him the benefit of guidance and discussion.

Twice a week the students met as a group. At each meeting some member of the government discussed a problem with which he was intimately connected that "lay along the frontiers of public law," such as control of the power industry, regulation of the coal industry, the Pullman antitrust case. In addition, Professor Hamilton was continuously in close contact with the students, thus providing active supervision of the training they received.

Upon its completion he concluded that the experiment had amply justified the time and energy spent. He listed, however, certain changes that he believed should be made in the future, particularly in the supervisory process. Many of the problems of supervision that had arisen are ones that schools of social work, for example, which require not only graduate-class instruction but extensive field-work experience in social agencies, long ago faced and have now solved more or less successfully. In spite of the not altogether satisfactory nature of small portions of the program, Hamilton suggested that the experiment be continued after the war; that the group be enlarged to twelve or fifteen; and that students from other schools besides Yale be included.

The Association of American Law Schools, to which he had turned for approval before initiating his project, subsequently asked Professors Ralph F. Fuchs and Herbert Wechsler to examine the method, significance, and success of the plan. They

[1] *Ibid.*, p. 122.

reported that certain dangers for legal education were potentially inherent in it, and that certain changes needed to be made before it was repeated.[1] Its significance, however, was unquestioned, and so far as the value of the project could be gauged by the opinion of the students, it was completely vindicated. Every student, except one, expressed the greatest enthusiasm for what he had done, and declared that, were it possible, he would again elect a similar type of training. This enthusiasm largely resulted, so Fuchs and Wechsler believed, from "seeing law operate," and particularly from "seeing it used as a directing factor in government and human affairs, rather than as a form of control which is supposedly non-purposive and which operates largely through judicial judgments after the fact. . . . The outstanding value of the Yale project was that it conveyed to the students an insight into the purposiveness of much professional activity to an extent that it would be difficult to equal in the classroom."[2]

"Experiment in Training Students by Assignment to Government Agencies," in Association of American Law Schools Handbook, 1943, pp. 113-120.

Ibid., pp. 116, 118.

PART TWO
NATURE OF WORK DONE BY LAWYERS IN FEDERAL AGENCIES

PART II

NATURE OF WORK DONE BY LAWYERS
IN FEDERAL AGENCIES

REFERENCE has already been made to the fact that the law-school world had no information prior to 1941 of the number of lawyers employed in the federal service. With the notable exception of a few individual professors, the schools seem to have had scarcely larger knowledge of what lawyers did in many of the executive departments, other than their litigatory work in the Department of Justice or their quasi-judicial functions in the "old-line" administrative agencies. The writer was frequently told that there was little need to emphasize training for public service as something distinctly different from private practice, since the work of the lawyer was much the same whether he was in a government or a private law office.

A professor of administrative law has admitted that he once thought that lawyers in relation to government, whether outside the government and dealing with it or within the government service, were concerned with those contacts which government has with private individuals. After having been employed by the federal government during the war, he realized that much government effort and much of its legal work does not, except in a remote sense, bear upon private interests. This is particularly true of some of the responsibilities more recently assumed by the political state. The state has become so large an entrepreneur, it performs so many public services, that the function of great numbers of federal employes does not extend beyond the government itself. Therefore, the distinctive function of the lawyer, in the historical sense of ministering to the contacts of government with private interests, has no place there. But the lawyer, as the interpreter of the laws or as the framer of new laws and regulations, has a very great place, and his role in the formulation and

43

effectuation of policy, in which he plays a leading part, is closely linked to that of other officials.

CLASSES OF LEGAL POSITIONS

To understand the importance of the place occupied by the lawyer in the executive branch of the federal government, certain factual information must be set down. In this connection the groupings of legal positions by the United States Civil Service Commission are instructive. From job descriptions of persons doing professional legal work in the federal employ, the Commission has grouped legal positions into ten *series*, which are defined as follows:

1. *Trial-Attorney Series*. Includes all classes of positions the duties of which are to advise on, administer, supervise, or perform professional legal work in the preparation for trial and the trial and argument of cases in court, or in formal hearings authorized by law before a board, commission, or local officer having quasi-judicial powers. Included within this series, among other positions, are those of professional legal employes who assist trial attorneys by conducting legal research, preparing briefs, motions, and other pleadings, interviewing witnesses, and performing other related duties, but who do not try or argue cases and who may or may not appear in court.

2. *Estate Tax Examining Series*. Includes all classes of positions the duties of which are to advise on, administer, supervise, or perform professional legal work in the interpretation and application of the federal tax laws relating to estates and their administration.

3. *Finance Examining Series*. Includes all classes of positions the duties of which are to advise on, administer, supervise, or perform professional legal work in the application of provisions of the interstate commerce laws relating to the financial condition and activities of common carriers.

4. *Attorney-Trial Examiner Series*. Includes all classes of positions the duties of which are to advise on, administer, supervise, or perform professional legal work involving the actual conduct of formal hearings as a part of the administrative procedure of a bureau, commission, board, or other body having quasi-judicial powers, and the preparation of reports of such hearings containing statements and discussions of fact and

law and presenting conclusions in the nature of decisions for adoption by such quasi-judicial body or other final authority.

5. *Legal Administrative Series.* Includes all classes of positions the duties of which are to advise on, administer, supervise, or perform professional legal work involving the direction and control of the administrative management and enforcement of particular laws and orders and regulations thereunder and including responsibility for the formulation and execution of programs and policies, or involving the conduct of studies relating to problems of business administration, organization, methods, procedures, and techniques arising in a government agency, where the work requires full professional legal training.

6. *Legal Assistance Series.* Includes all classes of positions the duties of which are to supervise or perform professional legal work arising in the operations of a government department or establishment, requiring full professional legal training but not requiring admission to the bar and not involving, as a regular and essential duty occupying a substantial portion of the time, professional legal work of a type specifically allocable to some other series in this group.

7. *Adjudicating Series.* Includes all classes of positions the duties of which are to advise on, administer, supervise, or perform professional legal work involving the examination, review, and adjudication of applications or claims for rights, privileges, gratuities, or other benefits conferred or authorized by various Acts of Congress, claims for property or personal injury damages, or other claims, where the work requires full professional legal training, but not admission to the bar.

8. *Attorney-Adviser Series.* Includes all classes of positions the duties of which are to advise on, administer, supervise, or perform professional legal work involving chiefly the study and analysis of assigned legal questions, problems, or cases, and the rendering of decisions or opinions thereon as a basis for executive action, including such activities as (a) serving as a legal adviser or consultant to administrative officials; (b) preparing authoritative opinions or decisions to be rendered by a government agency or official authorized by law to render opinions or decisions, or preparing advisory opinions for the guidance of administrative officials with respect to legal questions arising in the operations of a government agency; (c) searching statutes, decisions, opinions, and other legal authorities on specific points of law or assigned subjects and assembling, analyzing, and reporting upon the results to others for their use in the preparation of opinions or decisions; (d) examining transcripts of formal testimony and documentary evidence, and preparing findings of fact and conclusions of law based thereon for use of a judge,

board or commission member or trial examiner in the preparation of a decision; (e) studying and preparing reports and opinions on proposed legislation, drafting proposed legislation, or preparing interpretative and administrative orders, rules, or regulations to give effect to the provisions of governing statutes; (f) examining land title abstracts and title papers; (g) preparing, reviewing, or interpreting contracts, agreements, leases, bonds, deeds, notes, mortgages, and other legal documents which deviate from standard forms and require original phrasing to protect the interests of the government; or (h) performing other professional legal work requiring admission to the bar and of a type not allocable to some other series in this group.

9. *Attorney-Investigator Series.* Includes all classes of positions the duties of which are to advise on, administer, supervise, or perform professional legal work involving the investigation of alleged violations of statutes administered by a regulatory agency, including such activities as developing the facts, preparing reports, making recommendations, and participating in the preparation of cases for trial before the agency in such ways as securing and preparing evidence, examining witnesses, or writing briefs.

10. *Attorney-Editor Series.* Includes all classes of positions the duties of which are to advise on, administer, supervise, or perform professional legal work in editing, collating, and preparing for publication, statutes enacted by Congress, or decisions promulgated by a quasi-judicial body, including the preparation of indexes, head notes, syllabi, tables of cases overruled or modified, annotations, and cross references.[1]

Unfortunately the Commission does not have complete or current information as to the number of professional legal positions falling within the ten series. Such information would be of very real value. The agency knows, however, that the series which include the largest numbers of law-trained men occupying positions in the District of Columbia are the Attorney-Adviser Series, the Trial-Attorney Series, the Adjudicating Series, and the Attorney-Trial Examiner Series. It is probable that the greatest number of professional legal positions located outside the District of Columbia also falls within these four series.

[1] Handbook of Occupational Groups and Series of Classes Established under the Federal Position-Classification Plan. Government Printing Office, Washington, 1945, pp. 46–48.

Law schools have traditionally centered attention upon preparation for the function of advocate before appellate courts, and for counseling in connection with specific legal problems. Although the broadened curriculum of the last generation has tended to lessen this emphasis, comparable training for other functions has not yet been established. When it is realized that only one of the ten series established by the Commission is composed—and that only in part—of lawyers who "go to court," and that a considerable proportion of the legal fraternity in the federal departments is engaged in advisory, adjudicatory, and trial-examiner work in relation to problems far removed from the traditional legal categories, these facts would seem to indicate the direction in which reorientation of curricula might constructively move.

Representative Legal Activities

Important as are "series" definitions in outlining types of existing positions, they provide no clue as to the amount of work done, the reasons for doing it, the conditions under which it is done. They tell the reader almost nothing about the relationship of the lawyer to other lawyers, professional personnel, and administrative officials within the agency of which he is a part. These series are in fact only lists of positions, while what is needed is a picture in three dimensions of *lawyers* in the process of formulating and carrying out the legal program of a specific organization.[1]

Such a picture is difficult to obtain, in part because of the pronounced anonymity that surrounds most persons in the federal government below the level of politically appointed officials. Some of the annual reports of the several departments and administrative agencies contain sections devoted to the legal opera-

[1] The individual job descriptions, from which the Civil Service Commission compiles its "series" definitions, do attempt to record the duties involved in specific positions, the relationships of the incumbents to other professional personnel, and the responsibilities assumed by the incumbents. These job descriptions are so detailed and technical, however, that they are more helpful to the personnel specialist than to the layman. No adequate selection can be made from them that would illustrate, in this brief space, how the duties, relationships, and responsibilities assumed by lawyers vary at eight different grade levels and from agency to agency.

tions of these organizations. The information presented in them about the kind and volume of work undertaken during the preceding fiscal year is of considerable value. However, these sections are not so helpful as might be wished for the purposes of this study because emphasis is centered primarily on the work of organizations rather than of individuals: the *office* of general counsel or solicitor, or the *office* of chief counsel or solicitor of a bureau, office, service, or division. As a result, one gets the impression of a two-dimensional painting in which there is much and often varied action, but in which the landscape lacks depth and most of the figures are flat and undifferentiated.

In spite of this serious handicap, annual reports of two departments and one administrative agency have been selected. The Department of the Treasury is one of those chosen because its Legal Division is both large and extremely important. The Division is composed of the legal staff in the office of the General Counsel and the legal staffs in the Bureau of Internal Revenue, Bureau of Customs, Bureau of Narcotics, Bureau of the Public Debt, Procurement Division [now Bureau of Federal Supply], Bureau of the Comptroller of the Currency, and the Foreign Funds Control. Ordinarily between 400 and 500 attorneys are employed. Space does not permit description of the law work done by all the several bureaus. Following a brief résumé of the general program of the Division, therefore, a detailed statement has been given only of the Office of the Chief Counsel for the Bureau of Internal Revenue. The detail presented in this second statement reveals the scope and amount of legal work that comes before the federal government's tax office.

"Straight law work," either in the specialized field of taxation or in those several other fields that have received bureau status, engages the large majority of the attorneys. In addition, however, there is a relatively vast amount of work that requires far more than a knowledge of legal techniques. Such, for example, is the formulation and effectuation of policy concerning at least the legal aspects of broad monetary and financial questions both of a domestic and an international nature. As to these questions attorneys engage in essential advisory and planning functions, and their decisions exercise a profound influence over the economic and social welfare not only of this country but of the world.

Legal Division of the Department of the Treasury[1]

The General Counsel is by statute the chief law officer of the Treasury Department, and is directly responsible to the Secretary for the work of the Legal Division. With the assistance of his legal staff, he gives advice on legal problems to the Secretary, the Under Secretary, Assistant Secretaries and the administrative officers of the Department; exercises general supervision over the law work of the bureaus employing legal staffs; and serves as legal adviser to the branches of the Department not having legal staffs, such as the Bureau of the Mint, the Secret Service Division, Treasurer's Office, and the War Finance Division.

The activities of the Legal Division embrace all legal questions arising in connection with the administration of the duties and functions of the various bureaus, divisions, and other branches of the Department. These activities also include consideration of legal problems relating to broad financial, economic, and social programs, problems with respect to international co-operation in the monetary and financial fields, and problems relating to war activities.

In addition, the legal staff in the office of the General Counsel handles legal matters relating to legislation, including the drafting of legislation and preparation of reports to committees of Congress and the Bureau of the Budget; appears before congressional committees; prepares and reviews executive orders and proclamations; prepares formal and informal opinions and memoranda for the guidance of the administrative officers of the Department; performs the necessary pretrial work in litigation involving Treasury officials; makes recommendations to the Secretary in matters relating to compromise settlement of general claims of the United States; handles legal problems pertaining to gold and silver transactions and the administration of the stabilization fund; passes upon legal questions arising in the adjudication of Mexican claims; and handles the legal work in connection with railroad liquidations, receiverships, and reorganization proceedings under the Transportation Act.

During the fiscal year 1944, among the many special problems handled by the Legal Division were those relating to the collection of

[1] The following account has been taken from the Annual Report of the Secretary of the Treasury on the State of the Finances for the Fiscal Year Ended June 30, 1944. Government Printing Office, Washington, 1945, pp. 242–243, 239–241.

the revenues and related problems, the issuance of public debt obligations, the renegotiation of war contracts, the formulation of policies and procedures to govern the settlement of terminated war contracts, the establishment of policies and procedures to cover the disposition of surplus property, the formulation of proposals for an international monetary fund and an international bank for reconstruction and development, and co-operation with the military authorities on financial and monetary problems arising in liberated areas.

The activities of the Office of the Chief Counsel for the Bureau of Internal Revenue include the defense of all federal tax cases appealed to the Tax Court of the United States; the review of refunds, credits, and abatements in excess of $20,000; consideration of various administrative and internal revenue tax matters referred to that office by the Secretary and other officers of the Treasury Department, or by the Commissioner and other officers of the Bureau of Internal Revenue. They include also the preparation, at the request of the Department of Justice or of the United States attorneys, of data for use in the prosecution or defense of tax cases (civil and criminal) in suit, and compliance with requests for assistance in such cases; and the preparation, revision, and review of regulations, Treasury decisions, mimeographs, and rulings for guidance of the officers and employes of the Bureau of Internal Revenue and others concerned. The Office is made up of the Chief Counsel's Committee, the Engineers and Auditors Section, and the following eight divisions: Alcohol Tax, Appeals, Civil, Claims, Interpretative, Legislation and Regulations, Penal, and Review.

During the fiscal year 1944, 3,633 cases appealed to the Tax Court were closed. In 3,622 cases involving income, excess profits, unjust enrichment, estate, and gift taxes the appellants recovered $73,187,202 on claims aggregating $150,625,788; and in 11 cases involving processing taxes the appellants recovered $90,884 on claims aggregating $812,274. In co-operation with the Department of Justice, 781 civil cases in state and federal courts were closed, in which the amount claimed was $15,461,358; refunds aggregating $4,441,521 and collections amounting to $624,278 were made. There were also closed 1,131 cases involving liens, in which $678,523 was collected.

The Government was represented in 1,064 corporate reorganization and arrangement proceedings in which government claims amounting to $12,353,850 were settled for $4,878,908. In 3,948 bankruptcy and receivership cases disposed of, $3,399,726 was collected on government claims aggregating $9,895,218. In claims filed by collectors against the estates of deceased taxpayers and insolvent banks and in liquidation proceedings, including assignments for the benefit of creditors, 2,259 cases involving claims amounting to $8,187,810 were settled and $2,849,356 was collected.

The Office reviewed 715 cases involving proposed allowances for overpayment or overassessment of income, excess profits, estate, gift, and miscellaneous taxes, as well as deficiencies when coupled with tax reductions under review, where the amount of tax reduction in a particular case exceeded $20,000. Payment of $31,203,282 was recommended upon claims amounting to $57,183,582. Included in these figures are income, excess profits, estate, and gift tax cases involving overpayments exceeding $75,000, on which reports were prepared for the Joint Committee on Internal Revenue Taxation. Cases were reviewed involving claims for refund of amounts paid as processing and floor stocks taxes and unjust enrichment tax deficiencies aggregating $24,312,939. Final review of 3,275 cases involving compromise and closing agreements was made.

Claims for reward for information relative to violations of the internal revenue laws were considered and payments of $77,209 were recommended in 62 of the 212 cases disposed of.

In connection with the administration and enforcement of the internal revenue liquor laws and the laws relating to firearms, 5,669 memoranda, 181 briefs, 6,570 opinions, 252 libels, and 32 indictments were prepared. With respect to alcohol and Federal Alcohol Administration permits, 45 denials of applications for permits, 71 notices of contemplated denials of applications, 154 citations for revocation and suspension, and 52 orders in suspension and revocation proceedings were prepared. Reviews were made of 1,838 case reports, 480 claims of over $5,000 each, 7,447 compromise cases, and 135 petititions for remission or mitigation of forfeitures. In addition, 187 hearings were participated in.

During the year 528 internal revenue tax cases involving criminal liability were closed. Much of this penal work was performed in close co-operation with the Department of Justice and included consideration of offers in compromise and the preparation of opinions construing the criminal and percentage penalty statutes and whether certain cases should be reopened because of fraud or malfeasance, or misrepresentation of a material fact.

Work involving interpretation of internal revenue laws was performed in 2,592 cases, including the preparation or review of memoranda, correspondence, briefs to be filed with the Tax Court in key cases, actions on decisions in special cases, and closing agreements covering proposed transactions. Material submitted for publication in the Internal Revenue Bulletin was edited. The Office prepared or reviewed regulations issued under the internal revenue laws and tax conventions with foreign countries and reports on legislation introduced in Congress affecting the internal revenue. Consideration was given to suggestions for amendments of, and additions to, the various internal revenue laws, and reports thereon were prepared. The Office participated in the preparation of income tax and other forms and in the drafting of internal revenue laws and tax conventions.

In 159 cases, technical engineering and auditing advice and assistance were furnished revenue officials and the Department of Justice, principally in the fields of valuation and depreciation. Legal advice and assistance were rendered officials concerned with the salary stabilization regulations in 2,359 cases.

The second department selected is that of Labor. In 1944 it was still relatively small and its total number of attorneys was approximately only 150. However, the report of the Office of the Solicitor is particularly illuminating because the legal services performed are so grouped as to reflect the functional basis on which the Office had been organized.

Office of the Solicitor of the Department of Labor[1]

The Solicitor of Labor serves as legal counsel to the Secretary and to all the bureaus and divisions of the Department of Labor, both in Washington and the field. Legal services were rendered, during the fiscal year 1944, in the following areas:

1. *Litigation.* Although the Department of Labor publishes for the guidance of industry and labor interpretations of the Fair Labor Standards Act which are given great weight by the courts, the ultimate scope and application of the Act can be finally determined only by authoritative judicial decisions. The process of judicial interpretation and clarification continued during 1944 to furnish precedents from which the proper application of the Act to other situations may be ascertained. The most significant decision of the United States Supreme

[1] The following account has been taken from the Annual Report of the Secretary of Labor, Fiscal Year Ended June 30, 1944. Government Printing Office, Washington, 1945, pp. 71–77.

Court relating to the Fair Labor Standards Act was in the case of the Tennessee Coal, Iron and Railroad Co. vs. Muscoda Local in which the Court upheld the Administrator's position that hours spent by miners in underground metal mines traveling from the portal to the working face and in returning to the portal at the end of the day was work or employment compensable under the Act.

The appellate work of the Office required the preparation and filing of 19 briefs in the Supreme Court and 41 briefs in the United States Circuit Court of Appeals. Wartime pressure on child-labor regulations resulted in a substantial increase in the volume of child-labor litigation. One hundred and eleven actions for injunctions were filed as against 42 in 1942. There was also an increase in the number of proceedings under the Walsh-Healey Public Contracts Act. Forty-four complaints were issued in 1944 as against 19 in 1942. Proceedings for injunctions against future violations of the wage or hour provisions of the Fair Labor Standards Act were instituted in 347 cases, while the criminal penalties which the statute provides for cases of willful violation were invoked in 41 cases. Seventy-seven of the injunction proceedings resulted in contests. There is no record of the number of suits for back wages brought by employes; they probably exceeded a thousand. Because important questions of law were involved in many of these employe suits—for example, the Tennessee Coal and Iron case mentioned above, the Solicitor filed briefs *amicus curiae*, presenting his views to the courts.

2. *Administrative Proceedings*. Statutes administered by the Department, including the Fair Labor Standards Act, the Walsh-Healey Public Contracts Act and Executive Orders 9240 and 9248 require numerous administrative proceedings looking both to the issuance of regulations and to the adjudication of specific cases. The Office of Solicitor performs the necessary legal services in connection with such proceedings.

The Fair Labor Standards Act provides a procedure for raising the statutory minimum wage of 30 cents an hour to 40 cents by administrative action. In connection with this wage-order program, the Office participates in drafting industry definitions, acts as counsel to industry committees, conducts public hearings for the Administrator on industry committee recommendations, and drafts the Administrator's findings, opinions, and orders. As the result of new methods of securing evidence required for these proceedings, the legal phases of which have been worked out by the Solicitor, it has been possible to complete the task of bringing interstate industry on the mainland up to a universal 40 cent minimum wage well in advance of the statutory deadline of October, 1945. Puerto Rico and the Virgin Islands constitute special problems that cannot be quickly solved.

The Office also continued to perform the usual legal work in connection with the determination of reasonable cost of facilities furnished to employes in lieu of wages; the issuance of regulations for learners, handicapped workers, and apprentices, permitting their employment at wages lower than the minimum wage prescribed in the Act; the handling of cases involving the cancellation of certificates for such workers, and the issuance of regulations defining "seasonal" industries in which workers may be employed in excess of 40 hours during the seasonal period without payment of overtime.

Attorneys in the Office act as trial examiners in cases of formal complaint for violations of the Public Contracts Act, and others assist the Administrator and the Secretary in the drafting of their decisions. During the fiscal year 23 examiners' reports were filed, and 17 administrators' decisions were issued.

Under the War Labor Disputes Act, the Secretary of Labor, the National War Labor Board, and the National Labor Relations Board were designated as the agencies to receive notices of labor disputes threatening seriously to interrupt war production. A co-ordinating committee composed of representatives of these three agencies processed the notices. An assistant solicitor and the national representative of the Conciliation Service represented the Secretary on this committee. The Office of the Solicitor assisted in ruling on the validity of the notices and prepared the rulings issued by the docket officer.

3. *Interpretations and Legislation.* The Solicitor was called upon to provide advice and to issue opinions on numerous questions involving the meaning and application of the provisions of the various statutes and executive orders administered and interpreted by the Department. Requests for such opinions were received from individual employers and employes, from trade associations and labor organizations, from members of Congress, government officials in other departments and agencies, and state and local public officers, and from the various bureaus and divisions within the Department itself. Local service was given in many thousands of these requests by attorneys located in 27 regional and branch offices. In contrast to the requests that were previously received when the general provisions of the Fair Labor Standards Act and the Walsh-Healey Public Contracts Act were not widely under-

stood, the 1944 inquiries were largely concerned with problems of a difficult or complex nature. They usually involved questions upon which clarification of the law was needed either because of the absence of precedents or in order to resolve apparent conflicts between previous interpretations of the law by administrative officers and the courts.

There was a substantial increase in interpretative work relating to the child-labor provisions of the Fair Labor Standards Act. Because of the manpower shortage, employers who normally do not employ minors frequently sought to learn how they could do so within the framework of the Act.

The Children's Bureau, in 1943, undertook the administration of a program of grants to states for maternity and infant care and services to wives and children of servicemen in the lowest four pay grades. This program, for which nearly $54,000,000 was appropriated by the Congress in the fiscal year 1943–1944, required the establishment of new procedures. It became the duty and responsibility of the Office of the Solicitor to assist in drafting these procedures and to render frequent legal counsel to the Children's Bureau in their interpretation of the legislation and regulations.

The Office was called on more frequently than formerly to render legal advice to the Conciliation Service. This was the result of the increase in the number of regulations affecting labor. Much of the assistance was made available to arbitrators associated with the Service who required legal assistance or consultation regarding collateral judicial or administrative rulings in the field of labor law that bore upon their rewards.

The Women's Bureau and the Division of Labor Standards, which have extensive relationships with state departments of labor and with federal agencies, were often asked for advice in the interpretation and administration of federal or state labor laws. When such inquiries involved legal questions, they were referred to the Solicitor for his opinion.

The need for the development and maintenance of labor and social standards on an international scale resulted in the calling of a conference of the International Labor Office in Philadelphia in the spring of 1944. The Office of the Solicitor prepared studies and reports that were submitted to the international body in advance of the conference, and participated in discussions relating to the framing of policies of, and in the drafting of documents for, the United States government delegates.

A representative of the Office of the Solicitor was attached to the staff of the United States government delegation and served in the capacity of draftsman and legal counsel.

The Office prepared drafts of the Secretary's reports to the President on enrolled bills awaiting his approval or veto, and to congressional committees on proposed legislation. It aided the Secretary, bureau officers, and congressional committees in drafting legislation.

4. *Wage Determination and Wage Adjustment.* War construction demands kept the volume of work under the Davis-Bacon Act and the National Housing Act at a high level during 1944. A total of 7,768 wage determinations were issued, including confirmations and modifications based on Wage Adjustment Board action. The problems involved in making these determinations were intensified by the need for co-ordination with the wage stabilization program.

Wage stabilization for the building construction industry continued to be carried forward by the Wage Adjustment Board for the Building Construction Industry, which had been given jurisdiction over all labor disputes and voluntary wage or salary adjustments involving mechanics and laborers employed in the industry. The Board consists of nine members appointed by the Secretary of Labor, of whom three represent labor, three represent industry, and three, including the Chairman, represent the public. The Chairman is the Assistant Secretary of Labor, and the co-chairman is an Assistant Solicitor. The Office of the Solicitor performs the technical services required by the Board including the preparation of Board decisions, reports, and procedural regulations; presiding at public hearings and serving on panels of the Board.

The third selection for discussion is the Federal Trade Commission. The Commission is an independent administrative agency whose duties fall into two categories: legal activities in the enforcement of the laws it administers, and general investigation of economic conditions in interstate and foreign commerce. So extensive is the legal work done by the Commission that it normally employs between 200 and 250 attorneys. Before the war brought large emergency agencies and swollen staffs in its train, the Commission was appreciably exceeded in the number of its attorneys only by two cabinet departments and three or four administrative agencies.

Legal Activities of the Federal Trade Commission[1]

Legal activities of the Federal Trade Commission embrace administration of: 1, the Federal Trade Commission Act, which declares that unfair methods of competition and unfair or deceptive acts or practices in commerce are unlawful; 2, section 2 of the Clayton Act, as amended by the Robinson-Patman Act, prohibiting price and other discriminations, and sections 3, 7, and 8 of the Clayton Act dealing with tying and exclusive-dealing contracts, acquisitions of capital stock, and interlocking directorates, respectively; 3, the Export Trade Act, also known as the Webb-Pomerene Law, which, for the purpose of promoting foreign trade, permits the organization of associations to engage exclusively in export under stated restrictions; and 4, the Wool Products Labeling Act of 1939, designed to protect industry, trade, and the consumer against the evils resulting from the unrevealed presence of substitutes and mixtures in wool products.

The legal work of the Commission is under the supervision of its Chief Counsel, its Chief Examiner, its Chief Trial Examiner, the Director of its Radio and Periodical Division, and the Director of its Division of Trade Practice Conferences. The Chief Counsel acts as legal adviser to the Commission, has charge of the trial of formal cases before the Commission and in the courts, and supervises the foreign-trade work of the Commission conducted pursuant to the Export Trade Act.

The Chief Examiner is the principal legal investigating officer of the Commission and exercises supervisory direction over the investigation of applications for complaint filed with the Commission alleging violation of any of the laws administered by it. The Chief Examiner also conducts general investigations primarily of a legal nature. Otherwise, general investigations are the responsibility of the Division of Accounts, Statistics and Economic Investigations. During the war the Chief Examiner conducted numerous investigations, at the request of the War Production Board, of certain basic industries to ascertain the facts concerning their compliance with the Board's orders relative to the allocation of the supply and the priorities of delivery of materials.

Members of the Trial Examiners Division preside at hearings for the reception of evidence in formal proceedings and in certain of the general investigations conducted by the Commission. Other members negotiate settlements by stipulation of applications for complaint, subject to the approval of the Commission. The Division of Trade Practice Confer-

[1] The following account has been taken from the Annual Report of the Federal Trade Commission for the Fiscal Year Ended June 30, 1945. Government Printing Office, Washington, 1945, pp. 1-3, 5-6.

ences conducts the activities relating to trade practice rules for industries, including the holding of hearings and industry conferences, administration and enforcement of rules, and other staff duties incident to the trade practice conference procedure. This division also is charged with administration of the Wool Products Labeling Act and the rules and regulations promulgated thereunder.

The Radio and Periodical Division conducts office investigations in cases involving allegations of false and misleading advertising. Such cases usually result from the Division's continuing examination of radio and periodical advertising and, in a majority of instances, are disposed of by stipulation. Subsequent to Pearl Harbor, the Division also carried on a special continuing examination of war-related advertising for the War Production Board.

A considerable portion of the work of the legal divisions of the Commission is so highly technical that attorneys must be provided with the assistance of specialists. The Division of Accounts, Statistics and Economic Investigations, therefore, assists in the preparation of material and data in price fixing and other types of cases involving restraint of trade. The Medical Advisory Division furnishes professional opinions in connection with the investigation or trial of cases involving medical, chemical, or scientific questions relating to food, drugs, and cosmetics.

A summary of the legal activities for the fiscal year 1945 further indicates the scope of the work done by the Commission. One hundred sixty-four formal complaints alleging violations of the laws the Commission administers were issued; 140 orders directing respondents to cease and desist from such violations were entered; and 286 stipulations to discontinue unlawful practices were accepted, 66 pertaining especially to radio and periodical advertising.

More than 150 industries operate under trade practice rules approved by the Commission.

The Wool Products Labeling Act was given wide application during 1945. Field inspections were made of more than eleven and one-half million wool products subject to the labeling provisions of the Act, and of the labeling practices of several thousand manufacturers, distributors and other marketers. Compliance in cases of improper labeling was effected in most instances through co-operative action on the part of the concerns involved.

In May 1944 the Commission abolished its Export Trade Section and established an Export Trade Office. It conducted several investigations with respect to the operation of export associations, under the Export Trade Act. Investigation of the Florida Hard Rock Phosphate Export Association was completed, and recommendations for the readjustment of the business of the Association were issued. At the close of the 1945 fiscal year, 49 export associations were registered with the Commission. The Commission is continuing its observation of measures adopted by other countries looking to the regulation of trade and industry and the suppression of unfair competition.

Characteristics of Lawyers and Agencies

In an attempt to orient discussion around lawyers and what *they* do rather than around legal positions or the work of organizations, we have classified lawyers employed by the federal government in four groups. There are the "political appointees," the "top-flight" career men, the large but less dynamic career personnel, and those lawyers who, without reference to politics, serve the government on a temporary basis. This classification cannot be safely used for determining to which group a particular lawyer belongs. Judgments often differ about whether an individual attorney is a political appointee or not. A lawyer in whom one person would see a budding top-flight career man might be viewed by another as an almost undifferentiated member of the regular career personnel. The classification does, however, have considerable utility in revealing the extent to which the type of work done and the nature of the contribution made by lawyers to government differ according to group. It also suggests how lawyers enter the federal service, and what their probable tenure and mobility will be within that service.

Political Appointees. Concerning the political appointees it is most difficult to provide definite information. Since every lawyer comes to his job with training in law, it cannot always be determined whether political activity or recognition of professional fitness for the position has been the basis for his selection. The fact, too, that so large a proportion of legal positions has been outside the classified civil service has provided vast potential opportunity for political appointments.

Macmahon and Millett attempted to discover the immediate reason for selecting those persons who had held the positions of Solicitor General and of Assistant Attorneys General prior to 1938.[1] They found that political activity had marked the background of almost every incumbent of the post of Solicitor General, although many of the appointees had already or were later to achieve outstanding reputation in the legal profession. The average tenure in office was thirty-three months. Approximately nine-tenths of the 125 Assistant Attorneys General had occupied some public office prior to their appointment. Only five had spent a good many years in government service; forty others had had some prior experience with the activities of the Department of Justice. Their average tenure was forty-two months; subsequent to 1913 it was only thirty-eight months. The authors concluded that when so many men had been drawn from outside the government service on so temporary a basis, political activity rather than attainment in law—or at least as a necessary concomitant of professional attainment—must have been the determining factor in a preponderant majority of the cases.

Political appointments have supposedly always been frequent not only on the higher levels but throughout the Department of Justice. Policies concerning appointments vary radically from one unit of government to another. It is unlikely that the practice of political appointment of lawyers has been as pervasive elsewhere as in the Justice Department. Exception, however, should probably be made of the position of solicitor, general counsel, or chief legal adviser. Some of the principal legal assistantships are also filled, at least occasionally, through consideration of political as well as professional activities. Less prominent lawyers for whom the dominant political party feels that "something must be done" are scattered thinly through the various grades of the legal hierarchy. In general, they tend after their appointment to become a part of the regular career service which, as has been shown, grew up even in advance of the application of the civil service laws to

[1] Federal Administrators. Columbia University Press, New York, 1939, pp. 288, 279.

legal positions. Policies regarding appointments differ, moreover, at various times. During the emergencies of World Wars I and II and the economic depression of the 1930's, attention was centered primarily upon ability to solve difficult problems rather than upon any assistance the person under consideration might have rendered the party.

The top "politically appointed" lawyers are busied largely with advising executive officials about the legal aspects of problems encountered, and with representing such officials; acting as administrators of sometimes large legal staffs; and engaging in the formulation of program and policy not only for their own staffs but as assistants to administrators. They might be designated, therefore, as constituting part of that managerial class in government whose specialty is law.[1] Once their appointment has been confirmed by the Senate—if confirmation is necessary— their tenure is dependent upon their own pleasure and that of the head of the department or agency. Because they generally conceive of their term in office as temporary, they do not often provide the ripened experience and continuity that is a vital need in the management of vast enterprises. The modesty of the salaries received—$10,000 by a solicitor or general counsel and from $8,000 to $9,000 by the chief legal officer of a bureau or division —is a factor that militates against longer tenure. In recent tentative discussions by the Congress concerning a general increase in government salaries, the amounts allotted to these positions were appreciably raised.

Top-Flight Career Men. Although no figure can be given for the number of lawyers ordinarily found in the federal agencies who might be characterized as top-flight career attorneys, it would not exceed a few hundred. Prior to 1933 it was much smaller.

---

[1] A few lines on page 314 of Macmahon and Millett's Federal Administrators indicate how large is the managerial job in which these lawyers share. First is the task of operating the particular bureau or unit with its average of 1,000 employes. Second is the managerial job involved in the external relations of bureaus, as instruments of public policy, to the impinging activities of other agencies; to the management of the national administration as a whole; to the Congress; to the constellations of competing groups with which the bureau is immediately concerned; and to the interests of the public at large.

The attorney of this type generally comes to the federal service with a college education and sound professional training, as "sound" has been conceived of by the university law schools. His records in college and professional school will usually have been distinguished. He may have been attracted from private practice to take a particular government position or because the personalities and program of a particular agency engaged his interest. He may have been a teacher of law, a clerk to one of the justices of the Supreme Court, or an honor student just graduated from a national law school. Although he is generally still young, he often begins his government career in a relatively high position or in one where opportunities for advancement are favorable.

So marked is his creative ability, his initiative, his willingness to assume responsibility, and frequently his ambition, that the creeping paralysis which tends to affect all vast organizations scarcely touches him. He advances rapidly within a given agency. What is as likely, however, is that he will move not infrequently from one agency to another, often taking several other lawyers with him. His professional mobility within the government is marked. When the major problems of the first agency to employ him have been solved or their newness wears thin, another agency beckons him. The change, moreover, is usually accompanied by an increase in salary, prestige, and responsibility. In three or four such moves, the attorney raises himself to a position of considerable leadership. If a high administrative post in the legal hierarchy is filled on the basis of professional rather than political recognition, he is likely to be advanced to it. Thus he may become a member of the managerial class. As long as he has a sense of engaging in productive work and the political climate of opinion is not unfavorable, he is likely to remain with the government even though private law firms or corporations frequently offer him positions at double or triple the salary that he receives from the government.

These top-flight career lawyers are the ones to whom the federal service must look for much of the skill that raises legal work from the level of mere professional adequacy to that of social engineering. They are the persons who are responsible for a great deal of the planning and the formulation of legal policy just below, and sometimes on, the higher administrative levels. They handle important and complex legal problems for the solution of which far more than technical competence is needed. In supervising the work of other lawyers, they exercise broad critical judgment; they visualize new ways of attacking unsolved questions. Their judgment is sought by executives in other than legal matters.

Assistance in the development of such lawyers offers a distinct challenge to those law schools best prepared to train for professional leadership. Flexibility of mind and of personality is almost a prerequisite for the making of a top-flight career attorney. Wide educational background, highly developed judgment, executive and planning ability, intellectual curiosity, an understanding of the importance of non-legal factors affecting their work and of how to use legal doctrine and techniques creatively rather than in routine fashion—all these are likely to count heavily. In the cultivation of some of these desiderata the province of the law school may not extend beyond selecting students with such care that fundamental ability and substantial education are assured. In regard to most of them, however, even the best-equipped schools have not yet provided anything like the degree of assistance possible.

Permanent Career Service. The overwhelming majority of the lawyers in the federal service are members in a more modest sense of the permanent career service. Many of these men and women entered the federal service as clerks, attended the evening sessions of one of the several law schools in the District of Columbia, and, after obtaining a degree, succeeded in being appointed to legal positions. A larger proportion now come to the government already trained in law, and some have had long years of experience in private practice. When one recalls that no fewer than 13,000 lawyers took the written examination offered in 1942 by the Board of Legal Examiners for positions whose salaries ranged from $1,800 to $3,800, the readiness of members of the legal profession to accept even small positions in the federal career service is apparent.

Once admitted to a legal position in the permanent career service, advance both in grade and in salary generally comes through the carefully devised system of gradual promotion that the government utilizes. It may also come through promoting lawyers who have demonstrated ability to vacant positions of greater responsibility. By these two means hundreds of lawyers progress over a period of years from insignificant jobs to positions of considerable magnitude. The attorney, for example, who today—as an Assistant Solicitor of the Department of the Interior—is the legal Chief of the Indian Division and is also a member of the Department's Board of Appeals, began his federal career in 1916 as a clerk and stenographer at $900 annually. In 1925, after two advances in rank and salary, he received his first position listed as a strictly legal one, at a salary of $3,000. In 1933 he was promoted to an assistant attorneyship with a beginning salary of $4,800. Four years later he became a member of the Board of Appeals, his supervisory responsibilities were increased, and he moved to the $5,600 to $5,800 salary bracket. In 1939 he received his present position, the salary range of which is from $5,800 to $6,500. His work, if not his career, is now of the same sort in which the top-flight career man participates.

Because a lawyer belongs to the permanent career service rather than to that small top-flight group, it should not be imagined that what he does is relatively unimportant. Such lawyers are an indispensable part of the federal service. On them rests the responsibility for doing and supervising the doing of that stupendous amount of legal work without which both the federal government and this nation would shortly be in a chaotic situation. Their work varies enormously in interest and significance, from the routine processing of claims under a single statute to the drafting of important regulations or the conduct of major negotiations and litigation, sometimes ranging over many fields of law. For the most part they apply ordinary professional techniques to the solution of the problem confronting them, but policy considerations inevitably enter into the work of a goodly portion of them at many points. The caliber of these lawyers varies as greatly as the work they perform, but not always in conformity with the complexity of the work. Hence problems inevitably go unrecognized at times because those who handle the cases involving the problems are unable to transcend the limits of their restricted vision.

Since the nature of the ordinary legal operations of the federal government is difficult for the layman and even the attorney in private practice to visualize, the statement prepared for the writer by the Chief of the Indian Division is recorded here. Although it relates only to the field of Indian law and lack of space prohibits the reproduction of statements of other representative fields, it illustrates the variety of legal problems that may be encountered in one small unit of government and the care and detailed work involved in any satisfactory solution.

The field of Indian law, while highly specialized in itself, presents a large number of problems in other more or less specialized fields such as the law of oil and gas, probate law including the determination of heirs and the approval of wills, the law of taxation, irrigation and water right law, the law of domestic relations, and the law pertaining to real and personal property generally. In the Indian field the legal problems usually depend for their solution upon an examination of Indian treaties and agreements, acts of Congress, court decisions, departmental decisions and regulations, and Indian tribal law and custom. These problems embrace such questions as the constitutional power of the federal and state governments in the taxation of Indian property; the regulation of hunting, fishing, and other Indian rights; questions of jurisdiction; civil and criminal (federal, state, and tribal) questions; questions of enrolment and allotment; questions concerning Indian title, tribal and individual, based on aboriginal rights of use and occupancy; questions concerning the power and the authority of the Secretary of the Interior and the Commissioner of Indian Affairs; questions concerning the scope and extent of tribal self-government, prior and subsequent to the enactment of the Indian Reorganization Act of June 18, 1934; questions concerning the enforcement of the Indian liquor laws and law and order on Indian reservations; questions concerning rights and personal liberties of individual Indians and their interest in tribal property; and questions concerning the scope and effect of statutes imposing, removing, or reimposing restrictions against the alienation of Indian lands.

The various positions I have occupied, particularly since 1925, have required me to give consideration to legal problems touching all of the subjects listed above. Summarized briefly, the work required to be done involves preparation of memoranda, letters and opinions on Indian problems; preparation of pleadings and briefs in court cases; credit matters, including review of loan agreements and the drafting and review of loan regulations; Indian reorganization matters requiring a review of organization documents, ordinances, and resolutions of organized tribes and the interpretation and application of the review of organization documents; property transactions, highly diversified in character, involving the acquisition, use, lease, and sale of Indian lands, tribal and individual; contracts dealing with the employment of attorneys and other matters; matters relating to irrigation and water power development; miscellaneous matters relating to the interpretation, application, and drafting of departmental regulations of various aspects of Indian affairs, and the interpretation and application of statutes relating to the power and duties of the Department in relation to Indian affairs; probate work, including the determination of heirs of intestate Indians and the approval or disapproval of Indian wills; matters pertaining to Indian arts and crafts; correspondence with the Department of Justice on civil and criminal cases relating to Indian affairs; the drafting and review of legislation on Indian affairs prepared by the Department and reports on legislation pending in Congress; and review of correspondence, agreements, and so on, having relation to the war effort.

Temporary Government Lawyers. The fourth category of federal lawyers is composed of those attorneys who, without reference to politics, serve the government on a temporary basis. A few such men are always employed to handle important litigation cases, to serve as consultants, or to undertake some specific task where highly specialized skill is essential. During the war, however, the number of temporary lawyers was very large. Many volunteered their services "for the duration" or until they were called into military service; others were aggressively recruited by representatives of the emergency agencies that were obliged to build large staffs with dispatch. These attorneys were drawn not only from the private practice of law but from the faculties of the law schools. Nearly a hundred teachers from twenty-five law schools alone were to be found in Washington not long after Pearl Harbor. Others were employed in the field offices of the federal agencies. Although lawyers on temporary tenure varied in age, ability, and social philosophy, the statement made by an economist about the personnel of the Office of Price Administration might be largely applicable to them. The "relatively youthful staff were an energetic, dynamic, 'do things' group. When something needed to be done, they were quick to see it and not afraid to undertake it. When they saw a loose ball their instinct was to pick up the ball and run with it. They had taken the defense program seriously and they took the war even more seriously. They were aggressive 'activists.' "[1]

These attorneys came to their new jobs with little or no knowledge of government procedures. Most of them had never worked in so complex a setting, and many of them had had no experience in the kind of work to which they found themselves assigned. But they had not been worn down by a career service that sometimes deadens imagination and initiative. Predominantly they entered the emergency agencies where their zeal and freshness of outlook were tremendous assets and where their lack of knowledge of established procedures was somewhat less of a liability. They were found in almost every grade and salary level from those who began in the first grade at a salary of $1,800 to two law-school professors who were solicitors of departments with $10,000 salaries. The number, however, who entered at a salary of $5,600 or more was relatively very large.

Collectively these attorneys, like many of their forerunners who had flocked to the New Deal agencies during the economic depression, demonstrated the great value to government service of intellectual ability, substantial education, and social orientation. Had they not come on a temporary basis, the ranks of the top-flight career service would have been greatly enlarged. How

[1] O'Leary, Paul M., "Wartime Rationing and Governmental Organization," in the American Political Science Review, December, 1945, p. 1091.

government can recruit lawyers with such characteristics in considerable numbers for its permanent career service, and can provide them with the opportunity to widen and deepen experience while preserving initiative and imagination is a question worthy of the concerted attention of government, the bar, and the law schools.

Influence of an Agency Upon Recruiting Lawyers. The nature of the administrative program of an agency determines to no inconsiderable degree the importance of the legal staff, its size, and the caliber of the men and women attracted to it. The dynamic young lawyer who wants to make a place for himself in or through the federal service generally seeks connection with a youthful or very active agency whose program involves change and innovation. Or he seeks an agency where the experience gained will give him a decided advantage should he subsequently enter private practice. Thus the revivified Antitrust Division in the late 1930's, the new Securities and Exchange Commission, and several other New Deal agencies could readily engage the services of lawyers with ability, good legal training, enthusiasm, imagination, and a willingness to work long hours. The Bureau of Internal Revenue is generally able to attract excellent attorneys in sufficient numbers, both because of the scope and nature of its program and because the knowledge obtained of taxation policy and law provides a substantial foundation for later private specialization in tax problems. The war agencies, including the Office of Price Administration, the War Production Board, and the Board of Economic Warfare, stood high on the list of those with which lawyers wished to be associated. Admiralty lawyers and patent lawyers entered the service of agencies which needed their specialized skills. As commissioned officers, many lawyers served the War and Navy departments in professional capacities, and many others did so as civilians. So challenging was the element of innovation in most of the emergency programs that not even the excessive volume of work and the intense nervous strain to which many lawyers were subjected acted as deterrents in recruiting personnel.

But agencies, like human beings, reach their maturity and then tend to age unless aggressive leadership or the watchful eye of the over-all executive administration or the public spurs them on. The complicated problems of their youth generally reach solution; their programs often become stereotyped. Particularly instructive is the history of the changing role of the lawyer through the various stages of the career of the Resettlement Administration and its successor, the Farm Security Administration. The story was told the writer by Monroe Oppenheimer, the attorney who served for a time as chief legal officer of both bodies. During the summer of 1935 when the Resettlement Administration was launched, the staff in the District of Columbia consisted of almost a hundred lawyers. There was only a handful of lawyers in the field, most of whom were engaged in title examination. The Washington staff, large as it was, was scarcely sufficient to cope with the variety and complexity of problems confronting the new agency. In making funds available for its programs, the Congress had merely directed that they be spent for "rural rehabilitation and relief"—four vague words that contrasted sharply with the thousands of words prescribing the functions and powers of the Farm Credit Administration, the most nearly comparable agency.

From this broad charter, the administrative officials would have been helpless to develop consistent and legally feasible programs without the continuous and intensive co-operation of an experienced and imaginative legal division. To take but a few examples, it was necessary—in connection with the loan program —to prescribe rules and regulations governing loans for acquiring personal property and real estate, and the type of mortgage or other security incident to such loans. Similarly in connection with the resettlement program, it was necessary to develop mechanics for rapid land acquisition, and the organization of community co-operative or non-profit corporations; to develop contracts for public services both with private utility companies and with school boards and other public bodies; to prepare suitable contracts for building construction; to evolve techniques for assigning public streets and parks and their maintenance to appropriate public bodies.

This hectic period of initiating programs ended by the summer of 1936. "Beginning then," Mr. Oppenheimer interpolated, "our work was done by four-thirty in the afternoon [the official closing hour], and we developed hobbies." On December 31, 1936, the Resettlement Administration was placed in the Department of Agriculture, and was soon designated as the Farm Security Administration. Thereafter, the programs of the agency became more or less stabilized. The legal staff in the District of Columbia became smaller and smaller, while the staff in the regional offices tended to become larger and larger, thus reflecting a shift from consideration of novel and basic problems to decentralization of minor and largely routine questions.

For anyone acquainted with the picture of grueling work under great tension that is found in some of the federal offices and of leisurely undertaking that characterizes others, Mr. Oppenheimer's reference to four-thirty o'clock and hobbies is full of meaning. In some law offices it is almost always possible to lay aside work at the closing hour. Yet these offices may be essential units of agencies that are vested with enormous power to operate programs of wide social and economic consequence for the nation. Often they maintain considerable staffs of lawyers who receive the same salaries as do attorneys elsewhere in the federal service. But should an attempt be made to recruit top-flight career men for them, the result might not be highly successful.

The major problems of these offices were *supposedly* settled many years ago; they offer no real challenge. They are caught in the aging process that bears within itself the seeds of decay. Personnel for executive and planning positions is maintained largely by promotion from within the offices. This personnel has the important asset of thorough acquaintance with procedural techniques and long experience in handling the types of questions that customarily arise. But because of its extended association with one organization—and one which has lost momentum and flexibility—it tends to lack the ability to re-evaluate and revitalize its own programs. So long as fresh points of view are not energetically sought and those attorneys who are "activists" do not offer their aid, the aging process continues and these offices become progressively less able to attract lawyers who might adapt the programs better to contemporary needs.

Non-Litigatory Functions of Federal Attorneys

The federal government acts largely through the writing process. Statutes, regulations, executive orders, interpretations, contracts, applications, reports, letters, speeches, press releases, and other documents must be prepared in large numbers and a diversity of forms. It is widely assumed that, by virtue of his training, the drafting or at least the review of proposed statutes, regulations, executive orders, and contracts should repose in the hands of the lawyer.[1] Similarly, it is assumed that he should be consulted about, draft, or review letters, interpretations, and all documents where legal questions are involved. The amount of drafting alone that is required presents a formidable task.

In addition attorneys must write decisions and opinions that become the basis for executive action; they must do the research that is requisite for preparation of such decisions and for giving requested assistance to administrative officials; they must serve as legal advisers or consultants to persons in executive positions. Although litigation and enforcement play an essential role in many departments and administrative agencies, these responsibilities are in general greatly overshadowed by the non-litigatory ones that grow out of the writing and advisory process.

The Department of Justice furnishes an excellent example of the importance of non-litigatory functions. Contrary to the general assumption that its almost exclusive purpose is the enforcement of federal laws and the furnishing of legal counsel in federal cases, a considerable part of its program is not related or

---

[1] For an informal and interesting description of the way lawyers worked through the writing and conference method in the Office of Price Administration, see Professor Jacob H. Beuscher's "Law-Taught Attitudes and Consumer Rationing," in Wisconsin Law Review, January, 1945, pp. 63–76.

only remotely so, to enforcement and litigation.[1] One of its attorneys ventured the guess that, exclusive of the 500 lawyers employed in United States District Attorneys Offices, not more than 50 per cent of the work of the lawyers attached to the Department could be attributed to enforcement and litigation.[2]

The condemnation proceedings of the Lands Division, for instance, are handled largely through the administrative process with few cases contested; even the Antitrust Division has a relatively large volume of work that is not directly concerned with litigation; the Bureau of Immigration and Naturalization Service is an administrative agency that has been reposed, in recent years, within the Department of Justice. The twelve to fifteen attorneys who constitute the staff of the Office of the Assistant Solicitor General rarely enter the courts. In the fiscal year ended June 30, 1945, they handled, through a fortuitous circumstance, one case —the trial and appeal of the United States *v.* Montgomery Ward and Company, Inc. Their function is pre-eminently that of preparing opinions, preparing and considering legislation, and preparing executive orders. The annual report, which sets forth what this Office had accomplished in these areas during the preceding year, is reproduced here as concrete illustration of the significance of some of the non-litigatory functions performed by the Department.[3]

1. *Preparation of Opinions.* It is the duty of the Assistant Solicitor General and his staff to prepare for the Attorney General formal legal

[1] So useful would be a detailed analysis of the work done by attorneys in Justice, that the author attempted, with Senator Robert Wagner's assistance, to obtain such an analysis. The Department reported that it was unable to furnish the requested information. The data were probably not available, and the research necessary to collect and interpret them would have been considerable. It can only be assumed, however, that such analyses would be of immeasurable help to an organization employing more than 1400 attorneys in planning program, allocating responsibility and staff, and viewing its over-all personnel problem. Such analyses are even more needed if the American bar and the law schools of the country are to plan realistically for the future of legal practice.

[2] On October 31, 1945, the Department reported 1,457 attorneys in its legal divisions. The figure did not include a very large number of law-trained men employed by the Federal Bureau of Investigation, or those in the Bureau of Immigration and Naturalization Service.

[3] This unpublished report was made available to the writer through the courtesy of the Office of the Assistant Solicitor General.

opinions to be submitted to the President, the heads of the ten executive departments, and the Veterans Administration. He is also expected to give informal opinions and legal advice to the various agencies and instrumentalities of the executive branch. During the fiscal year 1945, he gave 93 formal and informal opinions. He also gives opinions to the divisions and bureaus of the Department of Justice on questions of law relating to the internal administration of the Department and to its relations with other departments. Thirty-nine such opinions were prepared.

2. *Preparation and Consideration of Legislation.* The Attorney General directed the Assistant Solicitor General to study the need for all proposed legislation relating to the war or to the problems of reconversion; to draft, or to assist other agencies in drafting, such legislation as was determined to be necessary; and to assist in clearing such legislation expeditiously through all interested agencies. As a result, the Office of the Assistant Solicitor General did a substantial amount of work during the fiscal year on legislation relating to the conduct of the war, the termination of war contracts, the disposition of surplus property, and the demobilization of industry.

In response to requests, the Office prepared and submitted reports to congressional committees and the Bureau of the Budget on a large number of proposed bills dealing with other subjects. At the request of the Bureau of the Budget, the Office also examined many bills passed by Congress and prepared reports which were submitted to the President before he considered these bills.

During the year the Office handled more than 700 legislative assignments.

3. *Preparation of Executive Orders and Proclamations.* The duty of reviewing and revising for form and legality executive orders, proclamations, and public land orders has been assigned to the Assistant Solicitor General. During the fiscal year the Office passed upon 226 such orders and proclamations. Many required extensive study of the statutory provisions involved. Advice was frequently given to the various departments and agencies about the preliminary drafting of orders, and sometimes the Office actively participated in the drafting process.

4. *Review of Customs Court Decisions.* It is the duty of this Office to recommend to the Solicitor General whether appeals should be prosecuted from decisions of the United States Customs Court to the Court of Customs and Patent Appeals. Recommendations were made in 23 cases of this kind. The Office also collaborated with the Assistant

Attorney General in charge of customs matters in several cases arising under the tariff laws that involved questions of reciprocal foreign trade agreements and treaties.

5. *Special Assignments.* The Assistant Solicitor General represented the Attorney General on the Postal Savings Committee, the National Archives Council, the Administrative Committee of the Federal Register, and on a number of temporary inter-departmental committees including the Surplus War Property Board. The trial and appeal in the case already mentioned was handled by the Assistant Solicitor General. Thirty-seven gifts or bequests to the United States or in aid of government agencies were supervised by this Office. During any absences of the Solicitor General, his duties were performed by the Assistant Solicitor General.

CO-OPERATION BETWEEN LAWYERS AND OTHER SPECIALISTS

To a degree unknown to the average attorney in private practice, the government lawyer is likely to find himself engaged in a division of labor with an economist, businessman, political scientist, engineer, soil expert, public health physician, social worker, or other specialist as his partner. In fact, he may discover that he is a member of a team composed of several experts. As such he generally must be prepared to accept assignments rather than initiate them, to work closely within the limits of the assignments, and to be content with anonymity beyond the confines of a small group. So large is the area of required collaboration with other technically trained staff members and so non-legal are the functions that he is sometimes called on to perform, that an occasional federal lawyer in the higher professional brackets has been heard to say that he was not sure that there was much law in what he was doing. Some lawyers have rebelled against being thus drawn into the context of public administration. They feared that it would destroy their identity as attorneys. But many a lawyer has derived "genuine exhilaration from assuming his place in an organization of manifold specializations linked together in order to give reality to a departmental program."[1]

[1] Marx, Fritz Morstein, "The Lawyer's Role in Public Administration," in Yale Law Journal, April, 1946, p. 500.

Henry S. Reuss, formerly Assistant General Counsel of the Office of Price Administration, has provided an excellent picture of what the lawyer who works through collaboration did within the Washington office of the OPA.[1] Mr. Reuss has illustrated the role of this type of attorney by describing how a typical, relatively simple regulation—that pertaining to pottery—was established.

The Price Department of OPA had discovered a threatened increase in the price of vitreous and semi-vitreous pottery. A letter of warning, to the drafting of which the legal division of the Price Department contributed, was sent to members of the pottery industry asking them to hold prices firm. Simultaneously work was begun on the preparation of a permanent price regulation of the industry. This task required numerous conferences between the legal, the price, and the economic research divisions about the collection of economic materials which would be necessary were the regulation to conform with the Price Control Act. When sufficient material had been collected to give some idea of the form the regulation was to take, drafting was begun by lawyers. The drafts were constantly reviewed with members of the price division.

A series of meetings with the pottery industry was then called, presided over sometimes by the executive of the price division, sometimes by the legal division. Prior to these meetings, tentative clearance of the program had been secured by the legal division from the Antitrust Division of the Department of Justice and from the Federal Trade Commission. After the regulation had been tested by these meetings with the industry, it was promulgated. Inquiries then began to arrive. Questions that had already been settled or that involved no legal problem were answered in the price division; all interpretations were handled by the legal division. Petitions for amendment, for adjustment, and for exception were referred to the legal division that processed them in conjunction with other divisions.

[1] "The Lawyer in the OPA," in American Law School Review, December, 1942, pp. 23–29.

Attorneys in the Rationing Department and the Rent Department also worked in a co-operative fashion, much as did those in the Price Department. It is therefore apparent that the OPA lawyer was expected to do more than serve as a drafting amanuensis, attempt to make certain that the regulation under preparation was legal, and decide—once the regulation was issued—whether a particular transaction violated it. His role was far more dynamic. He helped to decide what type of regulation could be most effectively administered and would be most equitable to the persons affected; what steps might be taken by those persons to evade the regulation and how to forestall such steps; what hardship situations might result and what relief, if any, could be granted.

The interpretation of a regulation and examination of petitions for amendment, adjustment, or exception often pointed to the need for improving the original draft. Here the lawyer was generally in the best position to make suggestions to economists, business experts, and executive officials. Sometimes a lawyer in one of the operating departments was convinced that action, either proposed or already taken, was illegal. Under such circumstances, he had the right to file a dissent from the point of view of his colleagues, which was examined in a review division. Thus illegal procedures were often checked.

In the Price, Rationing, and Rent Departments continuous interplay and cross-fertilization obviously occurred between lawyer, other specialist, and administrator. But the OPA maintained two other, smaller units both of which were staffed with attorneys who performed those types of work that have traditionally been considered as the lawyer's special province. In the court review, research, and opinion division of the General Counsel's office and in the Enforcement Department, including its division on litigation, attorneys "looked up the law," prepared opinions for the General Counsel, prepared briefs to be argued before appellate tribunals, planned and supervised the enforcement of OPA regulations carried out by a large staff of attorneys in field offices throughout the United States, and handled litigation of national significance and appellate cases.

It might be assumed that in such technically legal work, collaboration between lawyers and other specialists would cease to exist. Such was not the case. Even the "lawyer's lawyer" could not perform his task adequately without frequent consultation with economists, businessmen, and persons responsible for OPA policy, or without reference to materials which lie outside the traditional field of "law." Thus, in passing upon and defending the validity of a price or rent regulation, the attorney had to acquire full comprehension of the economic and business facts and considerations which underlay the establishment and operation of the regulation. Consequently, this phase of his work was different from that of the attorneys in the Price Department chiefly in that he had the added responsibility of translating nonlegal materials into evidentiary form and of interpreting to the tribunals the facts and policy determinations upon which the regulation was based.

Collaboration between lawyers and other specialists was carried even farther than in the OPA within the Office of the Stabilization Administrator. When visited early in 1946, the legal and economic staff of this small Office was engaged chiefly in reviewing certain policy decisions of agencies that attempted to control inflationary tendencies and in resolving disagreements among such agencies. Questions presented to it consisted of matters of policy involving a mixture of law and economics. Strictly legal questions rarely appeared. Consideration of the desirability of a flour subsidy, for example, required knowledge of the flour industry, of the relation between prices and wages, and of so many other complicated factors that neither the lawyer nor the economist could have worked alone effectively.

Because of the nature of the problems presented to the Office of the Stabilization Administrator, it had been deemed undesirable to attempt to restrict the function of the economic division to "economic" questions and the legal division to "legal" questions. Problems were, therefore, assigned to the two divisions without regard to a possible predominance of economic or legal aspects. Thereafter, the economist was free to consult the lawyer as often as he wished, and the lawyer was equally free to consult the economist. Because the economist had already learned from experience to deal with many of the less complicated legal aspects, and the lawyer had learned a considerable amount of economics, consultation about the more elementary components of a problem was unnecessary. Complex situations, however, always resulted in much conferring and checking of tentative conclusions. With a small staff this method of informal consultation and review worked reasonably well. However, the assistant general counsel had become so convinced of the essential interrelatedness of subject matter that he had recommended that *all* matters should be handled jointly by a lawyer and an economist. Had his recommendation been put into operation, pooling of effort would have been still further extended.

THE PROCESS OF POLICY-MAKING

When the President's Committee on Civil Service Improvement wrote its Report, it declared itself "forcibly impressed" by the pervasive role played by the lawyer in the administration of the American government. It concluded that "the lawyer, in contrast with the ordinary professional employe of the Government, is inevitably thrown into the heart of the policy-making process and of necessity has an important, and often a controlling, voice in the major issues of his department or agency."[1]

So exceedingly important is the question of the lawyer's participation in policy-making that some detailed consideration must be given to it. Policy is effectuated by attorneys on several levels and in a variety of ways. The policy-making function is most obvious when the general solicitor of a department or agency or the chief counsel of a bureau acts in an advisory capacity to administrative officials. But policy is made pervasively and continuously, although less conspicuously, on lower levels. It is made through the drafting of legislation, regulations, and executive orders; through

[1] Report of the President's Committee on Civil Service Improvement, House Document No. 118. Government Printing Office, Washington, 1941, p. 30.

interpretation of statutory and administrative law; through reviewing of work done by bureaus and divisions; and through the litigatory and administrative process. It is also made as the result of fortuitous circumstances whereby a lawyer, upon a particular occasion or in a particular agency, is given broad opportunity for planning and even administration which at another time or in another agency would be decisively denied him.

Policy-Making Through Drafting. In agencies that have any appreciable amount of legal work there are lawyers who devote all or a considerable amount of their time to the highly specialized task of drafting. In some instances they are expected only to put certain clearly formulated principles into legal form; again, as has been seen, they share with other specialists in the formulating of the pertinent principles; in still further instances, they carry almost the entire responsibility for the formulation of concepts as well as for the actual drafting. Even where their task is chiefly that of legal scribe, they inevitably determine in large measure how policy will be translated into operating programs through the degree of clarity, precision, and completeness, and through the exact nature of the methods and procedures for enforcement, which they succeed in incorporating into the proposed statute or regulation.

In some agencies legislation or rule-making assumes so important a role that a separate office is set up expressly to handle it. The Department of the Treasury, for example, maintains a permanent Office of the Tax Legislative Counsel to make legal and technical assistance continuously available to those who need advice about the *content* of proposed legislation, and to draft such legislation. The Office also reviews all internal revenue regulations; represents the Department in tax matters before congressional committees; participates in numerous conferences on taxation with individuals, private organizations, and other government agencies; handles recommendations for revenue legislation and inquiries about existing legislation; makes extensive studies, often in collaboration with committees of tax experts outside the government.

An article prepared by Reed Dickerson, a law-school teacher who had occupied various attorney positions in the Price Department of the OPA, emphasizes the policy-making function inherent in the drafting of regulations.[1] The administrative regulations of that agency not only determined the price of commodities, but a form of drafting was evolved that is believed applicable to other agencies where speed in preparation of regulations and readability are essential.

When the OPA was created in 1941, it found itself confronted almost overnight with the staggering task of regulating a major phase of the national economy. Regulatory problems pertaining to so complicated an economy and on so vast a scale had never before been faced. Rules had to be formulated with the utmost rapidity, applicable to day-to-day business operations. Yet they had to be legally sound. They had to be prepared, moreover, with such clarity that they could be understood by the layman without his having to employ counsel to interpret them.

From year to year appreciable progress was made in simplifying the style of the regulations and in achieving greater clarity through the use of such devices as explanatory material and examples. Continuing frontal attacks were also made on the problem of the structural organization of the complex body of regulatory law that was emerging. A legal device was evolved for co-ordinating a vast number of price provisions relating to many grocery products, without sacrificing the specialized treatment necessary to handling problems peculiar to individual commodities.[2] In Professor Dickerson's opinion this legal device, described at length in his article, was sufficiently successful to promise solution of some of the regulatory difficulties that are likely to

---

[1] "FPR No. 1, an Experiment in Standardized and Prefabricated Law," in University of Chicago Law Review, December, 1945, pp. 90–104.

[2] Those provisions that recurred frequently throughout the regulations and were generally applicable to the food industry were brought together, standardized, and published in a single autonomous pricing document, issued as Food Products Regulation No. 1. The non-recurring provisions that necessarily differed for each type of food commodity were stated separately from the master regulation and separately from each other according to their natural groupings. Each of these separate documents was issued as a "supplement" to the master regulation. Thus Supplement 1 covered macaroni products; Supplement 6, frozen fruits and vegetables; Supplement 7, canned fruits and vegetables, and so on.

accompany any further extension of direct government control over specific commercial operations.

Policy-Making Through Interpretation. The task of interpretation of statutes, regulations, and executive orders is both large and essential. No legal document can ever be so precise that it will specifically cover all contingencies. To quote Monroe Oppenheimer's graphic statement to the writer, "The draftsman, being human, cannot be omniscient nor delphic; and any documents, however clear they may seem when first drafted, soon reveal ambiguities and hiatuses which must be resolved and filled." Hence the preparation of interpretative memoranda is essential, and in such interpretation the opinions rendered by the lawyers are frequently decisive in determining how the statute or regulation is developed in actual operation.[1]

The importance of the interpretative function cannot be overemphasized. Here, the function of the lawyer is not unlike that of a judge. The interpretation of a statute has traditionally been thought of as an almost mechanical exercise of textual exegesis and logic. Actually, in genuinely doubtful cases a conflict between competing social, political, or economic desires is almost always involved. The lawyer interpreting a statute or regulation as part of the administrative process, no less than the judge in the event of litigation, must make a choice between these conflicting drives if he is to decide the case at all. How important intelligent and sympathetic lawyers can be in the effectiveness of an administrative program is illustrated by the remarkable scope of coverage relating to wages and hours that has been achieved by the Wage and Hour Division of the Department of Labor under an apparently narrow statute.

Policy-Making Through Review. When the review not only of legal but of administrative matters is entrusted to attorneys, they are in a position to exercise considerable effective control over the policy decisions of executive officials. In some cabinet depart-

[1] The Congressional Record for May 10, 1944, reported on page 4289 that between 1933 and 1942 inclusive, 3,565 executive orders were issued and 4,304 "public laws" were enacted by the Congress. These figures alone provide some insight into the magnitude of the problem of drafting and interpretation.

ments the general solicitor's office is expected to examine all documents, whether legal or administrative, that are submitted to the Secretary. Similarly, the chief counsel of each bureau or division of the department may be required to pass on material prepared by the non-legal as well as the legal staff. In such instances it is assumed that legal components are inherent in so large a percentage of matters dealt with and non-lawyers are often so unable to recognize those components that every document should be reviewed by an attorney. Such a procedure, however, tends to encourage the lawyer to include consideration of administrative as well as legal matters in his review. Thus he easily moves into the area of his making policy and administrative decisions that extend beyond the boundaries of the legal field.

Many students of public administration, and also the law offices of some departments and agencies have severely frowned upon placing this review function in the hands of lawyers. To specialists in administrative management who struggle to keep staff and line functions clearly differentiated, such an intertwining of responsibilities is greatly to be regretted. We cannot evaluate the validity of their disapproval. The important fact here is that lawyers *do* thus engage extensively, if indirectly, in policy-making and administration. It may fairly be said, moreover, that one ground of objection which formerly prevailed is tending to disappear. Two decades ago government attorneys were much more inclined than they are now to adopt a negative attitude in advising administrative officials. They were regarded as specialists in what could not be done. Today the situation has changed as a new generation of lawyers has applied a more dynamic concept in its work.

An unpublished study of the administration of the law work of the Department of the Interior, made a few years ago at the request of the Department by a highly responsible federal agency, provides documentary evidence of the control over administrative policy that was exercised through the review function.[1] The

[1] An examination of this study was made available to the writer through the courtesy of the agency.

makers of the study found that much of the work of the large and powerful Solicitor's Office was reconsideration of virtually all matters submitted by the bureaus to the Secretary. The Office had the authority of final decision over these matters, subject to reversal only by the Secretary and those who assisted him in the general supervision of the Department. Thus it was a review tribunal over the bureaus, not limited to questions of law. The study pointed to specific instances in which, as a review agency, it had opposed the administrative position taken by bureau chiefs.

The Office also exercised the function of detecting items that affected other bureaus where co-ordination and adjustment were needed, and often assumed responsibility for doing the co-ordinating and adjusting. Hence, in addition to performing law work, the Solicitor's Office acted as administrative supervisor and co-ordinator, and as an administrative assistant secretary.

Another major sphere of activity within the Solicitor's Office where the attorneys functioned both as administrators and lawyers was the hearing and drafting, and virtually the making, of decisions on appeals to the Secretary from bureau determinations. As an appellate body, it did not always restrict itself to passing upon the facts or legal issues as disclosed by the record. It sometimes conducted independent investigations of fact; it treated the appeal as a new administrative question.

In many of the bureaus of the Department, the law offices were used extensively as a check control over the operating staff. The attitude was prevalent that policy-makers and administrators should not engage in the making of decisions or in other forms of action without the sanction of an attorney. Assumption of the administrative function had been carried so far in one service of the Department that the office of the chief counsel participated actively in the formulation of general administrative policy, in the development of administrative programs, and in the operational conduct of administrative transactions.

Policy-Making Through Litigation. The litigation of a government agency may itself be made into an instrument for the development and effectuation of policy. This is obviously true of the administration of the antitrust laws, which are couched in broad terms and are given specific content only as court decisions are rendered. Since private litigation under the antitrust acts has been comparatively rare, the matters to be presented to the courts are determined almost wholly by the Department of Justice. An administration may, consequently, be either "tough" or "easy" in instituting prosecution. By its action or inaction it may go far in determining what business practices shall be sanctioned and what condemned. Even prior judicial decisions do not determine the law conclusively, for skillful litigation strategy may result in a judgment that serves to hem in an outmoded decision or dictum, or that reverses it.

Agencies, moreover, which are not wholly dependent upon the courts in dealing with their problems, must ordinarily function within limits set by court decisions. Indeed, the validity of an agency's entire operations may depend upon the outcome of a constitutional case for which it sometimes sets the stage. In comparing the fate of the National Industrial Recovery Act with that of the National Labor Relations Act, for example, the probable effect of public opinion, the Presidential "Court packing" proposal, the difference in scope of the two acts, and so on must be taken into consideration. But attention must also be centered upon the fatal weakness of the case of Schechter v. United States (popularly known as the "sick chicken" case) which was the first to reach the Supreme Court under the NIRA, and the relative strength of the steel and companion cases that initially established the constitutionality of the NLRA.

By pressing the right cases in the right order, also, both administratively before itself and afterward in the courts, an agency may establish its authority in obvious matters and lead from them to the less obvious in marking out the limits of its power. Thus it does not shock the courts, defy common sense, and risk failure by pressing an extreme claim in the first instance. Through the strategy of careful selection and timing of cases, the National Labor Relations Act and the Fair Labor Standards Act, to cite two outstanding instances, have been given enlarged application commensurate with the interstate ramifications of modern business.[1]

Policy-Making Through Counseling. Much of the most influential work of the attorney as policy-maker is done in the role of legal and policy adviser to administrative officials. The importance of this role is sometimes overlooked, because it varies greatly from agency to agency and because the advisory function is often exercised in so informal or highly personalized a way that little appears about it in annual reports or other published form.

Since a swarm of legal problems surrounds almost every question with which administrators and policy-makers are faced, they are likely to turn constantly to counsel for advice. They inquire if there *is* a legal aspect to the problem; they want to know *what* they can do in regard to a particular situation, and *how* it can be done. They frequently expect counsel to sit at the conference table at which questions of policy are decided. In such a close relationship the attorney almost inevitably comes, sometimes perhaps without realizing it, to express approval or disapproval of administrative policy. Even when he does not create, he at least strongly influences, policy.

The very fact, moreover, that an agency has definite objectives and continuing programs for the achievement of those objectives serves further to strengthen the lawyer's strategic position. Instead of being called upon for assistance only when a legal problem arises in affairs that normally run along without his aid, he is increasingly expected as a staff member of the agency to play an integral role in the effectuation of long-range programs. Sometimes, because the programs of an agency are highly technical,

---

[1] According to government attorneys, long-range litigation strategy is employed by industry and business too in tax and other matters where judicial authority is sought for contentions advantageous to business. An example of its use is said to be the labor litigation of the first thirty-five years of the Sherman and other antitrust acts, in which organized employers—taking the legal initiative and utilizing these acts, the injunction procedure, and common law concepts relating to employment— moved step by step to enmesh organized labor in ever tighter restraints. This situation was radically remedied by the Norris-LaGuardia Act of 1932.

because changes occur in the administrative personnel, or because the "high command" is largely occupied with interagency
matters and public relations, the general counsel is the only
person familiar with all aspects of the program. When such a
situation occurs, major responsibility rests upon him for maintaining the operations of the agency.

Fortuitous circumstances determine to no small degree the
magnitude of the lawyer's contribution. Some administrators
feel the need for counsel far more than do others. An occasional
operating chief develops the habit of dependence to such an
extent that the lawyer becomes his right hand. Some administrators respect lawyers and like to "have them around"; others distrust them and call on them only when it is unavoidable. In some
agencies, especially among certain of the older ones, the tendency
persists to keep the law office entirely separate from operating
units and to limit its program to strictly legal questions. In other
agencies, particularly emergency agencies where a large and involved program has to be developed and put into action with the
utmost dispatch, lawyers on the higher levels are required to
participate in policy-making. Many of the attorneys, moreover,
are members of the staff of the operating divisions and thus are
responsible to the administrative heads instead of the office of
general counsel.

This horizontal rather than vertical form of legal organization,
already noted in connection with the OPA, generally enhances
the lawyer's opportunity for co-operative endeavor with other
specialists and for policy-making through the conference method.
However, it is viewed as a disadvantage by some lawyers, because
they believe that it renders a uniform legal policy more difficult
and deprives the individual attorney who disagrees with his administrative chief of the support of a legal supervisor at a higher
level of policy determination. John Lord O'Brian, General
Counsel for the War Production Board, was so convinced of the
validity of maintaining a legal staff which was unified and independent that he required all attorneys working under him to
be salaried government employes who had already divorced

themselves from their own law firms or practices.[1] He also required that all attorneys doing legal work in the agency should be on his staff and report to him. After consultation with each executive, he assigned lawyers to the various divisions and branches as required. His attorneys were instructed to assist and advise but not to impede executive decisions, and not to act as policy-makers. Furthermore, O'Brian was given authority to review all proposed appointments of lawyers to executive positions. He frequently disapproved such appointments if there was evident intent to appoint a lawyer to an executive position where he would give legal advice and compete with the legal division.

Unlike the WPB and even more than the OPA, the Board of Economic Warfare (BEW) permitted fortuitous circumstances and organizational flexibility to determine the size of the contribution made by lawyers to its programs. As in the OPA, many of the lawyers were responsible to administrators, and hence were readily able to collaborate with the executives, economists, and business experts in their divisions. They were also able to transfer with relative ease, and were often encouraged to transfer, from legal to administrative positions. Because few agencies better illustrate how large a policy-making role lawyers may play, if circumstances are favorable to them, it is illuminating to review briefly the tasks performed by attorneys within certain parts of the BEW.

The General Counsel was expected to attend and participate in the Director's almost daily staff meetings of from four to eight persons who formulated policy. He was also called frequently in personal conference with the Director. In addition, he recruited most of the legal staff for the Board, drafted legislation and executive orders, and carried on negotiations in interdepartmental affairs. His work obviously lay in the very heart of policy-making.

In the Board's Office of Imports, whose function was the purchasing of critical materials, lawyers assumed an extremely active role. This resulted partly from the function of the Office, which

[1] Emmerich, Herbert, "The Search for Executive Talent," in Civil Service in Wartime, edited by Leonard D. White. University of Chicago Press, 1945, p. 35.

required preparation of complicated contracts. More important, however, was the attitude of the administrative head. He held in high regard the intelligence and judgment of lawyers, quite apart from their legal competence. The Associate General Counsel and the two Assistant General Counsels, who had been assigned to the Office of Imports, were present at his staff meetings. Their opinions were solicited on practical and business, as well as legal, problems. Assigned to each division and section of the Office were attorneys who engaged directly in negotiations with businessmen, drafted contracts, and interpreted contracts. One lawyer evolved the idea, made the initial draft, and promoted the desirability of the "labor clause," which although much debated was subsequently incorporated in many of the contracts. In general, both legal counsel and administrative staff worked closely together with little concern about separation of functions.

A considerable number of lawyers in the Board of Economic Warfare shortly moved into purely administrative positions. Some went to the London branch of the Office of Economic Warfare Analysis to assume executive duties, others were sent on economic missions to foreign countries. A still larger number of Spanish-speaking lawyers was recruited by the BEW to implement the program of freezing Axis funds and creating "black lists" in Latin American countries. Their work, done under the aegis of the Department of State, was partly legal, partly executive.

Administration and Policy-Making. The tendency, observed in the BEW, for lawyers to move into executive positions has been a clear-cut and definite trend throughout American history. Sometimes the lawyer begins his government career as an administrator. Sometimes he begins as an attorney, is attracted to executive work or to the occasionally better salary and greater prestige, and hence makes the change when opportunity presents itself. A large percentage of the persons politically appointed to administrative positions are lawyers. How many law-trained men occupy executive posts is not known, because of the fact that they are classified as administrators rather than attorneys. That their number is large is unquestioned. An earlier page has pointed to the fact that the board chairmen of some of the most important administrative agencies were formerly practicing lawyers. So were many of the executive heads and persons responsible for important determinations of policy in the various units of the cabinet departments.

The statistical evidence presented by Macmahon and Millett, who have surveyed the professional background of all Under Secretaries and Assistant Secretaries in the cabinet departments from the creation of those secretaryships until 1938, confirms how long-standing and pervasive has been the practice of selecting law-trained men for these high administrative posts.[1] Five of 10 Under Secretaries of State were lawyers. Of 7 Under Secretaries of the Treasury 5 were lawyers. All 11 First Assistant Secretaries and 18 of 21 Assistant Secretaries of the Interior and 6 of 12 Assistant Secretaries of Commerce were law trained. Similar posts in the Department of Justice were staffed exclusively with lawyers. Only in the case of the posts of Second Assistant Secretary of State (a position that existed from 1866 to 1924), second, third, and fourth Assistant Postmaster General, and second Assistant Secretary of Labor have the appointees from other professions equaled or outnumbered the lawyers. Interestingly enough no Assistant Secretary of Agriculture has been a lawyer.

Such law-trained administrators and hundreds of others in less exalted posts have been lost to the legal fraternity only by count. The professional training that they have had and their former experience as attorneys inevitably determine, to no small degree, the efficiency and social outlook that they will bring to the administrative post. Their task is a dual one: they must execute policies already made; they must engage in policy-making as a basis for further administration. The two tasks are inseparable. Policies are made and remade in the process of administration.

The public generally looks upon most legislation as policy-deciding. Hence it assumes that policy-making in the broad sense is not supposed to be part of administration. But this is true only

[1] Federal Administrators, pp. 293–294.

within very wide limits. Some legislative action, such as that—to use an extreme example—which provided funds for "rural rehabilitation and relief," is so little policy-deciding that the administrator is obliged to assume responsibility for deciding both *what* shall be done and *how*. Again, administrators may work under legislative mandates, as does the Social Security Administration, where the Congress had assumed that detailed policy could be evolved only as the result of experience in administering the act, and of research carried on concurrently for the purpose of aiding in the formulation of policy. Even when statutes are most specific and detailed, numberless policy decisions must be made in the mere process of translating the written documents into organizational programs. Thereafter, deciding *how* to implement the statutes becomes a necessary concomitant of every step in the administrative process.

PART THREE

IMPLICATIONS FOR LEGAL EDUCATION

PART III

IMPLICATIONS FOR LEGAL EDUCATION

IN Education for Responsible Living, Wallace Brett Donham has given the reader an opportunity to learn of the reorientation in philosophy that occurred in the Harvard Graduate School of Business Administration during his deanship of almost a quarter of a century. Essential specialized training needed "narrowly" by the business administrator was evolved during that period. But what was more important, in Dr. Donham's estimation, was the simultaneous study of the functions of the business administrator, public or private, in his wider relations to the national life, and the attempt to discover ways of relating the training of the School to such functions. Business administration in a technical and immediate sense is often extremely efficient. In its over-all public relations and in its handling of human problems, however, Dr. Donham believed it to be relatively weak.

Therefore, the primary objective of the School became not so much the training of specialists as the developing of "the student's capacity *to examine as many of the constantly changing facts and forces surrounding administrative situations in business as he can bring effectively into his thinking, and to use these facts imaginatively in determining current policies and action.*"[1] This capacity is an essential condition to socially sound performance of the administrator's most important functions. "Breadth of background and the ability to integrate many viewpoints at the point of action are," Dr. Donham concludes, "more important than specialization."[2]

These observations would certainly seem as applicable to those law schools that are in a position to prepare persons for the higher

[1] Harvard University Press, Cambridge, 1944, p. 6. (Italics are the writer's.)
[2] *Ibid.*, pp. 6–7.

93

levels of government service and for broad planning and advisory functions as to the Harvard Graduate School of Business Administration. Thomas Reed Powell is attributed with the satirical remark, "If you think that you can think about a thing inextricably attached to something else without thinking of the thing it is attached to, then you have a legal mind."[1] It is for the eradication of the "legal mind" wherever found that Dr. Donham argues, and for the substitution of the mind that has been trained to integrate many viewpoints.

On those levels to which the leading law schools would expect their graduates to rise, government lawyers are day in and day out confronted with intricate and important problems for which a solution must be found. The integration of many viewpoints at the point of action is almost indispensable for discovering a solution. Relatively few of these problems go to the courts for settlement. More often they arise and must be decided within the planning and advisory process; the review and interpretative process; the drafting process which David Riesman, Jr., has so aptly characterized as both the symbol and the technique of planning[2]; or the process of organizing and operating legal, and often non-legal, programs.

For such functions the case-by-case examination of selected judicial opinions and statutes cannot furnish adequate training. It must be largely supplemented by other teaching materials and methods. In skillful hands the case method is an incomparable tool for instruction in the analysis of problems. Something comparable must be found as an instrumentality for emphasizing synthesis, which is of equal importance to success in the solution of problems. Legal doctrine and highly specialized procedural knowledge of appellate tribunals are essential for the advocate. For the counselor, administrator, or draftsman who finds himself engaged in the formidable task of organizing opposed social forces, an understanding of those forces and knowledge of

[1] Arnold, Thurman W., The Symbols of Government. Yale University Press, New Haven, 1935, p. 101.

[2] "Law and Social Science: A Report on Michael and Wechsler's Classbook on Criminal Law and Administration," in Yale Law Journal, February, 1941, p. 638.

methods whereby their change can be effectuated are of primary significance.

How to teach the lawyer's role in social planning is the problem that confronts postwar legal education. For a generation before Pearl Harbor nearly closed all law-school doors for four years, a variety of individual, sporadic, and generally unco-ordinated efforts had been made to attack this problem. The schools had shown little interest, to be sure, in training lawyers for government service as such. But they had become increasingly aware of the fact that a nation moving constantly toward closely knit, gigantic industrialization and urbanization requires a wider range of legal aptitudes than had been necessary in the nineteenth century. Some of their efforts to bring the curriculum more in conformity with the economic and social pattern of twentieth century America had met with considerable success. Others were experiments which blossomed for a moment and died, leaving scarcely a trace upon the fabric of legal education. The following sections are an attempt to review and evaluate such of those efforts as seem to hold the greatest promise as training for government service.

REDUCTION IN NUMBER OF COURSES AND CO-ORDINATION OF TEACHING MATERIALS

Prior to the late 1920's, the curriculum of the average school appeared to be a collection of many and largely unrelated courses which had been added with the years, sometimes as a concession to changes in the nature of law and law practice but quite as often as a concession to individual teachers who wished to offer certain courses in which they had developed a particular interest.

It was not unusual even for law schools with sharply limited budgets and with faculties of only six or eight full-time instructors to list fifty or sixty courses in their bulletins. In spite of heavy teaching schedules, all of these courses could not be given annually, and many of them, when given, were elected by a mere handful of students. Such schools, moreover, could obviously not furnish teachers with adequate training in all these subjects. Hence many courses were taught by persons who had had no intimate acquaintance with those particular fields of law, but who contented themselves with presenting the judicial decisions of appellate courts and the legislative enactments relative to the subject that were found in the selected casebook.

Frequently a considerable number of the courses in the curriculum of a given school were further elaboration of a basic course. Some schools listed, for example, numerous specialized courses in property. Important as is the subject, many present-day teachers believe that the common law was elaborated upon to excessive length. Where this occurred, a professor of property law had generally succeeded in having one specialized course after another added to the curriculum without substantial faculty determination of policy of what subject matter is appropriate for the basic curriculum and what belongs in graduate courses, or how much instruction can be given in a particular field—no matter how important—without encroaching upon other fields that should be cultivated.

Aside from courses that represented elaboration of one subject, the curriculum was composed of fragmented portions of law so unassorted in arrangement that existing relationships were often not apparent. Some of the subjects were as broad in scope as administrative law; some as restricted as bailments, damages, or suretyship. The curriculum was not a *course of study* based on sequence or interrelationship of subject matter. It was rather a miscellaneous collection of offerings that tradition and individual opinion had decreed would be useful for practicing lawyers or interesting to teach. Curriculum construction by group planning was scarcely known.

One of the first indications of the intellectual ferment that began to work in the law schools before the close of the decade was the attempt of several schools to reduce the number of courses. Some were merely dropped from the curriculum. More often, however, the most important elements were culled from certain courses where relationships existed, and these elements were rearranged in new teaching units. Former courses in partnerships and in corporations, for example, or in agency, partnerships, and corporations were replaced in many schools by one substantial course in business associations.

This process of reallocation and reconstruction serves three goals simultaneously. It permits the saving of considerable time which may be used for the introduction of badly needed public law courses; it generally makes for much greater efficiency both in teaching and learning; it frequently enables the student to gain some knowledge of more fields of law than was possible under the old system of extensive elective courses, in no considerable number of which was he able to enroll. Professor Edson R. Sunderland's course in judicial administration at the University of Michigan, for which he expressly prepared teaching materials,[1] admirably illustrates the achievement of all three goals.

Prior to the introduction of this course the Michigan Law School offered fifteen semester hours divided among the following courses: common law pleading, five hours; code pleading, two hours; equity pleading, two hours; part of trial practice relating to jurisdiction, one hour; extraordinary legal remedies, two hours; federal practice, two hours; legal ethics, one hour. Professor Sunderland was permitted four semester hours for the course in judicial administration. Yet, in a letter to the writer, he stated that "the present arrangement is much more effective in many ways."

The three varieties of pleading, for example, involve a great deal of duplication when separately taught. Combined as they now are in one course, all duplication is avoided and the different problems in pleading are each discussed in the light of the varying solutions employed at common law, under the codes, and in equity. Extraordinary legal remedies, furthermore, are much more intelligible when treated in connection with ordinary common law remedies. Under the present arrangement ordinary common law remedies, which were formerly discussed as a part

---

[1] Judicial Administration: Its Scope and Methods. Callaghan and Co., Chicago, 1937.

of common law pleading, are immediately followed by material on extraordinary legal remedies, thereby making clear and intelligible the entire field of common law jurisdiction.

When a separate course was given on federal practice, comparatively few of the Michigan students elected it. Now that judicial administration is required, everyone obtains a fair working knowledge of the American system of federal courts. Finally something useful has been substituted for the course in legal ethics, which had never proved satisfactory. Professor Sunderland maintains that, for the sophisticated third-year student, it had only been "a course of instruction upon the problem of how far one can go in the direction of improper practice without being caught." When the subject is dealt with in the first year within the larger framework, students are easily given a clear idea of rules of professional conduct which are enforced by two kinds of sanctions: the first legal, carrying liabilities and penalties of one type; the second ethical, carrying penalties of another type but perhaps equally serious.

The process of selection and reorganization of materials may, of course, be applied to an entire curriculum. The new curriculum which emerged at the University of Chicago in 1937, and which received much attention and comment from the entire American law-school world, was made possible through extreme compression and shifting of materials taken from the traditional courses dealing primarily with private rights and their protection by the courts. Harry A. Bigelow, then dean of the Law School, stated to the writer that he believed overlapping and duplication had been largely eliminated in the interest of saving time for the introduction of other subjects, but that little truly essential had been omitted. Professor Malcolm Sharp questioned whether the process of compression could not profitably have been carried even farther in order to provide greater opportunity to study vital contemporary legal issues in their setting of philosophical and economic thought and experience. Although many teachers of law interpreted as drastic the cuts made at Chicago in the customary private law materials, the same general trend toward compression was going on in many schools, and no fewer than a half dozen in the midwest region alone had reduced the number of their courses but possibly enriched their curricula, or were in the process of doing it.

The College of Law of the University of Nebraska is the most recent school to publish a completely restudied curriculum. Casual comparison of the prewar and postwar curricula would seem to demonstrate that much of the training in private law had been eliminated in order to include more teaching in public law, legislation, and the great corporate business structures. However, by careful planning of a unified course of study, by reorganizing materials in large teaching units, and by making most of these units required rather than elective, students will receive almost as much, and in some instances more, instruction in private law than was received formerly.[1] Simultaneously they will be required to study other fields of law practice that have gained major importance in the last quarter-century.

INFLUENCE OF FUNCTIONALISM

At much the same time that teaching materials drawn from two to half a dozen courses were being coalesced in a single course and the curriculum itself had begun to be viewed as an appropriate subject for study and revision, legal cases came to be used by some instructors to serve different ends from those they had formerly served. Their purpose had earlier been conceived of as illustrating legal doctrine—a purpose the greatest usefulness of which was to advocates and judges of appellate courts. Even for advocacy and the judgeship, however, it was seen that more than legal doctrine is requisite. Hence cases began to be treated functionally; they were grouped along factual rather than conceptual lines. How did particular legal disputes arise? What was the economic, social, and philosophical or political setting in which these disputes had arisen? A few teachers particularly in the field of commercial law, moreover, began to ask what were

[1] Beutel, Frederick K., The New Curriculum at the University of Nebraska College of Law. Reprinted from the Nebraska Law Review, June, 1946, pp. 9–11.

the types of business transactions and the various situations in which the lawyer acted as counselor rather than advocate. How, in short, could cases be employed to provide training in the use of legal materials as well as legal doctrine both for advocacy and for counseling?

Professor Alexander H. Frey's statement to the writer in 1933 of his course at the University of Pennsylvania in business associations, the outgrowth of former courses in private corporations and partnership, suggests how he reoriented his use of cases.

My own aim is not merely to portray the rules which the present era of collectivism brought sharply to the foreground, but also to develop these rules with my students much more realistically than is possible through the medium of focusing attention upon legal concepts. Consequently, I classify my materials in accordance with the types of transactions with which business groups or associations are involved. For instance, instead of dealing with the activities of a functioning corporation under such chapter headings as powers and liabilities, directors, rights of stockholders, creditors, legislative control, and so on, I utilize the following groupings of materials: control or selection of the management, assembling funds, acquisition and disposition of property, short-term credit transactions, instituting and defending suits, employment transactions, accounts, compensation to managers and employees, distribution of "profits," distribution of "capital," allocation of losses.

A law-review article written some years later by Professor Karl N. Llewellyn around Roscoe Turner Steffen's Cases on Commercial and Investment Paper (Foundation Press, Chicago, 1939) indicates not only how large was the change made by Steffen over the older types of casebooks but to what degree law-school thinking was moving from emphasis upon legal doctrine to emphasis upon legal function or process. Llewellyn wrote in part[1]:

The book seeks to set its problems into our going economic institutions, past and current. It opens up, for training both in advocacy and in counselling, the problems of *using* legal materials. . . . It provides copious materials in the way of description of practice, presentation of problems, discussion, comment, and question. In a fashion happily be-

[1] "On the Problem of Teaching 'Private' Law," in Harvard Law Review, March, 1941, pp. 781–783.

coming usual, it presents a rounded collection of statutory texts (both domestic and comparative); it offers occasional cuts of forms, and repeated gatherings of clauses which raise and solve problems. I miss more cuts of the types of paper discussed. Those help students to *see* paper. . . .

Chapter I . . . strikes an unusual note, and a welcome one. It chooses as its thread neither the familiar "elements of negotiability," nor yet "the incidents of the contract." It is instead on "Types of Paper." . . . Steffen's Types are presented roughly in the historical order of their emergence, with effort to show first what each type was for, and second, what further uses it has since been put to; the legal problems *develop*, in consequence. . . .

The cases are seen functionally, the patterns of rule and concept are presented against the background of the time and the need which called them forth; that background is to be kept in mind as the formed pattern is then carried forward, to be tested out (and modified) as new backgrounds and needs develop. Thus the problems of court, counsellor, and advocate open up in terms of process—for process is the continuing phase of those problems. . . .

This functional approach to law has perhaps been carried farther at Northwestern than at any other law school. In 1931 Dean Leon Green produced the first edition of The Judicial Process in Tort Cases.[1] In earlier casebooks on torts, cases had been grouped under such traditional headings as proximate cause, negligence, contributory negligence, last clear chance, assault and battery, fraud, and so on. His chapters bore such realistic headings as threats, insults, blows, attacks, fights, restraints, nervous shocks. There were sections devoted to physicians, surgeons, and hospitals; treatment of ill, disabled, and irresponsible persons; traffic and transportation; builders, contractors, and workmen. Attention had been shifted from doctrine to the type of harm involved in the tort.

Dean Green stated in the Preface that his experience, first as a practitioner and later as a teacher, had convinced him that the significance which tort cases have for the law student is to be found in the numerous processes which courts employ in dealing

[1] West Publishing Co., St. Paul. The second edition was published in 1939.

with such cases. *How* does the judicial process operate? *Why*, in a given instance, does it operate in one way rather than in some other? On these two inquiries he thought that all of tort law could be hung. His emphasis upon the judicial process was evident in the title he gave the book.

In 1940 Dean Green issued another book, Cases on Injuries to Relations,[1] which was similarly unconventional in that it also dealt with factual situations. Furthermore, it was concerned with a field of private law that the schools had viewed only incidentally. Green argued that the protection available at law and in equity to those who enjoy the basic relations of society provides a convenient core for the study of the common problems of such relations, at a great saving of the time of student and teacher. Hence the book was designed to develop the form and content of the processes which are peculiar to the protection of these relations. Many of the materials had formerly been covered by courses on domestic relations, trade regulation, labor law, and equitable relief against torts. Other materials dealing with political and professional relations, general social relations, and abuses of governmental power, which had been inadequately treated in courses on torts, were added. Because protection against injuries to relations represents the freshest but as yet very incomplete growth of common law and equity, the degree of richness of the case material presented naturally had to depend upon the extent to which the courts have evolved principles for the protection of these several types of relations.

Professor Harold C. Havighurst, also of Northwestern, treated contracts functionally as Dean Green had treated torts. He made the nature of the transaction with which the contract is concerned his focal point. In the Preface to A Selection of Contract Cases and Related Quasi-Contract Cases,[2] he expressed the view that the grouping of cases according to subject matter rather than according to the doctrines employed enables the student more easily to master the facts of a case, and to see each situation as a

[1] The Lawyers Co-operative Publishing Co., Rochester, N.Y.
[2] The Lawyers Co-operative Publishing Co., 1934.

living problem rather than as dead material for logical dissection. He believed that rules and doctrines would thus be viewed in truer perspective, and that the student's power of analysis would be more rapidly developed. He divided his casebook into four parts. Contracts for services were treated first. (Labor contracts were not included; they were left to the course in labor law.) Then came contracts for gratuities to friends and relatives, and charitable subscriptions. Loans, including small loans, formed the content of the third part, and contracts for the sale of goods constituted the final part.

The following paragraph from Professor M. T. Van Hecke's review[1] of the book indicates his judgment of the success which Havighurst had achieved.

. . . The book is constructed with admirable skill and judgment. Here the case law of contracts is placed in its true perspective, allocated to the business situations in which the legal problems most commonly arise, and contrasted constantly with the opportunities afforded to business men to establish their own law through contract drafting, if their bargaining power is not too unequal. The book enables the student to acquire a skill in dealing with the application and construction of the more standardized contract provision, as well as in handling questions where no expressed intention of the parties is available. From their immediate juxtaposition, the comparable values of the appropriate judicial procedures may be accurately determined, and a sense of generalship developed. By frequent demonstrations of what the state has had to do by way of regulation of some contract situations, social-mindedness is directly encouraged.

In all of these instances an attempt was made to present teaching materials in such a manner that the character of the fact situation out of which the legal problem had arisen would not be lost to sight while the legal concepts involved were under examination. Difference of opinion has existed about the fruitfulness of the undertaking. Many professors like Llewellyn and Van Hecke have been enthusiastic in their praise; others have concluded that the results were far from altogether successful. However that may be, the broader implications of the appearance and

[1] In Illinois Law Review, November, 1934, p. 407.

application of functionalism should not be underestimated. Functionalism grew out of a dissatisfaction with legal education; it sought to find a way for bringing specific courses and entire curricula more in line with the demands of legal practice. Wherever it has appeared, it has generally been not only a manifestation of, but a springboard for further, attempts to view the role of law and the lawyer in contemporary society in a more realistic and dynamic fashion. Its motivation has led, often unconsciously, to unexpected and significant ways of conceiving of legal education.

As early as 1929 William Draper Lewis suggested to Justin Miller, in connection with the establishment of the Duke University Law School, that courses or groups of courses ought to be planned in their relation to industry, transportation, social conditions, international affairs, and so on. He argued that the formal classification of courses and the departmentalization of work which had characterized the law school had contributed largely to the failure of many lawyers and judges to realize that the law is not a formal thing, susceptible of such subdivision, but that it is a living thing inextricably interwoven in the fabric of social or industrial life and that it can be properly understood, interpreted, and applied only from that point of view.[1]

The recent reorganization of the curriculum at Northwestern University is in line to a considerable degree with Lewis' suggestions. This results largely from the exceptional interest that Dean Green has long shown in looking at the institutions of American society and then inquiring what the lawyer's function is in relation to each of them.[2] Therefore, in the curriculum which he and

---

[1] In his recent article, "The Lawyer's Role in Public Administration" (Yale Law Journal, April, 1946, p. 518), Fritz Morstein Marx suggests that perhaps a practical way of making progress in demonstrating the living, interrelated nature of law would be to build course sequences around institutional complexes such as enterprise, labor, and the family; or ideas such as liberty and representation; or major intellectual processes (methodology) employed in different disciplines. "Courses in jurisprudence, when cutting deep enough, have proved their value as a vehicle for conveying the essence of legal thinking and of legal thought. Mere accumulation of subject matter, of course, will never be enough."

[2] See his pamphlet, Institutional Life—The Lawyer's Role, published by Louisiana State University, 1938.

his faculty have recently devised, after extended conferences with members of the Chicago bar concerning the functions lawyers now perform and are likely to perform, third-year seminars are listed in agriculture, communications, insurance, patents, protection of health and general welfare, the power system, and transportation. Every student is required to select one of these seminars. Although much of the material that will be examined in most seminars has formerly been included in traditional courses, this functional realignment emphasizes institution and on-going legal processes rather than doctrine. Particularly gratifying, moreover, is the inclusion of seminars on agriculture, and health and the general welfare. In spite of the fact that government is now almost continuously in the act of formulating or administering policy relating to farmers' economic interests, health, education, housing, public assistance and social insurance, and the conservation of natural resources, the law schools have paid but scant heed to these areas of development.

Three required courses of the second year on corporate relations, employment relations, and competitive and consumer relations, are designed to broaden the base of legal preparation for dealing with industrial problems, and to guarantee that the student shall be oriented not only in corporate structure and function, but in management-labor relationships, and in questions of fair competition and protection of consumers' interests. A required seminar, given concurrently with the three courses in relations, examines particular industries from the point of view of their corporate organization, financing, labor relations, competitive relations, trade association activities, and price and wage policies.

It is obvious that beyond the work of the first four terms of the law school which are devoted to "basic concepts" and "procedures," Northwestern's emphasis is primarily on training attorneys to work with, within, or possibly against the great corporations of contemporary America, whether private or public. The program is based on the assumption that the task of most of its graduates will be largely one of formulating policy whether for industry, business, industrialized farming, unionized labor, or government, and that policy will be made more frequently by the lawyer in the role of counselor than that of advocate.

Another illustration of the kind of functionalism to which Lewis referred is to be found at the University of Chicago in the broad, inclusive course on law and economic organization that was planned as an essential part of the new curriculum. All students were to be expected to devote approximately one-half of their senior year to it. The course was formulated as a study of the effects of legal institutions upon the operation of the economic system and of the influence of economic factors in the development of legal institutions. The teaching materials were, in considerable part, a condensation and synthesis of materials designed for courses in industrial organization, labor organization and collective bargaining, credit and business fluctuations, bankruptcy and reorganization, and taxation. In fact, during the war and postwar reorganization when offering this course made more demands upon the school than could be met, its five components were substituted. The value of the course lay in the degree to which legal materials had been synthesized and economic materials had been interpolated, and in the way in which the functional approach pointed up the lawyer's task within our industrial system of "free enterprise" and its partial control by government.

Dean Katz has described the course as presented in 1940–1941.[1] During the first two months concentrated study was given to the antitrust laws and to labor law in the light of economic theory of prices and wages. The next two months were devoted to an examination of the marketing and employment problems of the steel industry. After an introductory view of the history of the industry and its major units, three lines of government policy were utilized as the focus for discussion. These policies might be described as "let well enough alone," "enforced competition," and "combination-with-regulation." The steel antitrust cases

[1] "What Changes Are Practical in Legal Education?" in American Bar Association Journal, December, 1941, pp. 760–761.

and the Supreme Court and Federal Trade Commission cases dealing with the basing point system of prices were studied in detail. The practicability of splitting some of the larger companies into competing units was considered, and students were required to explore rather concretely the difficulties involved in such a program. Attention was given to the types of decree entered in other antitrust dissolution cases and to the techniques being developed in the enforcement of the "death sentence" on utility holding companies. Some of the evidence and of the studies presented to the Temporary National Economic Committee in connection with the steel industry were considered. In investigating the policy of combination-with-regulation, the experience of the National Recovery Administration was discussed, as well as other proposals for a planned economy.

The study of the steel industry included a survey of labor history, with some attention to the early strikes and the NRA period. In dealing with current problems, the legal material was supplemented by discussion led by a vice-president of a steel company in charge of its labor relations and by an organizer of the steel union of the Congress of Industrial Organizations (CIO). The operation of the National Labor Relations Act was considered in some detail, including the report of the Smith Committee on the National Labor Relations Board and its work.

The second half-year was given to an examination of problems created by the economic depression. Bankruptcy and corporate reorganization were studied as types of legal machinery for dealing with failure in a profit economy. An effort was made to study the various economic roles which the law of insolvency administration might be expected to fulfill in guiding the allocation of resources, facilitating the transfer and abandonment of invested capital, and permitting the continuance of overcapitalized enterprises.

The first part of the course was under the charge of Charles O. Gregory with his especial interest in labor law, and David F. Cavers, then from Duke University, who was concerned with business regulation. Eugene V. Rostow from the Yale Law

School, as a specialist in reorganization and public control of business, was in charge of the second half-year. The late economist, Professor Henry C. Simons, assisted with the course; several faculty members attended the sessions and contributed whatever they could; and representatives of management and labor were invited to direct an occasional discussion. The organization and presentation of the course involved the Law School in a considerable outlay of time and money as contrasted with traditional teaching methods. The attempt was experimental. No one considered that it was the only, or necessarily the best, way to teach materials that would otherwise be offered in several courses. The course demonstrated its usefulness, however, to such a degree that the School wishes to return to it in the near future.

No reference to functionalism can be ended without some word concerning the growing emphasis that is being placed upon the policy-making function of the lawyer. A considerable part of the chapter about the work of lawyers in the federal government attempts to demonstrate the degree to which lawyers are engaged in policy-making, not merely when they act as counselors to administrative officials but when they draft or interpret bills, executive orders, and regulations. The policy-making function is similarly important in the private practice of law. That profession of society which is involved in advising, and in negotiating and drafting documents for, all the corporate undertakings of the nation, private and public, is engaged—year in and year out— in the making of policy.

Professors Harold D. Lasswell and Myres S. McDougal of Yale are the most insistent voices in demanding that policy-making be utilized as a basic, functional approach to legal education. In large part they are responsible for forcing many teachers of law to re-examine the purpose of law training. Their much-discussed article, which no one interested in legal education can afford to overlook, states their proposition thus: "If legal education in the contemporary world is adequately to serve the needs of a free and productive commonwealth, it must be conscious, efficient, and systematic *training for policy-making.*"[1] They would have legal education become realistic enough to consider every functional group in society, from the group which operates international cartels or determines international policy within the Department of State to the unskilled wage-earners. What policy-making services are, or need to be, performed by lawyers for each of these groups? What kind of lawyer is needed to perform them? How can lawyers be trained who will efficiently represent the legitimate interests of these special groups, but without putting their interests ahead of the general interest of society?[2]

One law school, that of the University of Minnesota, has been interested for nearly two decades in training lawyers to assume more broadly the policy-making function in regard to the larger issues of justice and the legislative process. Dean Everett Fraser vigorously stated in the late 1920's that the graduates of his school must be better prepared to serve society, not merely as private practitioners but as members of the bar and bench who could and would undertake greater responsibility for improvement in judicial administration and in statutory law. Hence a fourth year was added to the curriculum in which courses came to be introduced in judicial administration, jurisprudence, legislation including drafting, modern social legislation, and modern philosophies of social reform. Although the term "policy-making" was not used, all of these courses were definitely planned to produce a lawyer more efficient to make policy in the areas designated by Dean Fraser.

In general, however, the policy-making function has received little attention until recently. The bar has been fully aware of, and often blatant about, the size of the role it plays in the operating of American society. But it had defined its role in the broadly descriptive terms, advocacy and counseling, rather than in sharper functional terms which would have revealed the signifi-

---

[1] "Legal Education and Public Policy: Professional Training in the Public Interest," in Yale Law Journal, March, 1943, p. 206.

[2] McDougal, Myres S., "Policy-Making as the Center of Emphasis," in Association of American Law Schools Handbook, 1943, p. 53.

cance of policy-making. Only now are the implications of policy-making for legal education being given conscious recognition within the curriculum of any considerable number of schools. Courses in business units, public control of business, and labor law have probably illustrated, in varying degrees of consistency, the most generally marked orientation toward training for the making of policy. Some of this redirection had been made, however, without full comprehension of its larger significance. Now as new curricula emerge at Northwestern, Nebraska, or elsewhere, the element of conscious planning for "efficient and systematic training for policy-making" becomes more apparent.

THE SOCIAL SCIENCES AND OTHER NON-LEGAL MATERIALS

In a review in 1906 of Florence Kelley's Some Ethical Gains Through Legislation, Charles R. Henderson noted "the humiliating and discouraging decisions of some courts which set aside laws made to meet contemporary conditions by appeals to precedents drawn from ancient history."[1] The facts presented by Mrs. Kelley demonstrated the necessity, he asserted, for introducing social science into law schools. "One can hardly escape from the conclusion that a lawyer who has not studied economics and sociology is very apt to become a public enemy; and many a good judge would be hurtful if he did not get through newspapers and magazines a diluted kind of sociology which saves him from bondage to mere precedent."

Thomas Reed Powell, in an address in 1917 on "Law as a Cultural Study," remarked[2]:

From the desks of law teachers and from the Bench there has been much refinement of reasoning about the fellowservant rule, the doctrines of contributory negligence and assumption of risk, and the requirement that fault precede the imposition of liability for injury. The wisdom of these doctrines had been asserted in sorry neglect of the pertinent facts. It is far from complimentary to lawyers that it was a simple

[1] In American Journal of Sociology, May, 1906, p. 847.
[2] In American Law School Review, December, 1917, p. 336.

task for Crystal Eastman to shatter so much of this reasoning with her Work-Accidents and the Law. And much more of our legal reasoning needs to be subjected to the acid test of fact. Law as a cultural study will be intolerant of the reasoning based on the widespread ignorance that we commonly misterm "general knowledge." It will require exhaustive investigation of where we are and whither we are tending before it will listen to what to do or how to do it.

From Walton H. Hamilton's article, "The Ancient Maxim Caveat Emptor," come the two following paragraphs.[1]

The legislature of Connecticut . . . passed an act fixing minimum standards for motor oils offered for sale. The statute provided that vendible oils must meet the tests for quality and composition set down in Technical Paper 323B, issued by the United States Bureau of Mines. The legislation was challenged by a number of oil companies who prayed the federal court of the district of Connecticut for equitable relief. After an extended hearing, a special bench of three judges found the standards to be unreasonable, declared the measure to be a taking of property without due process of law, and pronounced the statute null and void.

The decision of the court provokes doubt rather than dissent. As the fortunes of law broke, the dominant issue came to be reasonableness of the prescribed tests. In an able and comprehensive brief, the attorneys for the companies recited chapter and verse from experts, and presented the results of technical experiments to show how fallible were the Bureau of Mines standards as an index to the practical worth of oils. The representatives of the state countered as best they could with an argument whose burden was largely "powers," "the nature of regulation," and "legislative discretion." If the testimony introduced by the companies had been subjected to critical examination by the state, or if an argument for the technical reasonableness of the disputed tests had been introduced, the result might have been different. As it was, the dialectic of legalism was of no avail against the recitation of technical fact.

These three excerpts have been chosen almost at random from numberless others as illustration that the necessity for drawing upon the social sciences to supplement legal knowledge and techniques has long been recognized. As late as 1931, however,

[1] In Yale Law Journal, June, 1931, pp. 1133–1134.

attempts to solve the problem of how to prepare lawyers to obtain and use social science data, theory, and methodology had been seriously undertaken in very few schools. The excerpts suggest, furthermore, that the bench and bar, which needed but generally did not have this knowledge provided by the social sciences to help them in dealing with broad questions of social and living conditions, also needed but did not have at their disposal the same aids for dealing with torts and with technical business disputes.

Probably no question facing legal education today approaches in importance that of how the prospective lawyer shall be given requisite non-legal information, or at least be given orientation in where to get such information and when and how to use it. Almost countless papers have been read and articles written about this problem. Scores of undertakings to find a solution have been made, but most of them have been small and half-hearted. As yet, accomplishment in the law-school world as a whole has been very unsatisfactory. Failure to achieve more is the result of two causes: the extreme complexity of the problem faced, and the inflexibility and aloofness from contemporary intellectual thought which characterizes the majority of law schools.

The relationship between law and economics appears more immediately obvious to the average instructor than that between law and the other social sciences. The courts have shown awareness of prevailing economic doctrines in cases on negotiability, price-fixing, freedom of contract, and responsibility for industrial risk. Much of the recent social legislation has made it imperative that the lawyer present economic facts and argue the legal implications of economic policies. Many lawyers employed by government and by corporate bodies find themselves faced with the solution of problems the economic component of which far outweighs the legal. For these reasons it might be assumed that the law schools would have made a concentrated, if not coordinated, effort to guarantee that the prospective lawyer have some knowledge of economic facts, theories, and methodology and how to use them.

But law schools rarely require that the student present credits in economics for admission[1]; not more than a handful of economists are associated with legal education; and most law instructors are not themselves "up to the job" of dealing constructively with economic materials, to say nothing of theory, or are making any formal effort to enlarge their horizon. With characteristic frankness, Professor J. H. Beuscher of the University of Wisconsin wrote in a memorandum: "We as teachers and law students are apt to go principally upon our *a priori* ideas of what the economic and social facts really are. I do not believe that we make sufficient use of the statistical data now available in some fields. In fact I am afraid that most of us are not qualified to read and handle such data and to pick the good from the bad." He might have added that when the law instructor attempts to employ economic theory, it is likely to be so outmoded that one recalls the pertinent statement of Ralph Linton, the anthropologist, "The ghosts of defunct theories have a way of haunting the halls of other disciplines for at least a generation after they have been given decent burial in their original homes."[2]

If further testimony is necessary, here is the report of Professor Cavers who, because of his undergraduate major in economics and his reasonably close contact with the subject for nearly a decade as editor of the distinguished Law and Contemporary Problems, might be considered one of the instructors best prepared to handle economics. Yet he maintains that his teaching of law and economic organization at the University of Chicago caused him to realize how deficient were his qualifications for instructing in a field where economics is as important as law. "I who had been able to give a moderately successful course in Antitrust Law soon found how painfully inadequate my preparation was once I was obliged to step from behind the shelter of

[1] The writer visited the first session of a class in labor law in a large, distinguished law school to which only college graduates are admitted. The instructor inquired how many students in the group of approximately fifty had had an undergraduate course in labor relations. Five hands were raised. He asked how many had had *any* work in economics. Only about half the hands went up.

[2] "Psychology and Anthropology," in Journal of Social Philosophy, January, 1940, p. 116.

Supreme Court decisions. . . . The law teacher in fields with a high economic content has been getting by with what may aptly be described as newspaper economics."[1] In a memorandum he noted, "Our attempts in the law schools to establish significant interrelationships between law and economic and social problems have failed because they have been scattered, incidental, and lacking in a sufficiently broad basis in knowledge on the part of both students and instructors."

Taxation is obviously a very important specialized course in the law school, and one where it would appear exigent that economic materials be introduced. Just as both lawyers and economists are employed by the federal Department of the Treasury to work together in the formulation of monetary and fiscal policy, so the law school would seem to need either the services of the two specialists or of a law teacher who possessed considerable knowledge of the economics of taxation. In planning for a reorganized course in federal taxation at the University of Chicago—a University economist who had been employed in the Treasury is now participating in the teaching—Professors Walter J. Blum and Harry Kalven were asked to draft suggestions concerning its nature. A portion of their memorandum is reproduced here because it indicates what has been the content of the best casebooks available, and what they believe should be the purpose of such a course. The large knowledge of taxation theory requisite is implicit in the statement.

The three leading casebooks in taxation appear designed to emphasize the following aspects of Federal taxation: (1) constitutional limitations; (2) history and development of certain portions of the statutes; (3) nature and scope of various concepts embodied in the positive law; and (4) problems and ambiguities involved in applying the positive law. The framework provided by this approach offers an opportunity to become acquainted with the existing statutes and to appreciate the background of particular clauses. In addition it exposes some of the difficulties involved in working out a tax which is both internally consistent and adapted to business and social practices. To a limited extent

[1] Education: The Law Schools' New Objective. Mimeographed paper presented before the Juristic Society, March 26, 1941, pp. 19–20.

it also permits some speculations as to what problems in statutory construction, and what new gaps in the positive law, might arise in the near future.

At best, however, the confining nature of such a framework is wholly out of proportion with the importance of taxation in an enterprise society. The orientation which it supplies almost necessarily results in looking primarily at the more technical aspects of the positive law. The underlying principles within the framework tend to be ones pertaining to statutory construction and legislative draftsmanship. In short, the basic philosophy of the course becomes, in the words of Dean Griswold, the admonition that "there is no use thinking great thoughts about a tax problem unless the thoughts are based on the controlling statute."

Although recognizing the importance of gaining some information about the present positive law, we believe that a law school taxation course can and should be given a scope which more nearly approximates the significance of taxation in our society. Any problem or point in Federal taxation acquires significance not only in respect to placing and characterizing it within the structure of the positive law itself, but also in one or more of four other contexts; and it is these which should provide the proper lines of reference in studying taxation. In fact, some of the best questions in taxation are involved in the most clearly settled positive rules.

The four approaches may be summarized as follows:

1. The role of taxation in national monetary and fiscal policy. This includes the relation of taxation to monetary stability, business cycles, and long-run contraction or expansion of national wealth and productivity. It seems particularly important to consider whether taxation is significant only in respect to the aggregate sums of taxes collected or whether the types of taxes collected and the allocation of the tax burden are also factors.

2. The regulatory effects of taxation apart from fiscal and monetary policy. This comprehends the bearing of taxation upon operation of the enterprise system and its function as a social control in other areas. The questions to be considered here are concerned with the proper relationship between taxation and managerial and enterprise judgment, and the advisability of taxation as a conscious or unconscious means of social control.

3. The political aspects and implications of taxation. This deals with constitutional limitations, political feasibility and expediency, and the

relation of the courts and Congress. Included is a consideration of painful versus painless taxation and the activities and accomplishments of pressure groups.

4. The equality or inequality of taxation among individual taxpayers—tax justice among persons. This concerns the general problems of achieving fairness in the distribution of the tax burden among real persons. It involves treating notions of benefit taxation, ability to pay, and redistribution of income and wealth through taxation. In addition it includes an analysis of taxing legal entities other than real persons.

If knowledge of economics is inadequate, the situation is even more unfortunate so far as the other social sciences, except political science, are concerned. Since the purpose of law is in considerable part that of exercising a form of social control over human affairs, the social scientist is likely to take it for granted that the bar and bench would have to have at their disposal the best information available about individual and group motivation and how motivation can be redirected; about social structure and how changes can be made in it; about broad social trends. "The individual cannot be understood," writes Professor Linton, "except in relation to his social and cultural environment, nor the processes of social response and cultural change without reference to the personalities of the individuals involved."[1] Hence it would seem that psychology and those relatively new but fruitful theories that have emerged from psychiatry and social casework, as well as sociology and social anthropology would be of vital concern to the law schools. But in general they are not. The average law-school instructor does not have in these fields so much as his newspaper knowledge of economics.

Teachers of criminal law have made many distinctive efforts to inform themselves about pertinent sociological and psychological theories and facts, and to integrate these theories and facts in their teaching. Jerome Hall's Theft, Law and Society; Michael and Wechsler's widely acclaimed Criminal Law and Its Administration; Professor Dession and Dr. Kahn's clinical seminar in

---

[1] "Psychology and Anthropology," in Journal of Social Philosophy, January, 1940, p. 115.

psychiatry at Yale[1]; Sheldon Glueck's seminar in criminology at Harvard and his and Mrs. Glueck's studies of juvenile delinquents; Professor Puttkammer's broadly sociological course in criminal law administration at Chicago[2]—these and other attempts illustrate what has been done to enrich criminal law within a relatively brief period of time.

In other teaching areas nothing comparable has been achieved. Courses in torts, it is said, could be immeasurably improved in the light of what psychology and psychiatry have uncovered and what sociological investigations might demonstrate. Sociology has been particularly productive in its studies of slums, slum clearance, regional and community planning, and housing. Yet, as will be seen later, most teachers of real property have not indicated interest in this fundamental problem of our industrial society, for which no solution is possible without large legal assistance. All of the social sciences have developed valuable methods of research that, except for the statistical method, are still little utilized or taught by law schools.

The question of how to develop even a speaking acquaintance with, not to mention specialized knowledge of, other disciplines than one's own is indisputably large. It forms the basic core of the difficulty encountered in weaving the social sciences into law teaching. But it must be said, in all intellectual honesty, that the problem is not so insurmountable as many law teachers would have one believe. The closed shop operated by the average school has been responsible for an appreciable amount of the difficulty encountered. First, most classrooms are closed, by sheer force of habit, to law professors other than the instructor. Thus the contribution of great teachers like Walton H. Hamilton or Huger W. Jervey is largely limited to students. Had it only been considered "good form" to visit classes at will, many law professors might have had an experience comparable to that of one

[1] See also George H. Dession's article, "Psychiatry and the Conditioning of Criminal Justice," in Yale Law Journal, January, 1938, pp. 319–340.

[2] See also Ernst W. Puttkammer's three public lectures published under the title, Criminal Law Enforcement, by the University of Chicago Law School, Reprint and Pamphlet Series, Number 1 (1941).

dean who met, as a graduate student in Hamilton's seminar, what he characterized as "the blinding vision on the road to Damascus." His deanship bore unmistakable witness to the broadened concept of law he had found.

Because classrooms have been so carefully guarded against intrusion, the occasional visitor to law schools is sharply surprised to find a Dean Green who "took" the late Walter Wheeler Cook's course in legal method *three times*, or a Dean Garrison who "did his lessons" and raised his hand in class to the much younger instructor exactly like other students in legislation. But the visitor would have had his greatest surprise had he arrived at the University of Chicago near the close of the 1930's to find Professor Simons giving a seminar in economic theory for the law faculty, or conferring with them about the use of economic theory in law courses,[1] and Dr. Max Rheinstein preparing materials in comparative law upon request for interpolation in various courses. He would also have noted the regularity and informality with which some half of the faculty visited and participated in each other's classes, and the vigorous discussions that ranged from the United States Steel Corporation to Adlerian philosophy in which faculty and students participated at will over a cup of late afternoon tea. Wherever such marks of informality have been found, they generally have been symbols not merely of freedom from customary restraint but of greater flexibility in communication that held further dynamic potentialities.

Second and more serious, the law school is largely closed to the university. Most of the approved law schools are supposedly integral parts of universities, some of which are extremely rich in cultural resources. But the contacts which the average law instructor has with his university library, museums, and lectures, and with the larger faculty, are negligible. Some teachers of law do not even recognize by sight nationally known social scientists who lunch daily in the same faculty dining room, and whose

[1] For a discussion of the relationship of economic theory to the study of law, see the December, 1946, issue of the University of Chicago Law Review, particularly Dean Katz's leading article, "Economics and the Study of Law: The Contribution of Henry C. Simons."

books are read by educated persons the nation over. Scores of teachers complain that the literature of their specialty in law is so large that they cannot read anything else. Yet, they do not avail themselves of the opportunity at hand to lunch with their social science colleagues. In fact many of them confidently assert that the social sciences are still so undeveloped or so badly taught that they have nothing to offer law.[1] Generally they speak on the basis of their own undergraduate work of twenty or thirty years earlier. They do not know that progress in the social studies has probably been as great or greater than in law during the same period.

At the first luncheon hour with a social anthropologist, the law instructor might discover that theories of culture have been evolved, and techniques developed for discovering and describing the rich matrix of interrelated institutions, both of primitive and advanced peoples, that have significant importance for law. In a year of such luncheons he might develop a reasonably good working knowledge of anthropology, while the anthropologist would profit equally from the law-teacher's interpretation of the social function and administration of law. It is even conceivable that these two men might decide to collaborate in some undertaking that would prove as valuable as has been the collaboration between Karl N. Llewellyn and E. Adamson Hoebel, which resulted in the joint publication of The Cheyenne Way: Conflict and Case Law in Primitive Jurisprudence,[2] and in Professor Hoebel's article, "Law and Anthropology."[3] Or perhaps the relatively untraveled law professor might conclude that the

[1] For a sharp rebuke of law teachers for their intellectual complacency, made by a member of the fraternity, see W. Willard Wirtz's "Investigational Possibilities in the Area of Curriculum Construction," in American Law School Review, April, 1942, p. 1321.

[2] University of Oklahoma Press, Norman, 1941. See the late Bronislaw Malinowski's "A New Instrument for the Interpretation of Law—Especially Primitive," in Yale Law Journal, June, 1942, pp. 1237–1254. This is at once a review of the Llewellyn and Hoebel book and an indication of the insights that anthropology can bring to law. As an example of fruitful collaboration between a psychoanalyst and anthropologists, see two books by Dr. Abram Kardiner: The Individual and His Society, with a Foreword and Two Ethnological Reports by Ralph Linton, and The Psychological Frontiers of Society, with the collaboration of Ralph Linton, Cora DuBois, and James West. These books were published by the Columbia University Press in 1939 and 1945 respectively.

[3] In Virginia Law Review, June, 1946, pp. 835–854.

preparation of a new edition of his casebook had better wait until he had made a little field trip to another culture that would perhaps help him to re-evaluate his own.

The belief is widespread and insistent that progress in understanding and using the social sciences has been retarded, not so much by the difficulty involved in the educational process, as because the bar has been oriented primarily toward the world of business and monetary gain rather than toward intellectual ideas and their use for the task of social engineering. Technical efficiency in dealing with relatively narrow problems of private conflict has been emphasized rather than the integration of many viewpoints at the point of action. Not long ago the writer attended a series of evening lectures on personality structure given by Dr. Erich Fromm at the New School for Social Research. Among the many persons, not psychologists or physicians, who attempted weekly to crowd inside the room, was one of the country's most able, dynamic, and broadly educated teachers of law. "Why don't the law schools," the writer asked, "*want* to incorporate teaching like this into their curricula, so basic is it to any understanding of the motivation of the individual and of group relationships?" "Because there is no money in it," was the lawyer's instantaneous reply.

If it be true that partly for this reason the social sciences have not been more cultivated, one can only conclude that the legal profession has been nearsighted in examining even the monetary value of the social sciences. The financial gain to be won from carefully considered use of economic facts and theory in litigation and counseling has already been demonstrated. The time may be fast approaching when it will be generally recognized that the success of the lawyer—who exerts any large leadership—depends to no small degree upon his ability both to determine current policies and action and to handle broad human problems, *including the ability to handle himself with emotional maturity*.[1] For the

[1] At the Yale Law School, Professor Harold D. Lasswell is now engaged in helping students to use their personalities more effectively in situations roughly comparable to those faced by the attorney in litigation, negotiation, and before hearing tribunals. A "soundscriber" records simulated conferences, trials, and hearings. Thus teacher and student are able to recapture later what was said and how it was said for the purpose of constructive criticism.

devising of policy and for dealing with human relationships, facts and theories and methodology gained from the social sciences are important instrumentalities.[1] Policy cannot be made or inter-relationships considered in an intellectual vacuum. Legal doctrine and a knowledge of the judicial process are totally insufficient, for their emphasis has been upon the search for controlling principles and certainty in judicial judgments. In these areas where uncertainty and interactions are dominant, a shift from a search for controlling principles to a search for facts, interpretation of facts, and how to utilize both with flexibility and imagination is indicated.[2]

Experiments in the Use of Social Science Materials. Attempts that have been made to experiment with social science and other non-legal materials may be roughly classified under four methods.

1. The first method is that of integrating these materials in existing, and often long-established, courses. Reference has already been indirectly made to integration, particularly in connection with functionalism, and other references will appear subsequently. Although integration is generally considered to be the most vital single way in which these materials can be used, such success as has been achieved has not come principally through effort planned and directed by the Association of American Law Schools, or even by individual schools except in a few instances. It has come largely through the knowledge and interest of individual professors. Hence it has been dependent upon the kind and degree of their particular knowledge and how they used it.

Integration has probably been most successful in the fields of commercial law, criminal law, labor law, and government control of business. One example from the field of government control will illustrate interpolation of economic facts, theories, and methodology. The course in public utilities as offered formerly by Professor Beuscher at Wisconsin supposedly contained more

[1] See N. S. Timasheff's "The Sociologist's Contribution to the Law," and Sidney Post Simpson and Ruth Field's "Law and the Social Sciences," in Virginia Law Review, June, 1946, pp. 818–835 and 855–867 respectively.

[2] See Wallace Brett Donham's Education for Responsible Living, p. 254.

non-legal material than any other course in that law school, with the possible exception of unfair trade practices. No instructor can talk intelligently about the necessity of regulating a public utility, argued Beuscher, unless he first has an understanding of the economic connotations of free and unrestrained competition in the public utility field. The regulation of public utility rates called for a careful analysis of utility accounting methods and of such economic concepts as going-concern value, goodwill, depreciation, and working capital. Another segment of the course was devoted to conflicting federal and state regulation of utilities, particularly in the motor carrier and interstate power fields. Here it was necessary to provide facts and figures showing the development of the trucking business in this country, its present status, and the expansion of interstate power transmission. Finally, part of the course was devoted to the public utility holding company, and again Beuscher found it impossible to handle the problems involved without considering in detail the economic consequences of the phenomenon of the holding company.

It is obvious from this statement that judicial opinions can be greatly clarified and the student given some comprehensive idea of the economic problems involved in public utility regulation if the professor has the requisite economic background and suitable teaching materials.[1] But the opinions of Beuscher and Cavers quoted earlier suggest how uncertain is the teaching ability of the average instructor in such courses. A survey of all law schools would probably reveal that the majority of schools were still teaching public utilities as an examination of judicial doctrine punctuated by a little newspaper economics. And the survey would unquestionably show, furthermore, that such accomplishments as had been achieved in a few specific courses had not been extended to other portions of the curriculum.

2. The second way in which social science and other non-legal materials have been used is to make them an important part of certain new courses that have appeared in a few law-school bulle-

[1] The importance of accounting and statistics is becoming so evident that a considerable number of schools now make provision for some instruction in them, either as a part of established courses or as brief, separate courses.

tins of the past two decades. Although these courses are viewed primarily as law courses and are taught by law instructors, the description of several of them appearing in the next section and elsewhere in the monograph indicates the extent to which emphasis is placed upon other than legal doctrine or procedure. Many of these courses and the methods of instruction are definitely encouraging. They represent an effort to move toward the goal well described in Yale's recent statement: "We take it to be self-evident that law is one of the social studies, and that the study of law will be most fruitful and critical when the skills and perspectives of history, economics, statistics, psychology, political science, sociology, and psychiatry are fully and effectively used in the work of the law schools."[1]

The world of legal education in general, however, still views these new courses as luxuries of unproved value which are, at least, expensive. They appear as amenities which the relatively prosperous schools can permit themselves, or even as "new-fangled ideas" to which some schools with limited funds have succumbed at the sacrifice of long-tested instruction. As yet, they have made no place for themselves within the national pattern of professional training. A few of them like Professor Cook's excellent course in legal method are, to be sure, so particularly the product of the scholarship, life experience, and philosophy of one man that they do not lend themselves to instruction by others. Their influence thus far has lain chiefly in making the traditionally minded schools less inflexible in thinking about curriculum. They have still to convince legal education that only a course of study that extends well beyond private law subjects and a few offerings in public law taught primarily from the advocate's viewpoint, will suffice to train lawyers for their tasks in the second half of this century.

3. Under the third method courses have been introduced in the law school which are not primarily law courses and which have been taught by non-lawyers. Reference has already been

---

[1] "Report of Committee on Curriculum," in Association of American Law Schools Handbook, December, 1946, p. 61.

made to the late Professor Simons, a specialist in economic theory. Besides aiding the faculty he regularly taught the course in economics required of all second-year law students at Chicago. He was only one, however, of several instructors whose services have been obtained from the University. Before the recent war a professor of philosophy, an accountant, a historian, and a political scientist were also offering work in the School. Since its reorganization Chicago has consistently been of the opinion that the curriculum should be enriched at every point by as many non-legal experts as the budget will permit. Unlike many schools it does not believe that all courses need to be taught by lawyers; in some instances it considers that other backgrounds are more important. At present two economists have been added to the School on a full-time basis to co-operate with some of the law instructors in a research program.

It should not be assumed that the initiation of non-lawyer teachers at Chicago introduced a new practice to the law-school world. Quite the contrary was the case. Columbia and Yale had already experimented largely with bringing non-legal specialists into their schools. From 1926 to 1928 the Columbia School of Law had made an intensive study of legal education, the details of which were set down in its Summary of Studies in Legal Education published in 1928. "A closer integration of law with the related parts of the other social sciences should not only improve the education of lawyers," wrote the School a few years later, "but it should make more effective valuable knowledge acquired by specialists in other fields."[1]

Extensive plans were formulated to introduce teachers from several of the social sciences, philosophy, and business administration—although principally to graduate seminars only; to lend law instructors to various departments of the University; and to prepare teaching and research materials through joint effort. In 1928 the School of Law listed among its faculty James C. Bonbright as professor of finance, John Dewey in philosophy, and

[1] Report of the Dean of the School of Law for the Period Ending June 30, 1931, p. 8.

Raymond C. Moley in public law. Three other members held the Ph.D. degree, as well as a law degree. Moreover, nine non-lawyers, five of whom represented specialized fields of economics, were being called upon to give further instruction in the School. Simultaneously co-operative research was assiduously promoted. Professor Albert C. Jacobs of the School of Law and Professor Robert C. Angell of the Department of Sociology of the University of Michigan were making a survey of the law relating to the family. A. A. Berle and Gardiner C. Means, the associated economist, were investigating recent trends in corporate development. Professor Michael and Mortimer Adler, then of Columbia, were analyzing rules of evidence in terms of formal logic.

A similar development evolved at much the same time at Yale. In an enthusiastic article written in 1933 on "The Educational and Scientific Objectives of the Yale School of Law," Charles E. Clark, then dean, exclaimed, "The law is awakening to the life around it, and the search for truth as it presents itself in its new and modern garb is fascinating and exhilarating."[1] He was able to report that for some years a well-known economist had been teaching topics in torts, constitutional law, and the public control of business as a full-time member of the faculty. The staff had included a psychologist for a period. In 1933 a member of the Department of Psychology gave regular courses in the School of Law: a seminar to third-year and graduate students on the judicial process from the viewpoint of social psychology, and part of a first-year course in professional practice and ethics.

A psychiatrist from the Yale School of Medicine was working with law instructors in the psychiatric aspects of crime. A sociologist with statistical experience from the Institute of Human Relations offered a course in methods of social and legal research, and was sharing in the field research being done. An instructor from the Department of Economics joined in teaching a course in legal accounting. Finally, the members of the law faculty who taught business units had associated with them a professor from

[1] In the Annals of the American Academy of Political and Social Science, Philadelphia, May, 1933, p. 165.

the Harvard Graduate School of Business Administration with practical experience in the reorganization of corporations and similar problems. Shortly afterward the Yale School of Law and the Harvard Graduate School announced a joint curriculum in law and business for the purpose of training men for the practice of law in those fields involving contact with or the handling of business problems. Such men were to spend the second of a four-year course of study in the Harvard Graduate School.

Obviously both Columbia and Yale had prepared to utilize the experience of social science specialists largely and with eagerness. A better case could scarcely be made for the correlation of law and the social sciences than was presented by Young B. Smith of Columbia in his 1931 Report of the Dean of the School of Law. It merits re-reading today, for it is as fresh and pertinent as it was then. Unfortunately, however, legal education has the capacity— to use Cavers' colorful simile—of absorbing new ideas much as the Chinese have supposedly absorbed invading races. "They come and create a little disturbance for awhile, but after a few years one finds difficulty in discovering the point where they had entered, unless one follows the footnotes in the case-books carefully."[1] So it has been in no small degree with the experiments at Columbia and Yale. Difficult problems of organization, instruction, financing, and divergence in points of view were encountered; enthusiasm began to wane, and energy to run thin. Although an important residue, particularly in teaching materials, remained from the fervor of the late 1920's and early 1930's at both schools,[2] the New Plan at Chicago seemed appreciably new in 1936, even in its inclusion of courses taught by non-lawyers.

This newness resulted in part, however, from the fact that the courses in other than law had been introduced as a substitute for,

[1] Comments by David F. Cavers, in American Law School Review, April, 1942, p. 1421.

[2] Word has been received of the appointment of F. S. C. Northrop, professor of philosophy in Yale College, as teacher of jurisprudence in the Law School. With Walton H. Hamilton and Harold D. Lasswell, the Yale School will have on its faculty representatives of economics, political science, and philosophy. Wesley A. Sturges, who was recently made dean, reports that the School will not be satisfied to confine itself to the anatomy of legal proceedings; that it will try to put the rules of law in their social setting.

rather than a supplement to, advanced undergraduate training in the social sciences. The trend initiated by the University of Minnesota to lengthen the professional curriculum from three to four years but to require only two years of college preparation for admission, was followed by Chicago, as it has been by several other schools, particularly in the Middle West. In every instance the question has arisen of how the additional time available should be utilized. Should the further courses present still more of the common law? Should they be broadly legal courses enriched by non-legal materials? Or should they be straight social science courses? Should the instructors be lawyers or not?

At Minnesota Dean Fraser decided that introductory college courses in designated social sciences should be required for admission to the four-year law curriculum,[1] and that the additions to the professional school should be, as noted earlier, either broad law courses that looked toward improvement in legislation and the administration of justice or courses, such as modern philosophies of social reform, whose implications were unmistakable. With only two or three exceptions, these courses have been taught by members of the law faculty. Although he would like to utilize the social sciences more fully, Dean Fraser has felt that some knowledge of law is almost indispensable for anyone to give effective instruction in the professional school. Hence he has been hesitant to call upon social scientists who have had no orientation in law.

Chicago moved to the other extreme. It did not require that specific courses in social science be presented for admission. Instead, it introduced a considerable number of courses which it believed important for the prospective lawyer's development.

[1] Of the twenty-three schools visited only the University of Minnesota Law School prescribed portions of the college curriculum which had to be studied as a prerequisite for admission. Pre-law students were required to take almost as much specified work in the social sciences as was possible in the two-year period and yet meet University requirements. As a result, they began their study of law with a better knowledge of social science than is possessed by many law students elsewhere who hold a bachelor's degree. The experience at Minnesota and that of certain other professions that have instituted definite academic requirements, lead one to believe that law schools, particularly those with the three-year curriculum, are extremely unwise in not demanding that the student enter with some prescribed minimum of proficiency in the social studies.

Most of these were in social science, philosophy, or legal history; one was the course on law and economic organization which, we have seen, combined law and economics about equally. For the non-law courses it engaged specialists who had had no training in law. It assumed that their energies could have been better spent in digging deeper into their own field than in gaining a partial knowledge of law. Its most difficult problem has been that of finding social scientists who are adequately acquainted with one social science in its entirety. Economics has grown to such proportions, the School discovered, that specialists were really needed in economic theory, land economics, taxation, banking, and labor relations. The situation was scarcely less complicated in the other social studies. Questions of financing or arranging with the parent university for the services of several such men are not easily solved.

The decisions of other schools that have initiated the Two-Four-Year Plan, as it is called, have been closer to the Minnesota than the Chicago concept. Additions to the curricula have most often represented efforts to enrich legal materials, frequently by the interpolation of social science data. The teaching has been done by lawyers. Rarely, however, have these schools been exigent, as has Minnesota, in making certain of the social studies requisite for admission.

Around the Two-Four-Year Plan questions of profound educational significance are involved.[1] Many law schools have consistently maintained that training in the social sciences on the undergraduate level is insufficient or not of the right kind as

---

[1] In a memorandum prepared before the war, Dean Bernard C. Gavit of Indiana University visualized a further extension of the Two-Four-Year Plan. He proposed a Six-Year Plan offered by the law school to high school graduates selected on the basis of an entrance examination. Students would begin the study of law simultaneously with the study of selected portions of the undergraduate college curriculum. All courses would be given within the law school, exclusively to law students. Instructors in academic subjects would be drawn from the university. College offerings in the social sciences and history would be emphasized. The physical sciences and the fine arts would not be omitted, but the number of possible credits would be sharply restricted. Languages would not be taught, although a reading knowledge of one language would be required for admission. An effort would be made to bring greater integration into the curriculum, and to provide more variation in instructional and examining techniques.

preparation for the law school. (This premise, however, has not been tested. No schools that enroll only students with the bachelor's degree have made specific requirements in the social sciences for admission, comparable to the requirements by the medical schools of extensive physical and biological science, and have then studied the results.) Because of the dissatisfaction, some schools found a possible solution in the lengthening of the law curriculum at the expense of the college. Where this has been done, responsibility has devolved upon the law school for providing any instruction given beyond the second college year in social science theory, facts, and methodology. But it has been seen that, on the one hand, grave doubt exists about the ability of law teachers to handle the social studies adequately. On the other hand, almost no schools except Chicago are attempting to employ any considerable number of social scientists chiefly because—so it is said—of their lack of acquaintance with law. The resulting dilemma is of such potential consequence for American education that it transcends the boundaries of the law school. It deserves careful consideration on the highest policy-making level of the university. If it cannot be solved at the conference table to which have been invited representatives of the administration, the law school, and the social scientists, then research techniques should be employed as a possible means for finding an answer. Certainly the question of how lawyers are to be made acquainted with the social and conceptual world within which they are to practice deserves more scientific thought than has yet been given it by most schools that have initiated the Two-Four-Year Plan.

4. The fourth method of using social science materials is through courses for which a law instructor and a social scientist share joint responsibility. Professor Sidney Post Simpson has well stated the raison d'être for this method. "The study of law in its relation to other fields of knowledge—government, business, economics, sociology, psychology, history—requires ability and expertness in separated fields which are seldom to be found in one individual. What is often needed is two men, each an expert in

his own field, who are willing to work together in attacking common problems."[1] Several values, in Simpson's opinion, are likely to be achieved simultaneously from joint undertakings: the student will profit from the seminar offered or the publication prepared by two specialists; the law teacher will broaden his knowledge and educational perspective; and bridges of mutual understanding will be built between the law school and the university.

It was on such an assumption that Columbia and Yale first engaged extensively some twenty years ago in joint seminars and research projects. On the same assumption, Professors Walter Gellhorn of the Columbia School of Law and John D. Millett of the Department of Public Law and Government are now offering a joint seminar in governmental administration which will be described at length in the section on "Administrative Law."

As yet, this method has not had wide acceptance. The majority of schools have never experimented with it. During the 1930's, however, a considerable number of institutions initiated the giving of at least one seminar in co-operation with some university department. Federal administration offered jointly by the Harvard Law School (under the dynamic leadership of Professor Milton Katz) and the Littauer School of Public Administration was a pre-Pearl Harbor seminar which attracted considerable interest. In it a single administrative agency was studied intensively for a semester. Subsequent to an examination of the Civil Aeronautics Authority, Professor Freund, who had viewed the progress of the seminar with interest, reported on the different but mutually profitable reactions that had been shown by the two groups of students.[2] The law students had been more preoccupied with the problem of reducing the issues under discussion to a narrow, manageable compass, and with safeguarding the private interests concerned. The non-law students had been more interested in building a body of standards and rules for the administrative

---

[1] "Function of the University Law School," in Harvard Law Review, May, 1936, p. 1080.

[2] Comments by Paul A. Freund at the December 29, 1941, Meeting on Training for Government Service, in American Law School Review, April, 1942, pp. 1420–1421.

agency that would carry out the necessarily vague definitions of public policy in the statute creating the Authority. They had also been interested in the application to this agency of economic theory and principles of administration. Professor Freund concluded that two purposes had been served by the seminar. From the association of law and non-law students had undoubtedly come a correction of focus helpful to both groups. Thanks to the subject matter of the course and the method of instruction, all the students had had an opportunity to examine the problems that trouble a representative administrative agency. In learning how to analyze and solve those problems, they had been given a technique that could be used in working with other administrative agencies.

The following brief references are samples of characteristic attempts at collaboration. At the University of Wisconsin members of the law faculty and of the Department of Economics experimented with seminars in labor relations and trade practices. These undertakings had the blessing of Dean Garrison who attempted in a wide variety of ways to bring the University's resources within the Law School and to make the Law School a source of enrichment to the University. At Virginia international law was taught jointly by a University lecturer and by Professor Hardy C. Dillard of the Department of Law. Only twelve students were permitted to enroll, although several times that number asked for admission. The schools of law, government, and commerce and business administration of the University of Southern California decided in the late thirties to offer a graduate seminar in government regulation of industry and government services to which four students from each of the three schools might be admitted. During the two-hour, one-semester seminar of the first year the Social Security Act was studied. In the second year the subject was government and credit. The Tennessee Valley Authority had been proposed for the third year, before the war brought all experiments to a sharp end. Shelden D. Elliott of the College of Law, who had been active in organizing the seminar and had been one of the three instructors, was convinced that the undertaking had been of vital educational value both to teachers and to students.

One other experiment needs to be mentioned. It was not an experiment in offering joint seminars but in offering a joint curriculum to a few exceedingly able and ambitious persons who wished to obtain the LL.B. and Ph.D. degrees. The plan was conceived in the middle thirties by Charles Aikin, a professor of administrative law and political science at the University of California who himself held the two degrees. He believed that training both in law and in political science or economics was extremely valuable as preparation for positions of high leadership, whether in university teaching, research, law practice, or government service. He believed, furthermore, that the study of law and a social science pursued simultaneously could be made far more fruitful than could the study of the two disciplines pursued in sequence. Hence he proposed that any student who showed marked ability in his first year of law or of graduate work in political science or economics and who wished training in two disciplines be permitted, after his first graduate year, to undertake a carefully planned and supervised joint curriculum. A minimum of five years was considered necessary to qualify for the two degrees.

The plan met with ready acceptance from Dean Edwin D. Dickinson who, too, had a Ph.D. as well as a law degree, and who insisted—in an era when many law schools were requiring only two years of college for admission—that the School of Jurisprudence be operated exclusively on a graduate level. He was interested in producing "top-flight" leadership, and he saw long and careful training of highly selected men as the most promising way of obtaining that leadership. R. D. Calkins, dean of the School of Commerce and professor of economics, also agreed warmly with the merits of the plan. The University administration expressed willingness to make necessary interdepartmental adjustments. It appeared, therefore, that an exceptional setting had been created for providing preparation in law and one of the social sciences.

By the outbreak of the war, however, only three students had undertaken the joint curriculum—two drawn from political science and one from economics. No student from the School of Jurisprudence had so much as requested admission. Professor Aikin was frankly disappointed that more men from the great University of California had not presented themselves. It must be assumed that much of the fault lay in insufficient cultivation of the proposal. Although Dean Dickinson described the plan to the writer with enthusiasm and pointed to its vast potentialities as preparation for the "high command," his faculty appeared to have little or no knowledge of it. Hence they were not on the constant outlook for able young men who might be encouraged to undertake the joint course of study. Plans like this which cut across traditional administrative boundaries and which require a large expenditure of time and money are not likely to receive much consideration by students unless extensive publicity or facilities for individual counseling are available. Even if a student hears about such a plan, how is he to evaluate its importance on the basis of his limited life experience?

Obviously the several efforts made to present joint courses or curricula have been useful chiefly as initial experiments. Even in the institutions where they have been tried, they have generally been available to, or have been accepted by, a mere handful of students. Often they have engaged the interest only of the law teachers who participated in them. They have not yet demonstrated their worth as an approved medium for integrating law and the social sciences. They will continue to fail, as will other efforts to broaden the curriculum, until legal education provides a climate of opinion in which the outlook on the purpose and function of the lawyer is immeasurably expanded. The situation at present is much like that of a distinguished national law school where ninety-six students elected the course in bills and notes, and only nine elected legislation in spite of the fact that it was strongly recommended. The philosophy of the common law and training for appellate court work so dominated the school that it is little wonder most students enrolled in the "bread and butter" course.

They did not know that legislation might provide equally valuable training for earning their bread and butter. Neither did they fully realize that statutory law had come to be an even more important tool than the common law for the great task of social engineering. Students inevitably tend to reflect the opinions of their teachers and the environment in which they find themselves. When the law school is able to furnish a pervasive atmosphere of being at one with the social sciences, the unresolved problem of interesting students in the social studies will probably cease to exist.

"New" Courses and Teaching Materials

In most of the schools visited at the turn of the decade at least one new course was being given or was under consideration. In a few, several such courses had been introduced. Generally speaking, these courses represented a radical departure from the traditional curriculum and from anything that had been offered in the particular school previously. Hence they are designated as "new" although some of them had been offered for a number of years. They differed as much from each other as Edward H. Levi's introductory course at Chicago on legal methods and materials and Elliott E. Cheatham's advanced seminar at Columbia on legal education.

The former was an attempt to provide first-year students with some knowledge of ideas basic to the law: the natural law, corrective and distributive justice, equity, legal acts; the structure and methods of the legal system: court and legislature, precedent, logic, and social policy; the growth and evolution of legal concepts: types of concepts, analytical concepts of the law, the relationship of law to the social sciences; some fundamental institutions: property, contract, the state, custom, and liberty; and rhetoric and the law.

The second course sought to acquaint candidates for the doctorate and third-year students who expected to enter teaching with the basic aims and methods of legal education in the

United States and with current problems confronting instructors and curriculum. Although both courses were unique, several schools were offering some kind of introductory survey to entering students, or made provision for consideration of many of the topics covered by Professor Levi in an advanced, elective course in jurisprudence. However, no other national law school besides Columbia made any formal effort—unbelievable as it may seem to educators—for systematic examination of the evolution, present status, and problems of legal education.

Certainly no description of all the various experiments that were going on can be set down here, and a mere cataloguing of them would serve no useful purpose.[1] Hence attention will be centered on a mere handful that seemed to the author particularly designed to broaden the horizon of lawyers by viewing law within its social and economic setting, or by emphasizing the social function of law and lawyers. References to several other new courses are scattered through this part of the book.

Modern Social Legislation was offered for the first time in 1939–1940 at the University of Minnesota by Stefan A. Riesenfeld. It replaced an earlier course in comparative social legislation that had been valuable but not entirely satisfactory because the students possessed too little knowledge of social legislation in the United States to compare it fruitfully with developments in other countries.

Professor Riesenfeld defined such legislation as that portion of statutory and administrative law that deals with the setting and enforcing of "minimum standards of living for the ordinary citizen." Hence his course focused attention upon the provisions of the Social Security Act, the Fair Labor Standards Act, the National Housing Act, the United States Housing Act, the Tenn-

---

[1] A first-semester course introduced at Chicago in 1946–1947 as part of the four-year curriculum deserves note because of the nature of the materials used and the teaching method employed. It was a reading course offered jointly by several members of the faculty. University professors, including the head of the psychiatry department, were invited for particular discussions. Erich Fromm's Escape from Freedom, Jerome Frank's Fate and Freedom, Ranyard West's Conscience and Society, and Elton Mayo's The Social Problems of an Industrial Civilization, together with selections from the writings of John Dewey and Frank H. Knight, were assigned for reading and discussion.

essee Valley Authority and rural electrification programs, and other legislation for the utilization or conservation of natural resources. Since courses with large registrations in administrative law, labor law, trade regulations, judicial administration, and legislation are also offered at Minnesota, the instructor sought to avoid duplication of teaching materials.

The course opened with discussion of the establishing of minimum standards of living as a new function of society, and of the development of that function in the United States. Then followed consideration of how the Constitution had been "adapted" to meet the requirements of modern social legislation. Standard cases decided by the Supreme Court were used to indicate judicial reasoning and methods of approaching the problem.

The second part of the course was devoted to an examination of the programs that have evolved from the statutes. Emphasis was centered upon *what* is done, *why* it is done, and *how* it is done in the several programs. Copies of all the acts and many administrative regulations were extensively used. So were Social Security in the United States by Paul H. Douglas, Labor's Risks and Social Insurance by Harry A. Millis and Royal E. Montgomery, the Roosevelt papers, and reports of congressional committees. The student was encouraged to familiarize himself with the legal materials, other than cases, that are indispensable to an understanding of this subject, and to use economic, statistical, and other non-legal source materials.

At much the same time Washington University School of Law in St. Louis was attempting to outline a course in law and economic problems. Professor Ralph F. Fuchs argued that the course should be designed to assist the student to develop an understanding of contemporary basic economic problems. Since no single course could focus attention upon all these problems, he suggested that one important subject be selected for detailed consideration. Without knowing of the course being given at Minnesota, Professor Fuchs recommended that legal provision for economic security be made the subject. In his outline more attention was centered upon historical developments than in

Riesenfeld's; less upon current practices in various countries and upon the techniques of administration. In both, however, the purpose and the major topics covered were the same. The war ended experimentation at Washington University before this or any other plan was tried in the classroom.

Judicial Administration, which has been taught by Maynard E. Pirsig for more than a decade at the University of Minnesota, is the direct outgrowth of Dean Fraser's desire that students be given some comprehensive understanding of the purpose and method of functioning of the judiciary and the legal profession as instruments of society, and some evaluation of the effectiveness with which bench and bar have achieved socially desirable ends. Because almost all law-school courses, procedural as well as substantive, have been primarily concerned with principles of law and courtroom techniques, the broader aspects of why and how law operates are often not brought to the student's attention in any systematic fashion.

Professor Pirsig began, therefore, the collection and arrangement of appropriate readings which were used in fourth-year classes at Minnesota in mimeographed form. In 1946 they were made available to other schools through the publication of Cases and Materials on Judicial Administration.[1] The readings open with a brief discussion of what justice is. No extended treatment of the question, which belongs to a course in jurisprudence, is intended. Rather is an effort made to establish the distinction, that permeates the entire course, between rules of law and the proper adjustment of human relations that these rules seek to accomplish. The criterion by which the administration of justice is to be measured is not the correct application of a given law but whether such application achieves the desired end.

Critical examination follows of the techniques, advantages, and disadvantages of law-making by judicial decision. Our method of conducting litigation as a contest between parties is considered, and the adversary method and the administrative method are compared. The doctrine of precedent receives extended consid-

[1] West Publishing Co., St. Paul.

eration. Then the problems involved in determination of the facts in a trial are examined, as are the qualifications of juries.

Detailed attention is given to the organization and administration of courts, and to the various remedies proposed for existent defects. The qualifications, selection, and retirement of the judiciary are discussed. Next follow nearly 200 pages devoted to the legal profession. Why is the practice of law restricted to licensed persons? The answer to this question necessitates an examination of the term "profession" and the obligations implicit in it. This examination in turn leads to an investigation of valid criticisms of the legal profession, and of possibilities for improvement. The final section envisages agencies and methods of reform in the administration of justice.

These teaching materials contain some illustrative cases, but they consist largely of excerpts selected from scholarly writings. (Nothing could have been more misleading than was the deletion by the publisher of the word "Materials" from the title on the cover of the book.) Wherever possible, both sides of controversial issues are presented, and students are encouraged through vigorous classroom discussion and otherwise to formulate opinions of their own. Copies of the Journal of the American Judicature Society are supplied to each member of the class. Current judicial elections, appointment of judges, and activities of local and national bar associations are examined, and visits are made to courts and to meetings of the bar.

One distinct shortcoming marked the book as published. It contained almost no notes, explanatory paragraphs, or illuminating essays of greater or lesser length written by Mr. Pirsig himself. He had had some twelve years in which to cultivate the subject. The book is likely to be used by instructors many of whom have had no such preparation. Fortunately, a teacher's manual is now nearly ready for the press. When available, it should furnish valuable supplementary aid in teaching so important but new a subject.

Five law schools besides Minnesota were using Cases and Materials on Judicial Administration a year after its publication.

One of these was the University of Texas School of Law where Professor Robert W. Stayton had already utilized the contents in mimeographed form for a considerable time. Because of Professor Stayton's particular concern with this subject, something must be said of his efforts before ending this section. He has long held membership in such policy-making bodies as the Texas Civil Judicial Council and the Texas Supreme Court Advisory Committee on Rules of Procedure. He also served for two years as judge of the Commission of Appeals in Texas. Hence his teaching has been enriched by his exceptional interest and experience. In addition to classroom discussion of Pirsig's textual materials, he has sought to give some of his students research training in questions of judicial administration through having them participate in various investigations. "A Study of Pendency in Texas Civil Litigation," by Robert W. Stayton and Philip P. Brown, in the Texas Law Review for December, 1939, is the published result of one investigation. This piece of research very effectively utilized charts and graphs as pictorial media for presenting data. The fact that the average period from the time a case was filed in the district court through disposition of the first appeal in the Texas Supreme Court was four and one-half years, thus emerged with such clarity that it became immediately useful for policy-making purposes in any attempt to reduce delay in the judicial process.

Function of the Lawyer in Reference to Civil Liberties. The outline of a course drafted by Professor Robert E. Mathews of Ohio State University just before Pearl Harbor reads as if he were applying the implications of Pirsig's course to one important but neglected area, civil liberties. Mathews intended that the first part of the course should deal with "liberty of personality in a democracy": freedom from oppression by the state; recognition of the rights of the individual and of groups in conflict with property interests; recognition of the rights of political, racial and ethnic, and religious groups; recognition of teachers' rights within the educational system. The second part of the course was to be concerned with the lawyer's function in preserving these liberties: his function as a citizen, drafter of legislation if not a legislator, officer of the court, judge, prosecutor and public defender, representative of clients, member of an organized profession. The materials to have been used in this course would have been taken from cases, statutes, rulings, briefs, reports of private organizations working in behalf of civil liberties, official investigations, political science, and history. Professor Mathews concluded that such a course would be of inestimable value in alerting the prospective lawyer to a concern about civil as well as about property rights.

Among liberal minded Americans it has long been believed that law schools, as well as the bar, have been primarily interested in property rights and only very secondarily interested in civil rights. If one were to consult the bulletins of the various schools, he would be certain that his contention was right. He would see one course in real property, and generally several, in the bulletin of every school. Aside from a seminar in civil liberties given at one time at Yale and perhaps in two or three other places, he would search in vain for any reference to the subject. He would even discover that Zechariah Chafee, one of the nation's foremost exponents of free speech,[1] was engaged at Harvard in teaching equity, while David Riesman, Jr., whose writing on civil liberties has been exceptionally stimulating and provocative, has been lost, at least temporarily, to the law-school world.[2]

There is another side to the story, however, which would do a little to alleviate the layman's indictment of law schools. Civil rights, at least from the angle of enforcement, are relevant to the content of many courses such as constitutional law, torts, labor law, and administrative law. To the degree that they are taught, it is generally within the framework of these courses, although some of the new courses include aspects of civil rights. The pedagogical device of integration has much justification. The question at issue—such as protection of picketing—takes on

[1] See Free Speech in the United States, Harvard University Press, Cambridge, 1941.

[2] See Civil Liberties in a Period of Transition, Harvard University, Cambridge, 1942; "Democracy and Defamation," in Columbia Law Review, May, 1942, pp. 727–780; September, 1942, pp. 1085–1123; November, 1942, pp. 1282–1318.

meaning and reality when presented within the course in labor law. But there are two weaknesses in this device, one potential and one almost unavoidable. Some professors show little interest or competence in developing related questions of civil rights. They are likely to center attention, as has been seen, on the "due process" clause at the expense of the Fourteenth Amendment as a whole. Even when their presentation is adequate, attention necessarily tends to be limited to questions of enforcement or to small segments of the subject of civil liberties. It would be unthinkable to restrict property rights solely to examination within the outline of other courses. The subject must be explored as an entity and by men who are specialists in it. Civil rights would seem to deserve comparable treatment.

Interestingly enough, a serious situation which has arisen in criminal law in recent years is peculiarly related to the question of civil rights and by implication to legal education. Numerous penal sanctions have been attached to a vast array of new laws, including social legislation. Thus a large proportion of the population has been brought into potential contact with the criminal law. Employers as well as employes, corporations as well as the unemployed, may be expected in the near future, said Professor Jerome Hall to the writer, to be hailed before the criminal courts. "The danger is that step by step the community, including the clients of the best lawyers, will find itself subjected increasingly to criminal laws which have been enacted through propaganda and the pressure of interested groups and superficial reformers." Even in the face of this situation which would seem to make immediate demands on legal education, if for no other reason than that important clients are potentially involved, law graduates are as ignorant of the Bill of Rights, Hall continued, as any man on the street. "Some of them have never heard it mentioned in three years of intensive law study."

In part, perhaps, because emphasis is not centered more squarely upon the vital question of civil rights, the law schools as well as the bar are slow to move if the nation is suddenly and unexpectedly challenged by issues of vast magnitude. In the summer of 1942 when social scientists were already engaged in field work on grants provided by foundations, a dean was asked if he knew what law-school professors were busied with the constitutional issues involved in the removal of some 70,000 American citizens to Relocation Centers. He replied bitterly, "The Supreme Court has not yet spoken. So how can *we* have any opinion? After a decision has been handed down, we may write law-review articles commenting on it."[1] Now when the country is not at war and civil rights, not merely of "minority groups," are nevertheless being flagrantly disregarded, will the law schools still assume that they have no special responsibility for "alerting the prospective lawyer" to a concern about these rights?

Legal Factors in Economic Society. This course, offered to a large number of second-year students and also at times as a seminar to third-year and graduate students at Columbia by Professor Robert L. Hale, has been unique in legal education ever since it was begun experimentally twenty years ago. Its instructor was formerly a teacher of economics in the University. He is also trained in law. The most surprising feature of the course is the large emphasis given to the question of individual rights within an economic system that Professor Hale views as being shot through with coercion. Property owners use coercion, but so do workers. All bargaining, in fact, is coercive. On the basis of this assumption of coercion, the first half of the course analyzes the coercion exerted by government and the rights of the people against it. The second half deals with problems of public policy that emerge in the process of conscious government intervention. The following paragraphs have been extracted from a digest of the course prepared by Professor Hale, as it was taught at the outbreak of the war.

Under the title Safeguards of the Individual Against Tyrannical Power, the mimeographed materials begin with brief readings on

---

[1] The law-review note, "Alien Enemies and Japanese-Americans: A Problem of Wartime Controls," in Yale Law Journal, June, 1942, pp. 1316–1338, indicates that one institution at least did not have to wait until the Court had spoken. Incidentally, the note came from a school that had devoted more than customary attention to the subject of civil rights.

liberty and equality. The cases on peonage which follow are presented not for the purpose of discussing peonage but of analyzing what is meant by "involuntary" servitude. They are intended to indicate the difference in the degree of compulsion when a man is compelled to perform a contract to work by threat of imprisonment, and when he is only subjected to a suit for damages. Under the subheading—Against What Types of Power Do Constitutional Rights Prevail?—official commands to act or desist are shown not to raise questions of constitutional rights if the commands are reinforced by no further sanctions; to raise questions if reinforced by threats of death, imprisonment, or fine. The problem is then discussed of ordinary legal duties when infringement results only in the payment of damages. This leads to consideration of why courts should regard some conduct as legally wrongful when simultaneously an injunction against it is thought too harsh, and what justification there can be for levying damages for conduct not considered wrongful.

The power to discourage the exercise of constitutional rights by taxation is examined, and the compulsory character of desistance motivated by desire to avoid the tax, even when the tax is held valid, is pointed out. Prices are shown to be as compulsory as taxes when they discourage the consumption of the article—but their necessity and economic function are indicated. Following cases discuss whether governments may grant privileges conditioned on the "relinquishment of constitutional rights," and whether the payment of money has a compulsory effect in making the recipient conform to the conditions (as with the federal payments to farmers under the Agricultural Adjustment Act, declared compulsory in United States v. Butler). Cases are then examined where constitutional rights are said to be infringed although the government does not directly act against those asserting the rights, but only compels third persons to stop dealing with them.

The course next turns to delegated power—power exerted in pursuance of a policy not formulated by the legislature. After a brief discussion of delegation to administrative officials, delegation to private groups is considered. Three types of cases are presented: where rules prescribed by the private group are held bad even if the same rules would be held good if prescribed by the legislature; where rules prescribed by the private group are held good if, and only if, the same rules would be good were they prescribed by the legislature; and where rules prescribed by private groups are held good even if the same rules would be held bad had the legislature prescribed them. Cases of the last type are shown to result in part from failure of the courts to recognize that there *is* delegation of legislative power. It is noted, however, that there are situations in which it is necessary to give the appropriate private group power to legislate free from constitutional limitations. The power of property owners to lay down conditions on which alone the use of their property will be legally permitted is shown to be an example of delegation of legislative power.

Under the next subheading analysis appears of the extent to which the law exposes an individual to, or protects him from, the adverse conduct of others. The judicial development of new legal duties and the refusal to protect against many forms of damages are traced, particularly the refusal of courts in the absence of legislation to protect the weaker party against the bargaining power of the stronger. Threats of non-feasance or causing others not to act are analyzed as measures to compel conformity to the wishes of those who make the threats. Finally, it is pointed out that most of the features of economic society are traceable to coercion and counter-coercion inherent in bargaining.

Inequality in Governing Power and in Subjection to Governing Power traces economic inequalities to inequalities in ability and in legal rights. Each person, so it is maintained, has a set of property rights that is wholly unique, and the sets of each are by no means equal. These inequalities are in large measure traceable to the laws.

The second half of the course, Public Policy and Political Guidance, deals, as has been stated, with certain problems that emerge in the process of conscious government intervention. A brief discussion of monetary policy is followed by consideration of labor arbitration, and the test of a "fair wage." Price regulation is examined for the object of showing that the ultimate decision in the fixing of a "reasonable" price rests upon assumptions as to economic policy. Taxation and public expenditures are viewed as instruments for altering economic relationships.

Who Furnishes the Political Guidance? In answering the question raised in this subheading, examples are given of government action which affects persons outside the boundaries of designated geographic units. Discussion is devoted to how the problem is met in the United States by removing certain matters from the hands of the states; to what criteria for determining state and federal spheres have emerged in constitutional law; and to the difficulties caused between sovereign nations by the power to govern with extra-territorial effects. Finally, the conclusion of the course which deals with political guidance as provided by different organs in the same geographical government, recalls the problems of policy that must be solved in any conscious government intervention. It raises the question of whether such policy questions can best be determined by expert commissioners, by courts, by legislatures, or by popular vote. The discussion ends with an examination of the merits of democratic majority rule.

Law and the Adjustment of the Individual. After Washington University School of Law in St. Louis had introduced the Two-Four-Year Plan, it tried systematically to discover what new courses might be offered to students, who had had only an introduction to the social sciences, that would enrich their thinking about law in its social setting. Two courses were planned for the first semester of the second year: law and economic problems to which reference has already been made, and law and the adjustment of the individual. In discussing the second course, Professor Fuchs maintained that the modern state attempts, through law, to make provision in a variety of special ways for those who fall below some kind of current norm of adjustment to society. It would be worth while to ascertain the reasons for such provisions and to raise questions about the adequacy and wisdom of what is being done. If the School of Law attempted, moreover, to integrate this understanding within a single course rather than to present it in fragments in many courses, he believed that the student would obtain greater perspective.

When Mr. Fuchs assembled materials and taught the course for the one and only time before he was called to Washington, the classes of persons whom he selected for consideration were the mentally deficient, the mentally ill including the "criminal insane," neglected and delinquent minors, and the recipients of public care or assistance. The subject of convicted offenders, whose handling by the state is increasingly that of treatment as well as of punishment, would have been included had it not been so vast and were at least certain aspects not covered in the course in criminal law. The readings demonstrated how ideas that have evolved about the worth of the individual, the desirability of making social provision for the less fortunate, and the proper role of the political state in caring for human needs, have been crystallized in legal provisions. Materials selected from an extremely wide variety of sources included those setting forth these ideas; pertinent doctrines drawn from the law of contracts, torts, and crimes; legal arrangements for the care of persons and property by institutions or public officers; and the statutory transition from poor relief to public assistance.

The course gave the student, as a by-product, much valuable information about the medical and psychological interpretation of mental disease and deficiency, and the sociological interpretation of the effect of environment upon the individual. But beyond this, it was particularly fruitful in giving him a conception of law as a living reality rather than a mass of partly dead, partly stern and fate-like rules. It enhanced the prospective lawyer's awareness of the law as evolution, of the still unexplored possibilities of his profession.

Legal History. "The American law school has neglected the development of that sense of the past, that perspective in time, which can conveniently be labelled 'history.' "[1] The inclusion of early cases in casebooks, the speaker continues, was never an adequate discharge of the law-school's responsibility to history. "The significance of history to law lies in its disclosure of the interaction of law and the social matrix in which it is formed. Cases reveal in a fragmentary way the adjustments in law; they are sorry clues to the forces which brought those adjustments about."

Thus Professor Cavers points to a shortcoming of legal education, which is almost as serious as that of failure to utilize the social sciences extensively, and which is more discouraging for the reason that even less of an effective attempt is being made to remedy it. Any person who pays prolonged visits to law schools is likely to come to feel that they are cut off in time and space. With a few notable exceptions, they seem not to be interested in the great body of experience that history or current developments in other countries might provide.[2] Their eyes are focused

[1] Cavers, David F., Education: The Law Schools' New Objective. Mimeographed paper presented before the Juristic Society, March 26, 1941, pp. 4–5.

[2] A handful of schools that can afford to provide such a luxury employ men who offer courses in comparative or Roman law. Generally so few students elect these advanced courses or use the prepared materials, that the effect of these professors upon basic legal education is negligible. Hence their courses are not considered here. Their contribution to legal scholarship, however, may be of marked significance.

upon the "here and now," and they do not appear to realize that the present and the future cannot be understood or safely planned for without a knowledge of the roots from which the present springs. Nor do they appear to recognize that a score of other countries—in struggling with legal and social problems comparable to our own—have often evolved methods, theories, or insights that could be of inestimable value to us.

It should not be inferred, however, that no references to history are made. On that score, at least, the schools do far better than they do in referring to developments in other countries. W. Willard Wirtz has recently reminded his listeners of the desirability of including discussion, in a course in labor law, of the pertinent techniques for labor arbitration developed in Australia and New Zealand, and the Scandinavian experience with labor courts.[1] Many teachers of the common law, by contrast, customarily begin their courses with a historical survey dating from the mediaeval period in England, and all of them utilize cases— which they think of, however, as legal rather than historical— from centuries preceding the twentieth. Unfortunately, both of these methods are often peculiarly ineffective. If one has ever heard the perfunctory way in which lectures on history are given as an introduction to certain courses and has viewed the complete lack of interest of the students, he concludes that the effort has been a waste of time. There is no living reality in history as thus presented.

Cases drawn from preceding centuries are frequently utilized to excellent advantage in demonstrating the evolution of a particular legal doctrine. A Karl N. Llewellyn will make of his presentation of selected nineteenth century judicial decisions regarding sales a great intellectual experience that will be recalled years later. The student will *see* the courts struggling to fashion doctrine to promote the interests of a rapidly expanding business economy. When cases are thus presented, their use is more than justified even if they can give only a limited perspec-

---

[1] A New Prospectus for the Labor Law Course. Paper read before the Association of American Law Schools, Chicago, December 28, 1946.

tive of the forces that caused the courts to act. Too often, however, such cases are taught not as steps in an evolutionary process but as rules of law, many of which long since ceased or should have ceased to have validity. Casebooks, so the writer has been frequently reminded, are cluttered with outmoded judicial opinions which serve no useful purpose in the contemporary world. History of this kind is more harmful than helpful.

In those few law schools which have permitted themselves to cultivate legal history as such, there has been a tendency to view the broad expanse of history and then to deal, in turn, with the growth of the law of contracts, of torts, of real property, and so on. Although the material produced is often extremely valuable, the effect of this method has been to encourage the study of legal history as an autonomous development rather than as an integral part of social and economic institutions and the fabric of intellectual thought.

At the Harvard Law School in 1939–1940, however, an interesting new seminar was given by Professor Daniel J. Boorstin, now of the University of Chicago, which sought to place legal history squarely within the frame of the life of a given period. Professor Boorstin would have preferred to treat some period in American history. But so fragmentary has been research in the legal history of this country and so limited still are the authoritative works on American economic and intellectual history, that he decided to select the period of the Industrial Revolution in England from 1750 to 1850. Because of the many important changes in social and economic life and the ferment of ideas that occurred, as well as the wealth of excellent source materials available, he believed that there lay a span of a century which could be used fruitfully as the basis for his experiment.

Materials were organized around the elements in the economy. Labor, technology, land, capital, and the structure of markets were considered in turn. The various legal institutions and doctrines that served the needs of each of these elements were treated in connection with economic factors, rather than primarily in relation to the development of legal categories. Thus, together with the changing place of labor in the economy, were discussed not merely problems in labor law, but also in criminal law (conspiracy), administrative law (wage regulation and poor law), and government regulation (mercantilism and laissez faire). The study of changes in technology introduced topics from the law of patents, administrative law regulating factory conditions, the law of unemployment (poor law and vagrancy laws), and the law of civil liberties (criminal libel and unlawful assembly), so far as these legal rules were occasioned by technological developments.

The changes in agriculture and in the importance of property in land led to a discussion of legal problems of the farmer (enclosures and the corn laws), and topics in the law of real property such as settlement and conveyancing. The study of the expansion of commerce provided the occasion for dealing with certain changes in the criminal law: false pretenses, embezzlement, benefit of clergy, and transportation as a punishment. An examination of the demands for the accumulation of capital introduced problems in the law of corporations: the unincorporated association, the preference share, the growth of freedom of incorporation, and limited liability. The study of commercial policy, markets, and the place of the consumer led to the legal problems of price regulation, competition, restraint of trade, cooperatives, and inviolability of property.

To illustrate the uses of the general stock of ideas in systematizing and rationalizing the legal responses to social needs, topics in intellectual history were treated at convenient times. Thus, readings on theories of population and of wages were assigned concurrently with materials on labor law, since these theories comprised the principal arguments for or against changes in labor law. A study of utilitarianism was introduced by problems of poor law, unemployment, and crime.

The course, conducted as a seminar discussion group that met for one evening weekly, was attended by a mere three or four students from the Law School and a small number of advanced graduate students from the Harvard social science departments.

The Law School made no effort to direct students to this seminar; in fact, the faculty seemed scarcely to know of its existence. In attempting to estimate the value of the completed course, Mr. Boorstin noted in a memorandum that the prospects for the future of such an undertaking must depend not only upon the instructor but to some extent upon the general atmosphere of the law school where the experiment is made. It was his belief that law students are willing to be encouraged to consider the law as a social science and to be made conscious of central historical problems. He did not believe, however, that students would readily enter such a course if they were led to think of it as a "cultural" digression. They are too busy; they feel that they "got their culture out of the way" in the academic college. If, on the other hand, legal history were offered to students as something which is essential to the intelligent self-consciousness of the lawyer in modern society—if they were pointed to the importance of understanding the process of legal adjustment to a changing economic order—then they might conclude that legal history is a rich field in which to work.

"Coursebook" on American Institutions. In an article published in the Harvard Law Review for March, 1941, Professor Llewellyn argued at length about the extreme desirability of a course which would, like Boorstin's experiment of the preceding year, center attention upon law and legal factors within their historical framework.[1] The setting, however, would be the United States; the time would be 1830 to the present. Mr. Llewellyn emphatically stated that no one person could prepare the coursebook alone. It would take a man ten years to get ready to do it, he wrote. Hence its preparation would need to be a co-operative undertaking in which perhaps several dozen instructors might participate, either in careful planning of the outline of the book, or in collecting materials and writing designated portions, or in criticizing the tentative drafts. Incidentally, Mr. Llewellyn insisted that materials for this book could not be "gathered" to any appreciable degree. They would have to be written. He estimated

[1] "On the Problem of Teaching Private Law," pp. 775–811.

that of a total of some 1,500 pages of text, 300 to 400 might consist of gathered materials, and another 200 to 300 of cases, statutes, and the like. So inadequate, however, has been American research, particularly research directed toward illuminating the forces that lie behind law and legal rules, that a large part of the course would have to be composed of essays written by men of sound scholarship and a capacity to portray interrelationships creatively.

Llewellyn based his telling case for a course in American institutions on two major arguments. First, "background" for problems of private and of public law must be "locked into law study," and background cannot be provided by present dispersed and unco-ordinated efforts, however skillful. Second, if perspective were provided through the medium of a required five-hour course given in the first semester of the second year, the amount of time devoted to private law courses could be appreciably reduced and the public law courses, where the need for perspective is especially felt, "could produce materially greater sharpness, both in sizing up need and policy, and in the diagnosis and handling of the resultant technical measures and problems."[1]

Part One, Our Law in the Pre-Industrial Era, would attempt to present a comprehensive, over-all portrayal of the functioning economy and the political and ideological structure of the 1830's and 1840's in their relation to law. The yet dominant agricultural and commercial economy would be shown as mainly responsible for the vigorous development of common law, common law concepts, and basic legislation. Although the common law still enjoyed leadership, required reformatory statutes began to appear dealing with such matters as land records, procedural changes, divorce, and married women's rights. The period would be seen as one of balance, and of relatively active contact between law, government, and people.

The presentation of political institutions would be designed to clarify the meaning of local government organization, the jury, structure of courts, the relation of common law to legislation and

[1] *Ibid.*, p. 801.

of the national government, including the Supreme Court, to the national economy. The discussion of economic and social institutions would strive to give a working meaning to selected basic legal concepts, such as: pledge, mortgage, equity of redemption, exemptions, land as a tax-base, recordation, condemnation; the "uncontrolled property" idea: neighbors, testation, preferences; the translation of "property" into control-for-profit: land-speculation; bill, note; contract; suretyship; insurance; the earlier corporation idea; the reviving "utilities" idea; family-law reforms; "wildcatting" (land and banks); special and general agency, and the extension of the latter into commercial bona fide purchase for value; criminal law codification; conditions of policing; procedural reform versus the factors which work against its effectiveness.

Part Two, Developmental Sweeps and the Consequent Legal Problems, 1860 to 1920, would assume a historical moving wholeness but would not attempt a comprehensive portrayal. Rather would it pick up special areas of growth and of problems for treatment, always emphasizing what they meant for law and lawyers. Mr. Llewellyn suggested that some twelve areas might profitably be sketched in about sixty pages each. Everyone would agree, he thought, that corporate development, labor, and the courts were three that should be discussed. As examples of others, he suggested integrating and nationalizing trends (from transportation through Americanization), cities and urbanization, taxation, the government machine, the family and consumption, the farmer, national resources, the succession of new government activities, the bar. The areas selected, however, would be less important than the sharp incisiveness of their treatment.

In Part Three, Legal Problems as They Now Open, integration rather than parallel lines of development would again be made the objective. So complex has society become, however, that it would obviously be impossible in a one-semester course to attempt a comprehensive examination of recent background. Hence Llewellyn suggested integration around the central theme of the machinery and processes of modern legal work. First, contemporary problems in the common law would be examined, such as: negligence law and the automobile accident; the friend-surety and the surety company; the single corporate scheme and the government corporation; "first mortgage" and Strauss mortgage-bonds; the bill of lading and what it has become under modern shipping conditions. These specific problems would be followed by generalized consideration of methods to be employed in using, reshaping, and supplementing older legal concepts when faced with new situations.

Next, broad legislative and administrative invention and intervention would be the focus of attention. Discussion would be devoted to various types of government programs: schools, parks, public hospitals, highways; tax assessments; regulation of fac-tories or mines and of combinations in restraint of trade; housing, social security, public assistance; the TVA. Thus the student would be led from those areas of governmental activity that have come to be generally accepted to areas that are more contro-versial or that represent recent attempts to solve basic problems. The question—paralleling that raised in connection with the common law—of how the legislative and administrative proc-esses can be used to meet modern needs would be emphasized.

It was intended that the course should end with an attempt to visualize emerging problems. Here Llewellyn would call attention to questions as varied as the native migrant, protection of natural resources, legal implications of the declining birth-rate, possible achievements through law revision commissions or congressional committees, and expansion of the availability of legal service. The student would be shown not what has been done, but what has *not* yet been done. He would be left with a picture of the way in which law and the lawyer's task open forward.

Law in Society. Prior to the war Professor Sidney Post Simpson was engaged at the Harvard Law School in preparing materials, under the title of Law in Society, designed for a third-year course in jurisprudence. If anyone thinks that Professor Llewellyn's pro-posed coursebook on American institutions was broad in scope and inclusive in content, it was as nothing compared to the scope of Simpson's materials. He drew upon cultural anthropology, history over the long span of time, and the social sciences to demonstrate the role of law in increasingly more complex types of society. The self-explanatory titles to the six parts of his book bear witness to this fact: law in a kin-organized society; law in an emergent political society; law and the rise of commerce; law and expanding industrialism; law in a complex economically organized society; law and society today. A short introductory essay preceded materials arranged under each part.

Space does not permit a résumé of the contents of this prodigious undertaking. Some of the main topics noted in Simpson's introduction to the part on law in a complex economically organized society, however, are listed. Like all topic headings they are tedious to read, but they have been set down as an indication both of their attempt at comprehensiveness, and of the extent to which they are generally comparable to topics noted by Llewellyn and Boorstin. Although there are scores of minor differences, the area of common agreement about the types of subject to be introduced appears large among these three men who were working simultaneously but independently to utilize history and the social sciences more completely for understanding law.

The greatest difference, perhaps, lies in the period of time covered. Simpson began with primitive societies; Llewellyn and Boorstin confined their examination to one century and one country. Both of the latter had insisted that the period should be brief enough to permit non-legal and legal institutions to be viewed in detail. They would probably have concluded that Simpson's effort was in the nature of an encyclopaedia, and as such was not best designed for teaching purposes. Certainly many such courses within the curriculum of a professional school would be deleterious. But more variety in teaching materials and methods than has formerly characterized the law school is desirable. Students, particularly in schools where highly specialized courses in the common law are predominant, might profit greatly from a broad survey which stretched their ability to see the relatedness of vast numbers of seemingly unrelated facts; which indicated something of the range of forces that created law and were created by it.

Professor Simpson's essay and the reading materials presented on law in a complex economically organized society include the following topics. Reasons for the breakdown of laissez faire. Curb upon individual liberty as outgrowth of increasing interest in general security: controls exercised in behalf of public safety, public health; regulation of economic enterprises such as public utilities, banks, securities. Entry of the state into certain enterprises to prevent their disintegration. Growth of departments of government to watch over and assist the operation of certain economic institutions. Development of the concept of the service state. Extension of the private-law principle of insurance to banking, to social security categories, to agricultural subsidies viewed as social premiums paid for the maintenance of a vital portion of the economic structure. Conservation and controlled utilization of natural resources.

Trend in public law toward regulation and supervision of economic institutions paralleled in private law by restrictions on freedom of contract, limitations on the use and disposition of property, conditioning of free activity *by liability* without fault.

Growth of collective contract in labor relations, government conciliation in labor disputes, accident and unemployment compensation, pension provisions, limitation of hours of work and regulation of minimum rates of pay. Growth of concern for preservation and improvement of *human* resources: compulsory education; private social work and public social welfare programs; parole, probation, and the indeterminate sentence; treatment for juvenile delinquents; elimination of legal incapacities, particularly those relating to women; growing recognition of a right of privacy; extension of remedies for injury to nervous susceptibilities.

New types of property: news, scientific discoveries. Transformation of old types like corporate stock, tradenames, trademarks. Growth of legal doctrines of contracts for benefit of third persons, restrictions running with goods. Separation of ownership and control in large corporations—most outstanding modern development in private property—made without legislative action. Demand for legal control of corporate actions to protect interests of helpless shareholders.

Changes in the technique of the legislative process. Growth of expert inquiry preliminary to legislative action. Demand for permanent agencies of investigation such as ministries of justice. Delegation of legislative power to administrative agencies and executive departments. The lobby as possible forerunner of provision for regular consultation between Congressional committees and organized interests concerned with particular legislative proposals. Abandonment in practice of doctrine of separation of powers. Administrative process as meeting-point of legislation and adjudication.

Creative nature of much judicial activity. Decay of concept of *mere* law-finding as appropriate function of courts. Increasing utilization by judges of legal standards—due care, public interest, public convenience and necessity—as instruments of social control.

Growing realization by legislatures and administrative bodies of necessity for some such standards which are essentially individualizing devices. Increasing tendency to employ non-legal experts in administration, adjudication, legislation. Trend much slower in courts except in field of criminal law.

Limitations on the scope of effective legal action: areas where religion and morals are still more successful than law; legal difficulties in dealing with interests of a spiritual, emotional, or psychological nature; areas where legal action is not supported by the mores; still uncharted fields of potential legal intervention.

REORIENTATION OF SELECTED PORTIONS OF CURRICULUM

Extensive changes have been made in recent years, as earlier pages have indicated, in the traditional curriculum of law schools. Nevertheless, there is a growing conviction that some of the courses most important either to the lawyer who enters public service or engages in newer and complex forms of private practice, have undergone insufficient alteration or been inadequately cultivated. As examples, three areas of the curriculum have been selected for somewhat detailed consideration. The first is real property. It was chosen because of its absolutely fundamental nature, and also for the purpose of discovering to what extent it has responded to the many changes in property concepts and in legal remedies that have occurred since the turn of the century and particularly since the economic cataclysm of the 1930's.

Administrative law is the second area selected. The pre-eminence attained by the administrative agency makes it a subject of ever-increasing importance both for the lawyer who is likely to work within it and for the private practitioner who will appear before it. The third area is that of legislation, legislative drafting, and the relation of legislation to other courses in public law. An attempt is made to indicate what training is provided for the lawyer's role not only in statutory interpretation but in other phases of the legislative process, particularly draftsmanship.[1]

Real Property. In 1941 a Committee on Curriculum of the Association of American Law Schools made a survey, through the use of questionnaires, of the teaching of property courses in schools belonging to the Association. The returns demonstrated, so it was said, the "established and routine method of teaching the subject, inherited from Gray, with little variation in essentials, little disposition to experiment, and few new ideas in the past two decades."[2] When teachers of property were asked to set down plans for future investigation and teaching, the replies could "best be described as complacent." Professor Myres S. McDougal wrote upon analyzing these answers, "No pen is dipped in bitter dissatisfaction; a dominant and recurrent note throughout the

---

[1] It had been the writer's intention to include a section on labor law, that field which has rapidly come to assume such importance not merely for legal practice but for national well-being. In December, 1946, however, W. Willard Wirtz of Northwestern University presented his paper, "A New Prospectus for the Labor Law Course," before the Association of American Law Schools in Chicago, to which reference has already been made. It succinctly portrayed the weaknesses of current labor-law courses; outlined a general plan for immeasurably broadening the subject as now taught to make it one in labor relations; and recommended that a workshop of teachers of labor law be convened to formulate conclusions as to how labor law and teaching materials might most constructively be offered. This paper was heard by a large group of law instructors, and has recently been published as the leading article in the Illinois Law Review for March-April, 1947, under the title, "On Teaching Labor Law." The workshop has now been held, but its results are not yet available. Hence the writer decided to omit further discussion here. Lay persons interested in labor law in its relation to current management-labor crises or in specialized problems of legal education should not fail to examine Wirtz's significant article prepared on the basis both of his experience as a teacher of labor law and as one-time member of the National War Labor Board and subsequently chairman of the National Wage Stabilization Board.

[2] Handbook of Association of American Law Schools, 1941, p. 257.

replies is that 'by and large, the present arrangement is satisfactory.'"[1]

The courses as offered since the time of Gray have dealt almost exclusively with private as distinguished from social interests in property, and have been built upon legal doctrines evolved by the courts. Yet the twentieth century has seen a prodigious expansion of concern about the social aspects of property, much of which became crystallized in statutes in the 1930's. The recognition had long been developing among official and private bodies engaged in studying the subject that natural resources must be preserved and improved through the use of legislative and administrative controls; that the chaos of unplanned cities and towns must give way to urban and regional planning; that the vast slums of America must be wiped out through slum clearance and the substitution of housing financed or at least controlled by government agencies. Education of the public regarding this recognition had progressed far. But it had been little reflected in the law schools, chiefly because the appellate courts had not yet been called upon to speak definitively about this broad social issue of the twentieth century. It is true that after the courts had belatedly and cautiously sustained zoning ordinances by evoking the police power of the state to curb "nuisances," these cases came to be incorporated in some casebooks in real property. Otherwise the student was given no opportunity to view the tremendous change in the property structure of the nation which was obviously in the making.

Then came the financial cataclysm of the late twenties with extensive paralysis of industry, including the construction industry, and countrywide unemployment.[2] In an effort to revitalize private enterprise and get men and women back at work, hurried legislation was enacted. Much of this legislation was built upon the philosophy of those studies that had already been made for

[1] *Ibid.*, p. 268.

[2] For an excellent brief statement of property problems prepared by a law-school teacher, see Professor Homer F. Carey's article, "Real Property: Post Depression and Future," in Journal of Legal and Political Sociology, April, 1943, pp. 101–114.

the reordering of the property structure, but to which the law schools had contributed little or even paid scant heed. Construction was set in motion by direct government loans for slum clearance and new housing for some of the nine million families earning less than $1,500 annually whose needs could not be met by the building industry. Construction by private enterprise was facilitated through another class of enactments, such as limited dividend corporation statutes, modifications of investment requirements of insurance companies, a National Housing Act, and a Federal Home Loan Bank Act.

But it was realized that the urban land problem does not surpass in social and economic significance that which concerns the use of rural property. The creation during the thirties of the Resettlement Administration which later became the Farm Security Administration, the enactment of provision for farm ownership loans under the title of the Bankhead-Jones Farm Tenant Act, the mandate to the Farm Credit Administration to make long-term and short-term credit available to farmers, the establishment of the Rural Electrification Administration to finance, through self-liquidating loans, construction of rural electric facilities—these were only some of the federal attempts to alleviate the condition of disadvantaged farmers. Because the utilization and conservation of rural property extends beyond the domain of agriculture, at least a third of the states busied themselves between 1929 and the outbreak of the war with the enactment of rural zoning and planning legislation which had as its objective the attainment of many social and economic ends essential to the welfare of the state. Finally, Congress created the multiple purpose Tennessee Valley Authority which has provided America's greatest demonstration of the intensive conservation, development, and use of the land, water, and human resources of an entire region.

In comparison with these numerous and sweeping congressional and state legislative enactments, the judicial decisions concerning real property seem relatively unimportant. Reference must be made to two decisions by state appellate courts, however, because they are not only of major significance to the future of city planning, but because they are likely to assume large importance for law schools which still feel far more at home in dealing with the judicial than with the administrative process. In the first case, which tested the strength of a zoning ordinance, the Virginia Supreme Court of Appeals maintained that the police "power is not limited to regulations designed to promote public health, public morals, or public safety, or to the suppression of what is offensive, disorderly, or unsanitary, but extends to so dealing with conditions which exist as to bring out of them the greatest welfare of the people by promoting public convenience or general prosperity."[1] To this strong affirmative statement which indicated how far the judiciary had progressed beyond its earlier reliance upon "nuisances" as a reason for evoking the police power, the Court added the self-evident observation, "The inalienable rights of the individual are not what they used to be." By refusing to review the decision for "want of a substantial federal question" the United States Supreme Court in effect approved the decision.

The second case was brought as an attack upon a statute which provided for a master-plan and official map of West Orange and for the regulation of subdivisions in accordance with that plan and map. The Supreme Court of New Jersey ruled that the police power extends to planning as well as zoning. After a sociological analysis of the objectives of city planning, unparalleled in any prior decision, the Court held that, "Planning confined to the common need is inherent in the authority to create a municipality itself. It is as old as government itself; it is of the very essence of civilized society. A comprehensive scheme of physical development is requisite to community efficiency and progress."[2]

A third significant development of the period was the appearance, in the spring of 1941, of the preliminary study of the Na-

---

[1] Walker, Robert Averill, The Planning Function in Urban Government. University of Chicago Press, 1941, pp. 82–83.

[2] *Ibid.*, pp. 84–85.

tional Resources Planning Board for conserving and improving the nation's natural public and private resources. A considerable part of the report dealt with maladjustments in the use of urban, suburban and rural lands, with recommendations for remedying both urban and rural blight. In this large and important research undertaking that received extensive publicity even though the Board received no congressional appropriation for further study, is set down the vast problem of land use to the solution of which legal skills are of paramount importance.

Faced with the logic of these facts, was it possible for the law schools to continue to stand outside the great dynamic current of change? Most of them succeeded in doing so. Although the legal profession carries wide responsibility for the drafting, enactment, interpretation, and often administration of statutes, its training schools had become so traditionalized that they could not free themselves from their own casebooks and their reliance upon judicial opinions.[1] Some of the teachers of real property most

[1] Among the several law professors who read all or parts of this book in manuscript were two teachers of real property. One of them, a distinguished specialist in his field for whose opinion the author has great respect, did not consider her presentation "a discussion of the teaching of property law at all." Because perhaps a majority of law teachers would subscribe to his point of view, it is being presented here, although necessarily in abbreviated form. This professor suggests that there are two distinct questions that should be considered: property courses; other courses that *should* be taught "which are not primarily property courses." He first lists types of judicial doctrines which lawyers need to know concerning the law of private property in land. He then turns to important matters of policy determination by government. Referring to the long citation quoted from Myres S. McDougal he writes "McDougal is discussing how far government can or should regulate the uses for land which is held by private persons, and how it should be done. This involves first, what can the government do under our constitutions (constitutional law); second, what within our constitutional framework, should the government attempt to do. This involves psychological, sociological, political, and economic factors. It is the task of the statesmen, guided by experts in these several fields. Third, how can these projects best be carried out. This is a matter for administrative law. These are the elements that enter into zoning laws, reclamation projects, TVA developments, and so on. Why McDougal should relate such matters as these to the teaching of property law I do not see. He is really arguing for additional courses in the law school which have little or no relation to the property courses."

The writer would completely agree with her critic's first point that the student *must* be given essential concepts of private property law. Even here, however, she would assume from the many discussions she has heard quite aside from McDougal's statement, that essential concepts might be presented more meaningfully, perhaps more expeditiously, and certainly more critically than is generally customary. Essential concepts appear, moreover, to have become greatly elaborated. In many schools visited several advanced courses, which proved popular electives, were offered. Can

Footnote continued on page 162.

interested in current statutory and administrative developments, moreover, were reluctant to introduce teaching in this area because they believed it would do nothing to fit prospective lawyers for practice. One trip to Washington alone would have demonstrated how many lawyers were then earning their living through practice, both public and private, in this very area. Similar work was going forward in local, state, or regional offices whose business related to land use and public housing, and in many private law offices.

It should not be assumed, however, that no changes had occurred. As the thirties came to an end and the forties began, small changes had become noticeable in many schools, appreciable alterations in at least two schools, and profound changes in one. Some of these changes appeared, however, not in courses in real property but in broad elective courses which reached only a very small portion of the student body. At the University of Michigan, for example, Professor Burke Shartel included—under

----

Footnote continued from page 161.

such elaboration be justified if it occurs at the expense of consideration of important statutory enactments relating to land use, housing, and so on? If the decision of one court upholding zoning is important enough to appear in a casebook on real property, is not the act of Congress that created the TVA, or the Farm Security Administration, or the Rural Electrification Administration? Did not these enactments result in work for substantial numbers of lawyers, both lawyers employed by government to translate the acts into operating programs and lawyers who served as counsel and advocates for opposing private interests? Is it not the function of courses in real property to train men for such work? Can it not be assumed that the future is likely to provide continuing, if not increasing, similar legal work?

Concerning the professor's second point of the place where broad questions of government policy should be considered, the answer seems less clear. The writer would favor experimentation within the property courses. She believes the law schools should attempt to create "statesmen," whether private practitioners, government lawyers, judges, or legislators, who can bring to the great contemporary issues of reclamation, irrigation, preservation and utilization of resources, "valley authorities," electrification, urban planning, housing, resettlement, and so on, the marked skill and the devotion that the bar has brought to issues in the private property field. Since she considers these as property questions, she is inclined to think that they might be better treated in property courses than in other courses where they would be viewed in fragments or would have to compete for attention with different and also large questions. She is, however, so opposed to rigid walls around courses that this is only a tentative judgment. Perhaps parallel courses should be given in private and in public property. Whatever the disposition, the matter is less important than the selection of teaching personnel. Lawyers need to be found who have had significant, responsible experience in developing such public programs. These men ought then to be given their exclusive time and that of assistants for formulating outlines of courses, and for assembling and experimenting with teaching materials.

jurisprudence—teaching materials both on zoning and the protection of natural resources. In his course on recent social legislation, as has been seen, Professor Riesenfeld devoted much attention to housing and other statutory provisions in the field of property. Professor Riesman, who had gained valuable experience from voluntary work with the Buffalo City Planning and Research Station, introduced into his property course at the University of Buffalo extensive consideration of land use. He was so convinced, moreover, of the fact that lawyers would be needed as counsel for housing authorities and as members of housing administrations, that he suggested that one law school set itself the task of building a specialized program to fit men for such work.[1] Professor John Ritchie of the University of Virginia is another teacher who made an essential place for problems of land use within his regular property courses.

Both of the leading law schools in Chicago reflected broadened concepts. At the University of Chicago Professor Sheldon Tefft introduced a one-quarter advanced seminar in 1940 on regulation of the use of land, in which were considered conservation of national resources, restrictive covenants, urban and rural zoning, eminent domain, and the police power. Under the sponsorship of the Law School, Professor Tefft also delivered three public lectures on the "Conservation of Land Values." Indicative of the interest created by the seminar, is a twenty-page note on "Public Housing in Illinois," appearing in the February, 1941, issue of the University of Chicago Law Review. In April, 1942, an equally long and significant note appeared in the same Review under the title "Amortization of Property Uses Not Conforming to Zoning Regulations." Much of the information was secured through extensive correspondence with zoning committees throughout the United States.

Since the end of the war, the seminar is again being offered. Professor Tefft reports that in 1946 he devoted attention to a historical study of the institution of property in land in England

---

[1] Riesman, David, Jr., "Law and Social Science: A Report on Michael and Wechsler's Classbook on Criminal Law and Administration," in Yale Law Journal, February, 1941, p. 639.

and the United States, in an attempt to ascertain the effect which the various rules of property law have had at various stages upon the use and development of land. Consideration was then given to modern problems related to the use and development of land and to relevant rules of law. Afterward, each student was requested to select one or more of these problems for intensive study during the remainder of the quarter. The titles of some of the reports submitted indicate the variety of the problems considered: Texas oil regulations, the Coulee Dam, taxation as an instrumentality in rural planning, public housing and the federal government, aesthetic considerations in zoning, racial restrictive covenants, soil conservation districts.

A current development of great interest and potential significance at Chicago is the research on problems of housing in which a recent law graduate and two economists, who have had considerable experience in fact research, are engaged. This three-man team has been asked to prepare for the law faculty a general over-all statement of the housing problem, that can be used as a basis for determining which legal problems require most attention if housing is to be improved. Many data employed in the preparation of this statement will be social and economic. It is assumed by the Law School that extensive portions of these data will be immediately utilized in several of the law-school courses—at least in property, constitutional law, and trade regulations—in order to describe, predict, or evaluate legal rules. By the time this statement has been prepared and an evaluation made of the priority of legal problems, it is hoped that an enlarged research staff will be available to begin work on the most important of these problems. Participating members of the law faculty and supervised students would assist the research staff. Service could then be offered the bench and bar in such form as statutory drafting, preparation of legal memoranda, and the filing of briefs by members of the staff as "friends of the court."

At the Northwestern University Law School Professor Homer F. Carey, assisted by two colleagues, offered a seminar in 1941 on public problems of real property to a small group of selected students. A systematic study was made of the statutory enactments of the 1930's. The legislative background, major objectives, and methods of operation of these laws were emphasized. Then each student was assigned a topic for investigation, such as city planning, rural zoning, or the effectiveness of the housing program. Professor Carey reported that never in his teaching had he seen such enthusiasm among students. The one problem was that of keeping them from seriously neglecting their other work. The experiment not only demonstrated that students enjoy struggling with significant contemporary problems, but it suggests that the third year of law school when student interest has frequently waned can be transformed into a significant educational experience. Because the postwar influx of students at Northwestern has overtaxed teaching facilities, the seminar has not yet been offered again.

At Yale University the teaching of property had undergone its greatest change prior to the war. The first-year course had been made into a survey course covering the whole field of property. About half of the time was devoted to possessory estates and future interests; ownership, possession, and rights in land; creation, transfer, and termination of rights in the land of another; and problems in the use and conservation of water resources. The second half was devoted to "land planning" and techniques of control, with much attention focused upon covenants and easements, zoning, legislation, and administrative action. Thus every student in his introduction to property was given an opportunity to view broadly the private and public interests involved in real property, and to see the role of the legislative and administrative processes as well as the judicial process in the regulation of those interests. The introductory course was followed by elective courses in vendor and purchaser and future interests, and in a seminar where Professors McDougal and Lasswell assisted their students in detailed examination of certain problems of "land planning."

This large shift in orientation at Yale resulted from Professor McDougal's vigorous dissatisfaction both with the customary teaching of real property and with many of the goals and much of the methodology of legal education. As his philosophy evolved, it was not only translated into change in the Yale property courses but was vigorously set down in print for colleagues to examine.[1] In the process he received much able assistance from the intellectually imaginative Professor Lasswell whom he had persuaded to come to his aid. Thus a two-man revolution was begun, and begun within that very part of the law-school curriculum where the hand of the past lay heaviest. The revolution soon extended out beyond the confines of real property, moreover, to an attack upon many of the basic assumptions on which legal education had long rested. McDougal and Lasswell were in the throes of attempting to discover those premises, already mentioned, which might form a new frame of reference within which the professional schools could train lawyers more effectively to meet contemporary needs.[2]

Before they had published the results of this larger task, however, McDougal prepared for the 1941 Report of the Committee on Curriculum a statement of what he believed teachers of real property should be seeking to achieve. Because it is the most comprehensive memorandum on the subject, but one that has not been available to the interested laity or even to many members of the bar, this powerful although highly controversial statement is reproduced almost complete.[3] Even if a few legal terms have little meaning for non-lawyers, the argument is clearly understandable. Furthermore, since McDougal is convinced that courses in property should concern themselves far more largely than in the past with the public aspects, little of the argument is confined to common law doctrine which makes such difficult reading for the layman.

[1] Review of William Ebenstein's "The Law of Public Housing," in Harvard Law Review, January, 1941, pp. 526–530; "Restatement of the Law of Torts, Volume IV, Division 10, Chapter 41," in Yale Law Review, June, 1940, pp. 1502–1507; "Title Registration and Land Law Reform: A Reply," in University of Chicago Law Review, December, 1940, pp. 63–77.

[2] See pp. 108–109.

[3] The following statement is reproduced with some abbreviation from pp. 268–277 of the Handbook of Association of American Law Schools, 1941.

It is McDougal's basic premise that teaching and investigation in property should be oriented toward the future and designed for the training of "policy-makers for action"—that is of "lawyers who are to be legislators and judges and administrators and counsellors who are not at the beck and call of every temporary selfish interest." To achieve such a goal, teaching and research, in his opinion, should seek the following objectives:

1. Clear definition and classification of problems in terms of *fact* and social objectives (i.e., in terms of social problems as opposed to overlapping legal concepts of high level abstraction).

2. Explicit consideration of alternative social objectives, general and specific, and of justifications for preferences and preference priorities.

3. Enough orientation in historical and contemporary trends to determine, considering probable future developments, what problems are important and what social objectives are practicable.

4. Consideration and use of, and efforts to add to, existing knowledge of cause and effect relations, which is necessary to the manipulation of existing, and the creation of new, social controls (forms of organization, rules, and practices).

5. Consideration and study of a repertory of controls adequate for the achievement of the social objectives specified.

McDougal now undertakes to test actual performance in the light of these objectives:

I. First our definition and classification of problems. To begin with, our master symbol "property" is itself a very poor and fuzzy focus of attention. It is used indiscriminately to refer to physical resources, to legal controls over resources, to claims to income from or beneficial use of resources, and to the whole social organization by which resources are exploited. Problems now considered under "property" could be, and in fact often are, indifferently subsumed under "contracts," "torts," "business units," or "public control of business," and so on. Indeed most of our books, as is well known, are organized not about problems but about "concepts" and "doctrines," and no principle of selection is offered for the latter other than that these are the concepts and doctrines which have been traditionally considered under the label property.

Take, for example, the orthodox course on Rights in Land (sometimes taught as a part of Conveyancing). Under some such label as "Natural Rights" of "Possessory Interests" we are treated to a diffuse mass of cases on "trespasses" on, under, or above the ground, on "nuisances," on "streams," on "surface waters," on "underground waters" and on subjacent and lateral support. Separate chapters ladle out cases on easements, profits, licenses, covenants that run at law, and covenants that bind in equity, with no apparent recognition that these words are but carriers for differing legal consequences about the same (though many diverse) social problems. Conversely, covenant cases from "landlord and tenant" and "vendor and vendee" are lumped together as if they had something in common beyond the words. In lieu of a functional treatment of landlord and tenant problems, we often get a chapter on Rent, which strings together a bunch of unrelated problems, united only by the curious notion that "rent" is something which spews out of the ground on rent day, as regularly as Old Faithful. A chapter on Waste may indiscriminately mix cases on landlord and tenant, vendor and vendee, mortgagor and mortgagee, and life tenant and remainderman problems without offering sufficient materials for the adequate treatment of any single relationship. Sometimes under the catholic concept of "public rights" there are included cases on fishing, muskrat hunting, and the use of the public highways.

.   .   .

II. Next, our specification and justification of social objectives. Here our sins have been largely of omission and unconscious assumption. Largely concerned with the teaching of "legal" propositions from appellate opinions, assuming apparently that these—however ancient— embody the preferred values of our own society, we have paid little conscious attention to what it is that we are trying to do. Legal concepts and doctrines, which at their best should be regarded as instrumental only, have come to be regarded as ends in themselves and our justifications of specific decisions have too often been not in terms of the key values of a democratic society but in terms of logical derivations from more inclusive, and hence even less meaningful, legal concepts.

Most general of the relevant questions to be asked here is, of course, how can "property" (resources, control, and claims) be used to implement our major democratic values. To be made meaningful, however, such values must be spelled out in terms which point unequivocally to specific and consistent goals. The task is not impossible.

The American Public Health Association has, for example, expounded in utmost physiological and psychological detail, according to present knowledge, the basic principles of healthful housing. (See Housing for Health, 1941.) How much more relevant it would be to the accepted values of our society if we appraised the landlord and tenant cases on "caveat lessee," no "implied covenants," "waste," "independent covenants," "constructive eviction," and tort non-liability in terms of these principles rather than in terms of that, in this context, phantom nonsense "freedom of contract." (A friend has suggested that a law school might just as well teach the techniques of creating, maintaining and exploiting slums. That is, of course, just what we have unconsciously been doing.)

Our community-planning experts have definite, intelligible, and generally accepted norms for building stable and livable urban communities and controlling blight. Our agricultural experts have similar norms for controlling soil erosion and planning the best use of our agricultural land. How much more relevant it would be for us to appraise "covenant" decisions in the light of these norms rather than in terms of those Eleusinian mysteries "touch and concern," "privity," "dominant estate," and "affirmative burden."

Our engineers have long known that the physical unities of a drainage basin are such as to make imperative the unified development of its water resources for flood control, soil conservation, power production, city supply, industrial use, irrigation, navigation and recreational use. How much more influential would be our teaching of "water law" if it were oriented toward such a goal rather than lost in the traditional trivialities of "stream," "surface," "subsurface," "riparian," "natural flow," "rule of capture," "prior appropriation," and "reasonable user."

Most of us would subscribe to the value judgment that the social function of the doctrines and institutions we study in Conveyancing should be to provide for the cheap, secure, and speedy transfer of land—free of adventitious hindrances without any basis in policy. Yet, if we ever actually and explicitly appraise doctrines and institutions in terms of such an objective, why is it that we continue to tolerate, and even to teach the virtues of, an elaborate, cumbersome machinery of transfer which requires both a "contract" and a "deed" and both a public recording system and a private, monopolistic recording system (with abstract or insurance company)?

For some time economists have been in substantial agreement that the institution of inheritance (taken in a broad sense which includes the dead-hand control of "future interests") is a prime contributing factor to our growing inequalities ("over-concentration") of income and wealth. The social and economic ill-effects of such inequalities are well known and are generally admitted to be inconsistent with our democratic values. Why should not our doctrines and practices about the transmission of wealth from generation to generation be appraised in terms of how much they contribute to the objective of reducing these inequalities and ill-effects? Why could not decisions under the "Rule against Remoteness," for example, be judged explicitly in terms of their effect, or lack of effect, on the maintenance of family dynasties rather than in terms of their logical consistency with the now almost meaningless symbols "vested" and "contingent"?

•   •   •

III. Next, our awareness and conscious use of developmental trends. . . . For better orientation in future probabilities our need is for careful and systematic disciplining of our common-sense hunches by reference to known social facts and trends. An abundance of relevant material lies ready to our hand: witness the recent studies of the TNEC and of the National Resources Planning Board. Further studies could be undertaken or encouraged and plans made for the more deliberate and comprehensive collection of data in the future. To collect the necessary data, to chart the relevant trends and probable future developments, and to appraise the effect of these on our traditional property doctrines and institutions and our distribution of property values will of course require monumental labor. But it is not difficult to indicate the kind of question which we should be asking ourselves. Some examples follow.

What is to be the effect upon our great cities of a declining rate of population growth? Of the heliocopter? Of the dive bomber? Of the diffusion of electric power? Of prefabricated and mobile housing? What is to happen to the fantastic land values, so generously underwritten by the federal government, which now support not only our antiquated local governments but also most of our banks, insurance companies, and other institutional lenders? What implications have our answers to these questions for the future "law" of community planning and housing?

What is to be the effect upon millions of agricultural laborers of impending changes in machines, animals, plants, land uses, and ways of processing and using farm products? Of the increasing concentration in the ownership of farm land? Of continuing soil depletion? Of a declining (or enlarged) foreign trade? What are the implications of our answers for the future "law" of landlord and tenant or mortgages? What are the implications for our whole economy and, hence, for other domains of "law"?

What is to be the effect on our institution of inheritance and, hence, on the "law of future interests" of ever-increasing governmental provision of capital for productive enterprise? Of continually more progressive taxation? (Chapter 2 of Richard R. Powell's Trusts and Estates, 1932, makes a good beginning in the use of relevant trends.)

On a more mundane level, is the transfer of land actually becoming simpler, cheaper, and quicker or is it becoming the monopoly of an exclusive group of dilatory and costly specialists (brokers, appraisers, recorders, "title" lawyers, insurance company executives)?

•   •   •

IV. Next, our efforts to use and expand scientific knowledge. The present undeveloped state of the social sciences is, of course, a matter of common regret and we need not reproach ourselves for not using knowledge which does not exist. But, however rudimentary the social sciences may be, are we actually taking advantage of what psychologists and economists, for example, know now? What, furthermore, are we doing to alleviate the sad state of the social sciences? Where is the Underhill Moore of Property?

The most cursory glance at our leading casebooks or our law reviews suggests that property "doctrine" (propositions from appellate opinions) is still the only variable of the many interdependent variables in any complex social situation which we seriously study. "Vested" and "contingent," to recur to a favorite example, are spun out in logical refinement ("vested interest in a contingent remainder," "vested subject to being divested," "vested subject to open," and so on) as if such symbols had some kind of predictable, somatic effect on judges. More exhaustive examination of any context in which the symbols are used would reveal a tremendous variety of variable: language in the dispositive instrument; factual reference of such language to person, time, and event; practical problem (destructibility, alienability, taxation, eminent domain, perpetuities); policy considerations and consequences (keeping in bloodline, free alienability, preventing tax evasion, control of dead hand); specific decision (for one set of donees rather than another, taxable or not taxable); place of trial; personality or class affiliation of judge; influence of parties or counsel; and so on. Our techniques of observation and analysis have not yet been, and may never be, sufficiently refined to take all of these variables into account.

But explicit and systematic study of some of them is possible and might yield startling results.

How much study, quantitative or qualitative, are we making of the effects of the existing distribution of "property" values (in terms of both income and power) on other values and on the "social controls" we invoke? What, for example, are the consequences of existing patterns of income and power distribution for housing, agricultural production, conservation, community planning, channels of communication, employment, and so on? Conversely, how much study are we making of the effect of contemporary social controls on the distribution of property values? Tillers of other vineyards have given us a study of *The Modern Corporation and Private Property*. Why have we had no comparable study of *The Modern Trust Company and Private Property?* Of the insurance company? Of the labor union? Of the public utility corporation? Of the government corporation? Why have we been content to leave the social effects of the institution of inheritance (including "future interests") so largely to nebulous speculation? Have we ever attempted to identify any, much less a persuasive, theory of social change for our society?

•   •   •

V. Finally, our conception and study of the relevant social controls. Here is illustrated most clearly our almost complete abdication of effort to be influential. Once again our attention has been too closely confined —too closely confined to one institution and an institution which in the total context of governmental activity is of diminishing relative importance: the appellate court and the norms it announces. Our failure has been a failure to observe the ineluctable trend even in "property" problems from the private lawsuit to some kind of administrative action as the method both of settling private dispute and of identifying the public interest. Our emphasis has been too much upon legal logic and not enough upon explicit presentation of major alternative methods by which specified objectives may be achieved.

Take again the problem of the use and conservation of our water resources in the interest of the consumer. The only contribution of the latest and most authoritative expression of scholarly opinion (the American Law Institute) here is an urgent insistence that the problem be handled not by property but by *tort* doctrines, apparently in complete indifference to the fact that the physical, engineering, and utilization unities of a drainage basin are such that every use—whether for city supply, power, flood control, and so on—affects every other use and that no distillation of *tort* doctrines can give a court the necessary staff, training, experience and powers to carry out the affirmative, multi-purpose programs which public and private interest require. (This is no aspersion on the courts; designed to settle private disputes by broad social norms, they are simply unable to perform all of the functions which must be performed.) Why do we get no survey of a variety of possible controls, from the most individualistic to the most collective, including along with the tort doctrines, state and federal flood control measures, the New England Mill Acts, the Western water boards, the state pollution control boards, the Federal Power Commission, interstate compacts, the federal-state Soil Conservation Districts, and regional authorities like the TVA?

Compare what we now do and what we might conceivably do with community planning. We teach "nuisance" here and "easements" and "covenants" there and allow zoning and subdivision regulation to go by default to teachers of Municipal Corporations; we have not even observed, if our casebooks are to be trusted, that the codification of procedure and the growth of the doctrine of notice have rendered practically obsolete the old common law doctrines of convenants. Why could we not begin with the "nuisance" cases to show not only the patterns of anarchy, the physical and utilization chaos, of our modern urban communities but also the inadequacies of any judicial, retrospective, small-scale, hit-or-miss handling of the problem by *tort* (or any other) doctrines? Having so defined our problem, we could then explore the possibilities and limitations of private agreement (easement and covenant) and then move on to newer and more effective controls: planning commissions, zoning, subdivision regulation, excess condemnation, set-back lines, reshaping of municipal boundaries, capital budgets for public improvements, public ownership, and so on. We might even discover that a large-scale public housing program is indispensable to effective community planning.

Suppose we should specify, as one of the key values of a democratic society, healthful and cheap housing? How could the necessary controls be marshalled for the achievement of this end? A beginning might be made in the antiquities of landlord and tenant, caveat lessee, constructive eviction, and so on. Having once again demonstrated that many of the functions which must be performed are beyond the reach of the judicial institution as it is now constituted, we could explore the consequences of certain timid invocations of the police power in the administration of tenement laws and building codes. These, too, having been found inadequate, we could then expand upon the abundant possibilities in tenants' unions, company housing, rent control, the use of the tax power for policy purposes, the use of the credit power (FHA, HOLC, and so on), co-operatives, limited dividend and urban redevelopment corporations, regulation of the building industry, and governmental construction, ownership, and management. Indeed our vision, though not necessarily our grasp, in this particular unit of study might extend even further. Obviously our use of land, and of other resources, for housing purposes is a part of our "whole economy"—that is, such use affects all of our other economic activities. Hence, it is possible that certain other general controls for expanding our "whole economy"— e.g., government spending and subsidies of all kinds, lowering of interest rates, changing of tax policies, removing tariffs, revising patent laws, enforcing antitrust laws, and so on—might be even more important for securing healthful and cheap housing than any of the more specific controls mentioned above. Such specific controls might, conversely, be of utmost importance in a general program for expanding the whole economy. Note already the emphasis in after-the-war planning on "housing" as a possible mode of maintaining full employment.

Administrative Law. The emergence, growth, and rapid expansion of administrative agencies in the past century is one of the significant phenomena in the social history of the United States. The fast development of gigantic industries and the mushrooming of densely populated cities made obvious the fact, before the end of the 1800's, that laissez faire must be subjected to considerable control in the interest of the public welfare. Neither the legislative nor the judicial branch of government, whether federal or state, was prepared to bring to this large and continuing task of control the technical competence, time, and quickness of action needed. Hence the administrative device, which combined legislative, judicial, and executive functions, was utilized to exercise public control over many of those private activities which the Congress and the state legislatures decreed should be subject to regulation.

The instrumentality employed was not new. On the contrary it was as old as the American government.[1] Its growth paralleled that of statutory law for the very reason that, as the federal and

[1] For a more detailed statement of the origin and early development of federal agencies, see the Final Report of the Attorney General's Committee on Administrative Procedure, Government Printing Office, Washington, 1941, pp. 7–11.

state legislative bodies enacted statutes, they resorted to the administrative device in the practical effort to meet practical needs. The First Congress enacted three statutes conferring important administrative powers upon the executive branch of government. Before the close of the Civil War no fewer than eleven of fifty-one of the now principal federal agencies or subdivisions of agencies had already been created, at least in initial form. Many lesser administrative powers naturally had been delegated. The trend in the various states was the same.

However, it was not until the creation of the Interstate Commerce Commission in 1887 for the purpose of regulating the railroads that the tremendous potential power and effectiveness of this instrumentality began to be foreseen. The establishment, in addition to several less conspicuously important bodies, of the Federal Reserve System in 1913, the Federal Trade Commission in 1914, and the United States Tariff Commission and the Shipping Board in 1914 was prophetic of the ever increasing and widening use to which the Congress would put this device in subsequent years. In the decade from 1930 to 1940 alone, it authorized seventeen administrative agencies.

Examination of the United States Government Manual, published periodically by the Government Information Service, offers proof of the extent to which the administrative agency has become the "fourth branch" of the federal government. Nor is the picture different on the state and municipal level. A Manual of State Administrative Organization in Michigan,[1] for example, is factual evidence of how far state government, irrespective of political party, has intervened in affairs once considered private.

The function of the administrative agency was initially conceived of as almost purely regulatory. Before long, however, the Congress realized that regulation was not sufficient. What was needed in certain enterprises was planned, co-ordinated activity to replace the lack of planning which had resulted in chaotic conditions within these enterprises. So planning, as well as regulatory, functions generally came to be vested in the administra-

[1] Published by Bureau of Government, University of Michigan, 1940.

tive agencies. With the years the Interstate Commerce Commission, for instance, was entrusted with increased powers until, after 1920, it possessed "less the appearance of a tribunal and more that of a committee charged with the task of achieving the best possible operation of the railroads."[1] The members of the Commission, as Mr. Landis has indicated, could no longer rest content to base the justification of their stewardship upon achievements that merely assured reasonable rates and the absence of discrimination. Instead, the ills of the industry had become their concern. The policies they were to formulate must "now be directed toward broad and imaginative ends, conceived in terms of management rather than of police."[2]

Together with the emergence of the concept of the planned society developed the philosophy of the service state. Government began to be viewed not as a potentially dangerous force that must be kept within close confines but as an agent capable of serving the unmet needs of large segments of the population. This concept of the service state has had profound implications for the evolution of older, and the creation of new, administrative agencies.

The United States Public Health Service provides a striking illustration of an agency whose once dominant regulatory functions of preventing the introduction and spread of disease in the United States have sunk into relative unimportance beside its broadly conceived task of protecting and improving the health of the nation. The Service, to be sure, continues to exercise responsibility for the administration of the laws and of its derivative rulings concerning maritime and interstate quarantine, and the control of manufacture and sale of biologic and analogous products. Its major program, however, consists of research and promotion of research relating to the causes, diagnosis, treatment, control, and prevention of physical and mental diseases and impairments; operation of a considerable number of hospitals and relief stations; and assistance to states, counties, and local

[1] Landis, James M., The Administrative Process. Yale University Press, New Haven, 1938, p. 13.
[2] Ibid., p. 13.

health districts in establishing and maintaining adequate public health service, including the training of personnel. Almost every Congress further enlarges by definition and appropriation its functions as a national health service.

In recent years several administrative agencies have been established expressly to provide those services that the Congress has designated as appropriate to benefit certain broad categories of the population. Any regulatory functions vested in these bodies are incidental to the major purpose for which they were created. The greatly enlarged Veterans Administration, the Farm Security Administration, and the Social Security Administration represent efforts on the part of the federal government to aid veterans, farmers, the aged, the blind, dependent children, the unemployed. The Tennessee Valley Authority, which is so far removed from the old type of administrative agency as to be scarcely recognizable, was set up not only to enlarge navigation; control floods; produce electric power, chemicals essential for war purposes, fertilizers and phosphates; but to carry on investigations that might further aid in the conservation, development, and use of the resources of the region.

The question now arises of the manner and the degree to which law schools have focused attention upon this instrumentality that has come to be a powerful implement both for social control and for providing specialized services. As early as 1911 Ernst Freund, who was for many years a distinguished professor of jurisprudence and public law at the University of Chicago, published the first edition of his Cases on Administrative Law. The book dealt with administrative power and action, and relief against administrative action. He endeavored, moreover, to free the course so far as was possible from purely constitutional problems. His influence over a small group of disciples was very great; they, in turn, were the teachers of some of the present instructors of administrative law. In spite of the influence he exerted, however, his book remained virtually the only teaching tool available until 1932. Bruce Wyman, a professor at Harvard between 1901 and 1914, did much, both through teaching and several published works, to direct law-school attention to the more specialized subject of public utilities.

Regardless of the early contributions of Freund and Wyman and subsequently of a larger number of persons, the difficulty that most law teachers experienced in freeing themselves from myopic concentration upon the courts made them extremely slow to give adequate recognition to the administrative agency as such, even though it renders far more decisions annually than do the federal courts. In fact, when Felix Frankfurter and J. Forrester Davison's Cases and Other Materials on Administrative Law appeared in its first edition in 1932, it was not a book on "administrative law" in the sense of law produced by administrative agencies. It was a specialized work on constitutional law which dealt with the delegation and separation of powers and judicial control of administrative action.

Close consideration of judicial opinions, moreover, caused instructors to emphasize that functional aspect of the agency, namely the judicial or the "quasi-judicial" as it is often called, that most nearly resembles the function of the court. Legislative and executive functions were sadly neglected, in spite of the fact that some of the multitudinous regulations issued and the programs administered affect the very core of the nation's economic life and liberty. To the extent that training in administrative law was offered, its almost exclusive purpose was to prepare private practitioners to act as advocates for clients before administrative bodies. Few planned efforts were made, even to the giving of a series of introductory lectures, to help the student to view administrative agencies as an important social institution vested with responsibility for discharging certain public functions. During the 1930's, however, broad first-year courses began to appear in a considerable number of schools, some of which served to acquaint students with administrative agencies and with other modern aspects of law and administration.

Because most of the attention devoted to administrative agencies was centered upon the judicial function, only those generally independent regulatory commissions or boards where adjudication plays an important role came within the ken of the average law school. "Administrative law" was often taught as if it were something peculiar to, if not the exclusive possession of, these regulatory bodies. The same narrow meaning was carried into such rather general terms as the "administrative process." From a realistic point of view, however, as Dr. Marx has indicated, the administrative process must be regarded as the basic device through which administrative agencies *of every kind* attain their ends. "Correspondingly, administrative law must seek its aim in furnishing guidance and imposing restraint in the exercise of authority wherever the administrative process affects the individual."[1]

The tendency to focus consideration upon independent regulatory bodies made it appear that the task of the agency lawyer is that of regulation. But the legal function has long since passed beyond duties restricted to regulation. Even in the independent commissions and to a marked degree in the newer agencies, the lawyer is tied into the execution of a large variety of service functions administered for the benefit of some social group. For such responsibility scarcely a law school offered so much as general orientation prior to the recent war.

These broad statements of the way in which legal education has viewed administrative agencies must be examined in more detail. For the person unacquainted with law schools, they do not provide an adequate picture either of how insufficient—even for private practice—was former training or how relatively dynamic and subject to change is the current situation.

As late as 1937 when Arthur T. Vanderbilt made his presidential address before the American Bar Association, he announced that only 55 of the 94 law schools then approved by that Association offered any course in administrative law and administrative tribunals.[2] Such courses as were offered were said to be generally

[1] Marx, Fritz Morstein, "The Lawyer's Role in Public Administration," in the Yale Law Journal, April, 1946, p. 500.

[2] "The Bar and the Public," in American Bar Association Journal, October, 1937 p. 871.

one-hour electives. He concluded that the law schools made little attempt to give their students an adequate grasp of what he has often publicly stated to be the outstanding legal development of the twentieth century.

Although Dean Vanderbilt's assumption was doubtless essentially correct, it must be said in all fairness to the schools that the situation was not so unrelieved as the layman might conclude from these figures for one specific year. He happened to speak at the moment when courses in administrative law were being rapidly introduced, and the time devoted to them was being appreciably increased. As a result, 88 per cent of the 74 schools for which Professor Clark Byse subsequently obtained information, announced administrative law in their 1939–1940 bulletins.[1] Twenty-nine of these schools noted that their courses were two-hour credits, 19 were three-hour, and 10 were four-hour.

A second consideration must also be kept in mind by the lay reader. Law-school courses dealing, for example, with industrial organization, labor law, corporate finance, and public utilities could scarcely fail to consider the procedures evolved by administrative agencies that had been created expressly to control those areas of economic life and labor relationships. The University of Chicago, which was about to introduce its carefully planned new curriculum and which was well aware of the dominant role played by the administrative agency, did not then or subsequently—in spite of the influence Freund had exerted— offer a course in administrative law as such. Rather did it attempt to make administrative law an integral part of many of its courses.

Integrated instruction certainly has much to recommend it. One cannot safely assume, however, that the absence of specific courses in administrative law, or the election of an offered course by a mere handful of students is substantial evidence that such integration is being effectively carried on in the majority of schools. Neither can one assume that law schools have fulfilled

[1] "Administrative Law—Cases and Comments," in Iowa Law Review, May, 1940, pp. 840, 842.

their responsibility for the training of prospective lawyers even where administrative law in its regulatory aspects *is* made a part of the fabric of other law courses.

What was the content of administrative law in those schools that gave a course in it in 1937? A Special Committee on Administrative Law of the American Bar Association declared that most schools taught the subject from casebooks that were largely *limited to opinions of the courts reviewing administrative decisions.*[1] Although the Committee's interest in administrative agencies did not appear to extend beyond adjudicatory functions, it considered those functions so essential that it professed grave concern with the narrowness of courses that featured only the opinion of the courts. It maintained that little, if any, attention was being given to matters of such paramount importance as how a particular controversy originated in the administrative machinery of the federal, state, or municipal government; the administrative process which such a controversy followed before it became a case in the courts; and the method of presenting the issue to the various administrative officers or boards required to decide the matter.

If a case can be settled properly by the administrative process, the Committee argued, there is no need for litigation. Experience has shown that with the proper machinery for getting the facts in such controversies, with the aid of briefs and oral arguments by attorneys skilled in the compilation and use of economic and scientific data, the vast majority of the cases can be—and are— satisfactorily settled by the departments, boards, commissions, and other agencies of the federal government, and need not be taken to the courts.

Yet little radical change in the teaching of administrative law was achieved prior to Pearl Harbor. Professor Walter Gellhorn's Administrative Law—Cases and Comments (published in 1940 by the Foundation Press) did constitute a significant advance over earlier teaching materials and has been used extensively

---

[1] "Report of the Special Committee on Administrative Law," in Advance Program of the Sixtieth Annual Meeting of the American Bar Association, 1937, p. 180.

since then in many schools. Texts on judicial opinions constitute less than half of the book. The remainder of the volume endeavors to focus attention on some of the practical workings of the administrative process. In spite of this fact Gellhorn noted, in a memorandum addressed in 1946 to his colleagues at Columbia, that administrative law as taught at Columbia and elsewhere has to do principally with judicial appraisals of the legality of administrative procedures, policies, and decisions. Thus the Columbia course considers the circumstances in which notice of hearing must be given, the adequacy of different types of notice, the various minimum ingredients of a fair hearing, the process of proof in administrative proceedings, the necessity of findings, the methods of obtaining judicial review of decisions, the time at which review may be sought, and the extent of judicial review once the court's attention has been properly invoked. Gellhorn concludes that in such a course, where time and emphasis are centered upon procedural questions, there is little opportunity to consider how administrative judgments are formed in the first instance.

Increasingly attorneys, law-school teachers, and political scientists, who have had personal acquaintance or association with administrative agencies, have expressed dissatisfaction with the pronounced limitation of such training in administrative law. O. R. McGuire, formerly counsel to the Comptroller General of the United States and chairman in 1937 of the American Bar Association's Special Committee on Administrative Law, pertinently inquired in a forceful article whether the neglect of and indifference toward administrative law, showed by many law schools, was not depriving the nation of a source of men at least partially trained to operate the administrative machinery of government.[1] He maintained, furthermore, that such neglect and indifference resulted in failure to develop that knowledge vitally necessary for members of the bar, if bar associations were to carry out any needed reforms in the machinery for the administrative

[1] "Reforms Needed in the Teaching of Administrative Law," in George Washington Law Review, January, 1938, p. 176.

settlement and adjustment of controversies. The situation seemed
so totally unsatisfactory to Dr. McGuire that he suggested giving
teachers of administrative law, who had had no practical experience in the federal government, a sabbatical leave from the law
school in order that they learn something from work in the administrative branch of government about how agencies actually
operate.[1]

The same year A. H. Feller, then special assistant to the Attorney General of the United States, wrote a significant article in an
equally pessimistic vein. He declared that the small group of
scholars of administrative law had divided their time between
writing apologies for the system and studying in elaborate detail
the relations between administrative tribunals and the common
law courts. What was needed was to learn what each administrative agency was doing (as had Gerard C. Henderson in his invaluable study of the Federal Trade Commission, published by
the Yale University Press in 1924); what the remediable defects
were; what should be preserved and what discarded.[2]

In his carefully reasoned, thirty-page article Feller was not
primarily concerned with the teaching of administrative law or
even with the broad over-all purposes served by administrative
agencies. Rather was he concerned with having research done on
problems of organization and procedures of, and enforcement by,
administrative agencies, which might be used as a foundation
for the subsequent formulation of policy. Obviously, the results
of such research would be of very great assistance to attorneys of
the various agencies; they would provide the facts requisite, if
members of the bar were to participate in carrying out some of
the reforms to which McGuire referred; they would have profound implications for teaching purposes.

The problems which Feller posed as questions relative to organization, procedures, and enforcement are reproduced here as
a demonstration of the "unfinished business" of creating the

[1] *Ibid.*, p. 179.
[2] "Prospectus for the Further Study of Federal Administrative Law," in Yale **Law
Journal**, February, 1938, pp. 647, 649.

"fourth branch" of government, and equally as a demonstration of how far removed from these realities was the teaching of administrative law. Unfortunately, it is not possible to reproduce the rich matrix of illustrative material which he laid down as proof that each problem was important, and which incidentally gives much insight into the complex difficulties encountered by administrative agencies in their day-to-day operations.

The first question of organization which Feller asked was, What is the appropriate form which an agency engaged in administrative adjudication and legislation should take? Which functions are peculiarly adapted for exercise by an executive department, by a regulatory commission, by an adjudicative commission, or by an administrative court? Is it possible to make a reasonable distinction between legislative and adjudicative functions? If so, to what extent should those functions be segregated? To what extent may adjudicative functions pertaining to different subjects be consolidated in one agency? To what extent should legislative and adjudicative agencies be independent of the executive branch of government?

The second organizational problem related to *how* an agency should be organized. Should it be centralized, or decentralized through regional offices? Should the commission or board operate through individual members, through small divisions, or *en banc?* In the executive departments should the legislative and adjudicative functions be conferred on the head of the department or on subordinate officers? Should every agency be required to have a board of review?

Under procedural problems, Feller asked when administrative hearings should be required in connection with legislative (rule-making) as contrasted with adjudicatory functions. What are appropriate requisites for hearings? Who should participate in them? How can the presentation of "findings" in adjudicative actions be improved? Are "findings" necessary as a prerequisite to administrative action? In what form should the issues be presented for decision by the administrative officer or commission? Has the vesting of prosecuting and adjudicative functions in the same agency impaired the judicial quality of administrative acts? Would efficiency suffer if the two functions were separated?

Finally, under problems of enforcement, he inquired how the various enforcement devices actually work out in practice, and how a more orderly system of enforcement can be devised.

Obviously no over-all answers to these questions were possible. Instead, a variety of solutions had to be found to fit different specific situations. Once found, assistance needed to be provided the government in accepting and utilizing them. Hence Feller maintained that only research that was both subsidized and co-ordinated would be of any considerable effectiveness. Individual persons, dependent upon their own resources or those of the average law school, could make scarcely a dent upon formulating the necessary policy, or influencing its application once it had been formulated. He advised therefore that the American Law Institute sponsor and finance research projects utilizing the co-operative efforts of a number of scholars. For the practical application of the findings and recommendations of these scholars, he suggested the creation of a Conference of Senior Law Officers of the various agencies.

While attorneys like McGuire and Feller were struggling to enlist understanding interest in administrative law, political scientists and others concerned with the field of general public administration were pointing to functions, often performed by lawyers, for which some knowledge of administration, as contrasted with knowledge of administrative law, is essential. Dr. Comstock Glaser, for example, undertook to show what scientific management had already accomplished when applied to public business offices, and how much more might be accomplished by the further application of scientific methods.[1]

Reeves and David, although emphasizing personnel rather than scientific management, came to the same implied conclusion. So complex is government machinery that every new top-ranking administrator must rely upon "those who know the

[1] Administrative Procedure, American Council on Public Affairs, Washington, 1941. See also Arthur C. Millspaugh's Democracy, Efficiency, Stability: An Appraisal of American Government, The Brookings Institution, Washington, 1942.

rotations of wheels within wheels, how to start and when to stop them, and how to make them mesh with the smooth perfection that will keep administrative matters in the field appropriate to them."[1] A corps of highly competent career persons immediately subordinate to the High Command should therefore be regarded, maintained Reeves and David, as indispensable to the successful functioning of the executive branch.

A previous section has pointed to the frequency with which attorneys occupy these immediately subordinate positions. Even when they are employed on a considerably lower level, their tasks often transcend legal work, as that term has been traditionally used, or tend to cut across the activities of the line agencies. For such functions training in administrative law, no matter how broadly given, is insufficient.

From the Office of the Director of the Bureau of the Budget, Dr. Marx had an exceptionally good vantage point for viewing lawyers in the executive branch. He concluded that three basic qualifications are desirable in the government attorney. The attorney should be a trustworthy source of legal counsel; that implies sound professional training in the law. More distinctively, he should have a sure touch in the fine art of human and institutional relationships. Proficiency in such relationships with many different persons and groups inside and outside his agency is a crucial factor in his equipment. "And finally, in his nearest approximation of the ideal, he should be what is best described as a clear-headed philosopher of democratic governance, quietly effective within the institutional framework of public administration."[2]

The prospective government lawyer is now not brought up on a formula of mental nourishment especially appropriate to his subsequent tasks, Marx observed. "More often than not it is only after his entrance into public service that he begins to learn about

[1] Reeves, Floyd W. and David, Paul T., Personnel Administration in the Federal Service. President's Committee on Administrative Management, Washington, 1937, p. 63.

[2] Marx, Fritz Morstein, "The Lawyer's Role in Public Administration," in Yale Law Journal, April, 1946, p. 513.

government as a going concern, as an embodiment of needs, ideas and symbols, as a synthesizing force in the social order, as a spearhead of things new and simultaneously a defender of things old."[1]

How are law schools then to provide work in administrative law which visualizes the administrative agency as engaged in significant executive and legislative, as well as judicial, functions; and as concerned not only with its relationship to the public but with those inter- and intra-agency relationships of which the intricate machinery of government is composed? How are law schools, furthermore, whether through administrative law courses or elsewhere in the curriculum, to give their students that knowledge of the purpose and method of operation of an on-going government that is increasingly imperative for all attorneys, whether in public or in private practice?

Answers to these questions are beginning to emerge. The Attorney General's Committee on Administrative Procedure, appointed by Attorney General Murphy in 1939 with Dean Acheson as its chairman and Walter Gellhorn as director, did a vast amount of valuable spadework within the limits of responsibility with which it was charged, namely, the procedures and the procedural practices of administrative agencies, and general methods provided for the judicial review of administrative decisions. Perhaps the two principal contributions of the Committee were: its reduction of the consideration of administrative procedure from one which emphasized constitutional problems and stereotyped concepts of government functions to a discussion which deals with present actualities in the light of needs to be met; and the formulation of specific recommendations as to concrete aspects of procedure, most of which could be administratively applied, but a few of which were recommended for legislative adoption.

From an educational standpoint, the work of the Committee was also of major importance. The very fact that three deans and three professors of administrative law, besides the director, were

[1] *Ibid.*, p. 518.

members could scarcely fail to emphasize the importance of the subject in the law-school world. The series of monographs and the Final Report of the Committee supplied a rich body of material for study in administrative procedure courses, and stated realistic criteria by which existing procedures can be judged and improvements be considered. These criteria took into account the public purposes of the legislation setting up administrative agencies, as well as the protection which affected interests are entitled to enjoy.

What is of more importance for the future of legal education than the Attorney General's Committee, however, was the hegira of teachers to Washington, federal regional offices, and foreign countries during the recent war. As has been noted earlier, appreciable numbers found themselves in the midst of those staggering problems of administration and policy-making, which had to be faced by emergency agencies attempting to build organizational structure and staffs and to begin operations simultaneously. So absorbing in time, energy, and interest were many of these positions that the average law teacher perhaps had little opportunity to view analytically the over-all job which he or his agency did, or the relationship of his agency's program to that of others. But from those hectic war years, law instructors have returned to teaching with an intimate knowledge of what it meant to be a participant—intellectually and emotionally—in a going government concern. Thanks to the worldwide upheaval, scores of teachers, not merely those in administrative law, received unplanned sabbatical leaves that stretched into years to engage in government work. The full impact of that experience cannot be evaluated within a decade, but its effects are certain to be profound both for administrative law and for the reorientation of many other courses.

Already proposals for change or additions to curricula are being translated into action in some schools. One of these, which antedates the war, is the emphasis—on the graduate level—upon public law at New York University School of Law. So convinced was this university that all possible assistance should be given to training competent administrators and technicians for the nation's "largest industry," namely government, that in 1938 it created a Graduate Division for Training in Public Service. Graduate training for administrative and public law, labor law, and taxation, together with other fields of concentration, are offered in the School of Law in association with the Graduate Division. The courses listed in administrative and public law, which carry credit toward a master's degree or a doctorate, are the administrative process, administrative law including a comparison of American with English and Canadian experience, municipal corporations, housing law and administration,[1] public administration,[1] public-utility law,[2] public utilities, statutes and their interpretations, and trade regulation. Five courses are currently scheduled under labor law, and twelve under taxation including a broad general course[1] in fiscal policy and intergovernmental finance.

In addition, short institutes are held periodically on some topic of particular significance to attorneys and administrators. A one-week institute, for example, was offered in February, 1947, on the Federal Administrative Procedure Act and the Administrative Agencies. So important was this Act of 1946 for all administrative agencies and attorneys practicing before them that the institute was planned to set forth changes being made in the administrative process.

The courses and institutes given by New York University School of Law are obviously designed to benefit practitioners, whether attorneys or administrators. So large is the number of persons employed in New York City in public offices that the University is strategically situated to make this important contribution to the public service.

Another entire curriculum which has appeared is that of the School of Public Law created in 1946 by the Washington College of Law.[3] F. Morse Hubbard, formerly of the New York bar, is the

[1] Course given by Graduate Division for Training in Public Service.

[2] Course given by Graduate School of Business Administration.

[3] Washington College of Law, Preliminary Announcement of the School of Public Law, 1946–1947.

full-time director. An extensive panel of attorneys, administrators, and judges, who either serve or have served the interests of the federal government, is available for participation in seminars or group discussions. The purpose of the new School is twofold: to give practical instruction and training in legislative and administrative procedure; and to develop a graduate and research center for the study, at the source, of substantive and procedural problems involved in the legislative and administrative activities of the national government. The School is to be open to undergraduate students of other law schools, graduate students, clerks in law firms, practicing lawyers, representatives of business concerns, graduate students and teachers in political science, and persons interested in comparative government procedures. The administration wishes particularly to develop a "clinical" training course, available to the first-named group, that can be conveniently integrated with the undergraduate courses in public law of various schools. Hence it hopes that arrangements can be made whereby students specially interested in this field of law will be permitted to spend a term in Washington for which they will receive credit at their own institutions.

Encouraging as are such undertakings, the most important question is that of how less specialized, basic training can be made readily available to undergraduate law students everywhere. Hence the report is particularly gratifying that Thomas I. Emerson, who has had exceptionally valuable experience in at least three federal agencies, has been appointed to the Yale School of Law for the purpose of building up the curriculum for the training of lawyers who may plan to enter government service.

Also gratifying is the emergence at Columbia of one experiment in such training which is being offered as a two-semester seminar in legal problems of governmental administration. Although the seminar is offered to a mere handful of students, it will be described in some detail because it appears to combine, perhaps as yet to an unprecedented degree, a realistic formulation of representative problems which government lawyers have to handle, and a method of instruction that promises to provide the maximum value as training. What is even more needed, as will be seen from the section on "Legislation," is emphatic recognition at the beginning of the curriculum rather than at the end of government as a functioning institution. This course has made a beginning, however, where it is most feasible to begin, and its implications for a broader and earlier approach to the institution of government may be considerable.

The seminar, which had a trial run just before the war with Professors Gellhorn and Paul R. Hays at the helm, is now being given by Gellhorn in collaboration with Professor John D. Millett of Columbia's Department of Public Law and Government.[1] Graduate students in public administration, as well as law students, are invited to enroll in it. Thus a co-operative effort between prospective lawyers and political scientists has been established in the hope that differences in methods and points of view will emerge which will enrich the thinking of both groups.

The purpose of the seminar is totally unlike that of the "regular" course in administrative law at Columbia which has been described above. Emphasis has been shifted from legal requirements enforceable through the courts to "legal aspects of intra-governmental administration" and "to suggestive problems arising out of relationships between private interests and public agencies." *Planning* rather than litigation is made the central core of the seminar, although Gellhorn notes that planning must be done with an eye to possible later litigation. Policy determination is discussed not in terms of "what will get by"—a central question in any administrative law case—but in terms of "what seems to be the best thing to do, all factors considered."

The problem method of instruction is used. Although the problems that have been formulated are hypothetical, they deal with situations such as government lawyers actually encounter and for which they are expected to find some solution. All students in

[1] All factual material pertaining to this course has been taken from Professor Gellhorn's mimeographed memorandum to the Columbia law faculty, dated August 19, 1946, and entitled Seminar in Governmental Administration.

the seminar generally work simultaneously on the same fundamental problem, but often on different facets of it. In connection with some of the problems, groups of students are assigned to represent each of the several interests affected by the government issue under consideration. To the extent that these interests clash, students will gain insight into the contentious atmosphere which sometimes marks actual government discussions.

The projects have been planned to give the student participation in a variety of roles. In some projects he is a law clerk; in others, the draftsman of regulations; in still others, an advocate representing a party in contested proceedings. In instances he must plan policy for a broadly defined program. The problems have been formulated, furthermore, to offer practice in working in harness with other prospective lawyers and non-lawyers. Group undertakings are stressed as themselves training for future positions where, particularly in government, the lawyer is most often an inseparable member of a team.

Except for some omissions, particularly in Problem III, that have been made to conserve space, the problems that follow are in the form in which Gellhorn presented them to the Columbia law faculty in the summer of 1946. A few had not then been translated into specific projects. The intention in each, however, is entirely clear. In connection with a number of the assignments, it was expected to ask administrative officers or attorneys, now or formerly connected with specific agencies under consideration, to assist the seminar in discussing designated problems.

SEMINAR IN GOVERNMENTAL ADMINISTRATION

I. The Lawyer's Function in Government
   Prescribed readings, class discussion.

II. The Personnel Status of the Lawyer in Federal Administration
   Project: The President requests the Civil Service Commission to report to him concerning the present status of lawyers as to methods of selection, tenure, and so on, and to make appropriate recommendations for the future, having in mind the

obligations of the Civil Service Commission under present statutes and executive orders.

> This project will furnish some knowledge concerning the Civil Service Commission and the statutes and orders which affect government attorneys. The demand for recommendations will force the group to explore problems relating to recruiting and examining public employees.

III. Legal Aspects of Control over Government Funds, Property, and Personnel

Eight representative projects have been formulated by Gellhorn relating to government funds, property, or personnel. They are based on problems constantly arising in government business and which are assigned to junior attorneys for solution. Each problem requires exploration into appropriation acts, decisions of the Comptroller General, executive orders, and like materials.

> Familiarity with the use of such sources is important for government lawyers. In this instance separate problems will be assigned to individual students or small groups for investigation and class report. Pertinent relationships uniting the several projects should result in class discussion rather than recitation.

IV. Planning of Operations and Methods Within the Confines of "Red Tape"

Project: During the war the Government was the largest user of the railroads. Freight charges to the government were computed according to the same tariff classifications as were used for private shipments. Much time and personnel were consumed in classifying the freight and arguing about the correct classification. The War Department concluded that the classification system should be eliminated in connection with government shipments, and that a single freight rate should be created, computed on the basis of the weighted average freight rate for all government shipments during some stated period. This proposal has been outlined to various interested parties. A conference has been arranged among representatives of the War Department, the Interstate Commerce Commission, the Comptroller General, and the Association of American Railways. Representatives will come to the conference prepared either to deal with the indicated problem or to demonstrate that it should not be dealt with.

This project is designed to shed light on the interplay between government fiscal controls and operating efficiency. It will introduce students to problems of inter-agency negotiation; it will show the interest of private parties in matters of government management as distinct from direct regulation.

V. A Problem in Federalization of Administrative Activity Previously Carried on by the States

Project: The Federal Security Agency wishes to replace state systems by a federal system of unemployment compensation. Assume that no doubts exist about the constitutionality of the proposal. The Federal Security Administrator summons the General Counsel to inquire concerning the taking over of the several state administrations and their respective funds. Problems such as personnel transfers and separations, and existing contractual arrangements for office space and supplies are involved. The General Counsel is asked to explore the matter both from the viewpoint of drafting a bill to formalize the proposal and of planning the action that would be necessary were the Congress to enact the bill. The Administrator proposes that a staff conference be held at a designated place and time, and that the General Counsel complete his studies and prepare his recommendations for presentation at a further meeting on a given date.

This project will illustrate some of the clashes of vested interests which may occur when one government unit seeks to absorb the operations of another. To assure full exploration of the peculiar difficulties which such absorption may entail, one group of students will be assigned as counsel for the Federal Security Administrator, and another as counsel for the New York Division of Placement and Unemployment Insurance.

VI. Administration of an Unemployment Compensation Law

Project to be worked out to illustrate process of initial adjudication and appeals. Lawyers generally think of adjudication as necessarily adversary in tone, with nice attention to trial techniques and formalities. By selecting an agency with a heavy volume of claims, it can be demonstrated that facts are often found, informally and rapidly, with fairness to all affected interests. Then the factors necessitating different types of procedure in various adjudicating agencies can perhaps be identified. Thus it may be seen that a uniform administrative procedure to govern all adjudicatory processes is not feasible.

> Attention is here centered on a state agency as a demonstration that important government work is done on the state, as well as the federal, level.

VII. The Use of Governmental Authority to Achieve Possibly Desirable, But Not Necessarily "Legal," Objectives

Project: Lem Botkins, a giant heavyweight recently released from the Army, had quickly knocked out most of the leading heavyweight boxers of the world. Hence there was tremendous popular demand for a championship match between Joe Louis and Botkins. Mike Smith of the Century Sports Club announced that he had both men under contract, and that he would promote a match between them. He predicted a $3,000,000 gate. He added that he would "put on the show where it will make the most money. Maybe that will be in New York, maybe not. I just don't know yet." He mentioned Indianapolis, and also Philadelphia where he would save the five per cent New York State tax on motion pictures of prize fights.

At this point State Athletic Commission Chairman Jones was interviewed by a newspaper reporter. In a copyrighted story, the paper reported that Commissioner Jones had said: "We will battle all the way to keep this fight in New York. If Smith wants to keep on promoting fights in this State, he had better watch his step. If he likes Philadelphia or Indianapolis so much, maybe he will find himself doing all his promoting there. And maybe he will have to move Madison Square Garden out there. After all, we issue licenses and we revoke them, too. . . ."

Jones and Smith now consult their respective attorneys, the former to discover how he can assure that the match will be presented in New York, the latter to discover how to retain freedom of present action without untoward consequences in the future.

> This project will force the student to explore substantive and procedural state law, and will expose him to problems of possibly abusive exercises of government author-

ity. He may discover that "abusive" means only that power is being used in a fashion not contemplated when the authority was initially conferred. Conceivably, the "abusive exercise of power" may serve a legitimate public interest. The government ethics of this situation needs discussion. Finally, the student may discover that a law suit is not always the solution of a business man's difficulties with an administrator. The business man might win the suit only to find he had lost the war.

VIII. The Scope of Municipal Authority Under a Modern Charter

Project: The Mayor of New York summons his Corporation Counsel and says that he is convinced that Harlem and the other Negro ghettos of the city are the number one problem. "The congested housing conditions create health and morality problems. The social conditions create tension and community unrest. The enforced segregation of a large part of the population perpetuates inequities contrary to a progressive democracy. I am under tremendous pressure to do something about these ghettos, or at least make a dent on the housing patterns built up here over the years. But I don't know what I *can* do. I can put in a few new schools and playgrounds, but those aren't the fundamental answers. I wish you would have your staff make a study, and tell me what the city can do legally, practically, and politically. I want to avoid going up to Albany if I can. I don't think the Legislature would put through any new legislation, and, anyway, I'd like to work this out as a strictly New York City enterprise."

> This project would stress the interrelationship of "public law" and "private law," for Harlem is in part perpetuated by the use of restrictive covenants. The possibility of overcoming these covenants would have to be examined. Students would need to acquire some familiarity with the New York State Constitution, the New York City Charter, and the Administrative Code, important legal materials of which they are largely ignorant. They would have to consider municipal taxing power, housing laws, financing, power of excess condemnation, public housing projects, and so on. They would have to speculate about the integrated utilization of government powers to effectuate a single program. They might discover at the end that the city was powerless to deal with this problem. If so, it would demonstrate that a government of delegated powers cannot

perform miracles which the people themselves, the
source of power, are not yet willing to have performed.

IX. Federal-State-City Relationships in the Execution of Public
Housing Programs

    Project: Assume that additional federal money has been made
available for low-cost housing and slum clearance under the
Wagner Housing Act. The Federal Public Housing Authority
proposes to make a loan of $200,000,000 to the New York City
Housing Authority for three large housing projects. It also
offers an annual grant to insure that the project will be "self-
supporting." Although New York State will not contribute
any financial aid to these housing units, the State Housing
Director informs the New York City Housing Authority that
before any contract is signed with the federal government,
he must review the terms of the contract and approve the proposed project. The New York City Housing Authority and the
Mayor question the power of the State Housing Director to
insist upon such review under existing state housing laws. The
New York City Housing Authority asks its counsel to examine
the question, with a view to forestalling any action by the
State Housing Director that would cast doubt on the legality
of a contract between the Authority and the federal government.

    Upon receiving a copy of the letter which the State Housing
Director addressed to the Authority, the FPHA immediately
looks into the matter in order to plan its own action. When the
State Housing Director realizes that the city challenges his
authority, he too spurs his counsel into activity to support the
position he has taken.

> This project again raises the question of the relations of
> New York City to the state government under the
> home-rule amendment as interpreted by the courts.
> Involved is an examination of the state housing law,
> the state law authorizing New York City to establish a
> housing authority, and the federal law. Profitable dis-
> cussion should arise about the desirability of state ad-
> ministrative supervision of housing activities, even
> where no direct financial subsidy is involved.

X. Problems of Policy and Method

    A. The Use of Publicity in Administrative Proceedings

    Project: The Health Department of the State of Columbia has
undertaken a vigorous campaign to stamp out trichinosis.

Under the laws of the state, the Director of the Department has authority to issue complaints against food processors, food sellers, and eating places, charging them with unsanitary practices. If, after formal hearing, the Trial Board of the Health Department finds the charges true, the Director may issue whatever order—including revocation of license—he deems necessary to end the unsanitary practices.

After investigations and scientific tests, the Director (Mr. B.) decided that the XYZ Sausage Company was manufacturing and selling trichinae-infested pork frankfurters. He thereupon issued a complaint. Simultaneously he gave out a strong press release which set forth the allegations about the XYZ Sausage Company, the nature of trichinosis, and the date on which the formal hearing would occur. The release contained such sentences as: "We are not going to be lenient with those who disregard public health in order to make a few extra pennies," and "We are going after the big fellows as well as the little fellows."

This press release gave rise to a story in the Columbia City Times, headlined:

XYZ COMPANY SELLS
SPOILED PORK, MR. B. CHARGES

Health Department Complains
Products May Cause Trichinosis

One week later the Health Department completed an investigation of the DeLuxe Restaurant. According to the inspector's report, the restaurant had during the rush hour served inadequately cooked fresh pork, thus exposing its patrons to the risk of trichinosis. Having heard through a friend that the Department would probably issue a complaint against DeLuxe, the restaurant owner hurried to his lawyer. He declared that if his restaurant got the same bad publicity as XYZ Company, he might as well close his doors without waiting for the result of the Trial Board hearing. XYZ's business, he said, both in pork and beef products, had been cut in half since the appearance of the Times story. He would suffer as badly if a similar story were published about DeLuxe. He seemed confident that at a hearing he could prove precautions were habitually taken to assure proper cooking of pork, although he acknowledged to his lawyer that there might have been carelessness on the day the restaurant was inspected.

On a designated date, by appointment, counsel for DeLuxe are to meet with Mr. B. and his staff for discussion of the De-Luxe situation.

> This project is designed to introduce discussion of the broad subject of government publicity, with special emphasis on publicity relative to disciplinary proceedings. Some agencies rely upon the threat of publicity as their major sanction. Is this good or bad government? Since the press release is not an administrative order subject to judicial review, what controls can be exercised over it?

> In this particular case, counsel must give sharp attention to tactics as well as to theory. Are there any legal steps available to DeLuxe to stave off publicity? What sort of negotiation will best serve the interest of the private client, while appealing to the official guardian of the public interest?

B. Choices in the Planning of Enforcement Programs

Project: In the administration of the Fair Labor Standards Act of 1938, the Administrator must make choices suggestive of those encountered by administrators of many other statutes. Such important questions as the following must be answered by the Administrator's legal advisers:

From the point of view of enforcement, what are the advantages of relying on amicable restitution? injunction? criminal proceedings? What are the advantages and disadvantages of the employe suit, a privately-administered law enforcement device? Should the Administrator issue interpretative opinions cautiously with some assurance that they are correct, or should opinions be issued in great number and therefore with more risk of error? Should major reliance be placed on routine inspections, "enforcement drives," or investigations only on specific complaint of probable existence of violations? As to coverage of the law, how does one draw the line between the logic of the commerce clause extensions and the need of practicable administration?

> This project should demonstrate to the prospective lawyer that laws are not self-executing, and that administrators must struggle with methodology. Questions

such as those listed above emerge in almost any enforcing agency.

C. Centralized Versus Decentralized Administration

Project: Discussion of centralized versus decentralized administration, with emphasis upon areas where policy-making
as well as operations might be decentralized. Review of issues
relating to the organizational development of actual administrative bodies would give specific content to the discussion.
A comparative study of texts of delegations of authority within
different agencies would show various degrees of internal
delegation of similar sorts of functions. It may be useful to
raise the question whether this or that authority should be
delegated by the head of some newly-created agency, then
leaving it to counsel to draw up the appropriate regulations.
Perhaps the problem can be stated in terms of regional versus
departmental administration, as for example, the proposed
Missouri Valley Authority versus the Department of the
Interior.

XI. Planning a Major Law Enforcement Campaign by a Non-
Regulatory Agency

Project: Mr. A. has been elected governor of State X. He is an
earnest believer in "white supremacy," and publicly urges
that Negro voting be discouraged by "whatever means may be
necessary." He has told local law enforcement officials to concentrate attention on "crooks, thieves, and murderers," and
not to divert their energies by trying to "enforce a lot of laws
that don't make sense in X and that we don't want to bother
with."

Perhaps as a consequence, an inordinately large number of
violent offences against Negroes are occurring in X. Many
Negroes who voted in the last election for state or federal
officers have been beaten by unidentified white men; others
have been discharged by employers who have been urged to do
so by unknown visitors. Negro passengers on interstate buses
and interstate Pullman cars have been forcibly ejected at stations within X by white persons, despite protests by bus opera-
tors and conductors. An effort to organize the Negro workers
in a lumber mill was discouraged by the beating of several
union members. The assailants were unmasked but unrecognized white men who had no known relationship with the
employer.

Repeated appeals to state and local officials have produced no action. Governor A. is quoted as having said, when questioned by reporters, "Our people know what is right and what is good for X. If anyone don't like the way we do things here, let them go back where they come from. In my opinion, the police and the sheriffs are doing the job the people pay them for. I'm satisfied we've got the best people and the best sense of what's fit and decent of any state in this nation."

The National Association for the Advancement of Colored People, the American Civil Liberties Union, and similar organizations now begin a vigorous effort to move the United States Department of Justice into attemptimg to protect Negroes in X. Whether out of conviction or because of the pressure exerted on him, the Attorney General of the United States decides that an attack should be made on this problem. He calls an Assistant Attorney General and says, "We ought to look into this mess in X and see if we can do anything about it. I don't want to start a second civil war, or get into political trouble with Congress. But if we can straighten things out there, we ought to do it. I wish you would figure out what to to and how to do it. Maybe you can draft some instructions for me to go to the United States Attorney or the Marshal or the FBI. Let's talk it over again on such and such a date."

> This project involves the planning of a delicate program that has not been defined legislatively. An important by-product will be familiarity with the structure and powers of the Department of Justice, both in Washington and in the field. Another by-product will be practice in drafting intra-organizational instructions, and then devising feasible means for supervising their execution.

XII. The Conduct of an Adversary Proceeding Before an Administrative Tribunal, Involving the Use of an Established Procedure

> Project: The seminar would be divided into three groups, one constituting the staff of the National Labor Relations Board, and the two others constituting law firms. The instructors would constitute themselves a labor leader and an employer, respectively. Between them, they would fabricate a labor dispute with sharply defined issues. Then the labor leader would retain one of the law firms to press his demands on the employer, who would at once retain the other law firm. The two firms would negotiate until an impasse was reached, when the

labor firm would file charges with the NLRB. The NLRB would issue its complaint and, after the pleading stage was completed, the case would go to hearing.

This project will require the students to familiarize themselves with the somewhat conventional procedural regulations of the NLRB, in order to plan and conduct an adversary proceeding before that body. In carrying the case forward, the students will gain experience in negotiating. The negotiations will not succeed because of the intransigence of the principals (the instructors). They will have to draft the necessary formal papers to meet the Board's procedural requirements. Those students who constitute the NLRB staff must become familiar with the inner workings of that agency, if they are to proceed intelligently when called upon to enforce the Wagner Act against the alleged violator.

XIII. The Interplay of International and National Considerations in Shaping the Policy of a Domestic Administrative Agency

Project: The Civil Aeronautics Board supposedly has before it an application by the X Company for a certificate of necessity and convenience permitting it to operate regularly scheduled flights from Philadelphia to Glasgow via New York, Boston, and Reykjavik. The application is opposed by the American Y Company which already operates between Philadelphia and Boston via New York, and by the Z Company, another American line operating between New York and London. The British Government, moreover, has formally proposed that neither the United States nor Great Britain should authorize the establishment of further international routes or schedules by domestic lines; instead, the British propose the creation of an international company to own and operate trunk lines extending beyond the boundaries of a single country. The British also remind the CAB that a British-owned line now operates a schedule from Halifax to Glasgow via Reykjavik. How should the CAB proceed?

This project is designed to introduce students to the processes of an agency which importantly controls entry into business; to make concrete the concept, "public necessity and convenience," so that one may perceive the difficult technical, political, and economic elements which give content to that easy phrase; and to demonstrate that the decisions of a national administrative agency are today often affected by international considerations.

XIV. The Expression of a General Policy Determination Through the Drafting of Detailed Regulations

Project: Hypothetically the Interstate Commerce Commission concludes that in the interest of national defense every railroad and interstate trucking line operating domestically under ICC control should be wholly owned and controlled by citizens of the United States. It desires that all directors and major officers be citizens and that the companies' securities be held exclusively for the benefit of citizens. Having reached this general conclusion, the Commission requests its General Counsel to devise laws, regulations, or orders, and to outline the necessary administrative steps, to effectuate the policy.

This project involves preparation of regulations or legislation that will prove surprisingly complex, since the stated policy has a delusive simplicity and is even of present doubtful legality. To give it any sort of practical expression will require much ingenuity.

XV. Administrative Control of "Propaganda"

Project: Assume that the America First Foundation, Inc. of Detroit, of which G. L. K. Jones is hypothetically founder and president, has applied in due form to the Federal Communications Commission for the assignment of a standard broadcast frequency and for a frequency modulation station as well. As indication of the type of programs to be offered, the applicant submits scripts of addresses given by Mr. Jones over a period of years. The applicant further alleges that Detroit does not have any truly independent stations and that "public convenience, interest, and necessity" require additional competition there so that the listening public will not be limited to stations linked to "monopolistic chains." No engineering difficulties are presented; a frequency is available and will not interfere with reception of signals from other stations. The Commission's Accounting Department is satisfied that the applicant has adequate financial resources to meet the requisite standards. The matter has been set for a hearing before the Commission.

This project should be handled as an adversary proceeding. Some students would be assigned to represent the applicant, some the Commission, some the inter-

vener. Perhaps the National Association of Broad-
casters or the American Civil Liberties Union would
appear as "friend of the court." Emphasis would be on
determining the competing considerations that will
influence ultimate policy choice.

Legislation, Legislative Drafting, and Other Public Law Courses

Legislation is now generally thought of as the pre-eminent
instrument for law-making. However, this method which
appeared at an early period in English history was used but
sparingly both in England and the United States until comparatively recent times. Professors Durfee and Dawson have dramati-
cally demonstrated this fact with figures from the English record
where the span of Anglo-Saxon history is longer than in the
United States.[1] The first volume of the Statutes at Large covers
the 115 years from 1225 to 1340. The next three volumes embrace
two centuries, averaging 66 years to a book. The next three
average 38 years each, and bring the legislative record to the
Restoration of 1660. The remaining 40 years of the century
almost fill three volumes, averaging 13 years to the book. It required 31 volumes to cover the eighteenth century, or approximately three years to the volume. The nineteenth century filled
95 volumes. Since then there has been a volume for each year.
Durfee and Dawson might have added that the trend in the
amount of *delegated legislation* emanating from administrative
agencies is the same. The size of the British Statutory Rules and
Orders is greater even than that of the Statutes at Large, and so
far as the public is concerned these rules and orders have the same
effect as legislation.

Why was this method of law-making utilized so little in earlier
centuries and is now utilized so extensively? A variety of answers
comes to mind. In a relatively static and uncomplicated society,
the adjudication of disputes on a case-by-case basis undoubtedly
worked reasonably well. There was probably little felt need for
laying down rules, other than the precedents growing out of

[1] Durfee, Edgar N. and Dawson, John P., *Cases on Remedies*, Book I. Mimeographed, pp. 2–3.

judicial decisions, that would be applicable to future similar controversies or that would prevent such controversies from arising. As the body of judicial doctrine developed, furthermore, and was strengthened by scholarly exegesis, the scales were increasingly weighted in favor of the judicial process as an established institution.

No defined concept of the service state had arisen. The church, in fact, provided in rudimentary form many of the social welfare services now performed by the state. Hence there was no occasion to enact a multiplicity of statutes charging the executive branch of government with performing designated functions in behalf of society. The legislative process, moreover, is a difficult one. It requires thorough knowledge of the particular situation which should be remedied, imaginative ability to devise practical means for remedying the situation, and skill in drafting a rule stating those means which will be understandable to persons charged with administration. Only a society prepared to engage in scientific research, broad social analysis, formulation of intricate policy, prediction of probable acceptance and success, and highly technical drafting can use this instrument of law-making effectively for the solution of more than simple problems.

The events of history reversed the balance of power between the common law and statutory law. With the economic and social complexity that the Industrial Revolution introduced, the common law was often unable to cope. Its concern was with the *broken* contract and a variety of other kinds of *wrongdoing*. It could not impose affirmative duties in an era of unprecedented expansion which called for planning and organization, and supervision of those processes. The judiciary did not even have the machinery necessary for obtaining the facts, other than those relating to a particular controversy, whereby it might determine desirable policy.

Because many of the judges, furthermore, failed to bring to the bench the ability, experience, sociological outlook, and non-partisan courage needed, the judiciary was frequently unable to reinterpret common law doctrine to meet new exigencies, even in areas where adaptation to changing conditions was possible. The common law, in fact, had become impotent to grapple with the enormous problems of the late nineteenth and twentieth centuries. It was slow, expensive, and uncertain.

Thus legislation came largely to replace the judicial process as a means for rapid and radical change of law. The legislature has machinery, such as the standing committees, the appointed investigation commission, and the special investigating organizations within the executive branch for securing requisite information. Many *types* of law-making and many sanctions are available to it which the courts do not possess. Thus it can regulate those areas which it has become convinced should be brought under supervised control. It can engage in social planning of long-term, wide-range policy in fields such as taxation, housing, penology and prison reform, child welfare, co-ordination of production and purchasing power, improvement in the structure and procedures of government, reorganization of the administration of justice. The paramount issues of our time lie within its domain rather than that of the common law.[1]

Obviously so tremendous a shift in power from the common law to statutory law has profound implications for legal education. The statutory development of law, however, has been neglected by the law schools just as has administrative law, and for much the same reasons. Attention has remained primarily concentrated on the casebooks of judicial decisions; it has not been adequately shared with the statute books. Although much improvement, to be discussed presently, has been made in the thirty years since Professor Thomas Reed Powell wrote the following paragraph, a considerable residue of the thinking of that period remains even now.

Our law schools have thus far given but slight attention to the law that Legislatures have made or ought to make. Both the field and the mechanics of legislative law making seem to have been regarded as outside the pale of professional law training. This neglect has doubtless

[1] See Harno, Albert J., "Social Planning and Perspective Through Law," in Handbook of the Association of American Law Schools, 1932, pp. 8–22.

been a factor in producing the attitude towards legislation which is characteristic of many lawyers. There seems to be a widespread notion that statutes are wanton interferences with the legal natural order. The mesh of the due process clause must therefore be woven fine, so that few statutes shall pass through. Law should be the distillation of a tradition from a remote past, rather than the application of a judgment as to the needs of an immediate present. Its exemplar is theology, rather than the practical judgments of the president of a corporation or the head of a family as to what will further the interests committed to his care. Its source is something higher than man, and its credos must not be altered by man. This is an attitude not uncommon among lawyers. It is reverential, rather than scientific; emotional, rather than intelligent. And our law schools have doubtless contributed to it, by devoting so much more attention to the doctrines revealed in judicial decisions than to the practical adjustments made by legislation.[1]

Professor Powell might have observed parenthetically that this preoccupation with the common law at the expense of statutory law has had serious practical consequences for private attorneys, to say nothing of its consequences for the development of the legislative process. Many advocates are so unacquainted with statutory law and so unaware that principles and trends can be deduced from legislative acts that they prepare cases which carefully consider all common law decisions but leave statutes uninvestigated. Their lack of training in the appropriate function of the legislature versus that of the court, moreover, has kept them from aiding the court, as they should have been able to do, in not exceeding its proper function and in making use of statutory regulations as well as judicial decisions in rendering judgments.

Some of the reluctance of law schools to introduce more training in statutory law stems, in Professor Riesman's opinion, from the problem of how to make statutes teachable. The case method continues to hold sway partly because cases make easy reading. They are discursive, concrete, and, especially in criminal law, dramatic. Statutes are abstract, unliterary. They require imaginative and creative spelling out, not routine condensation. "A statute cannot be skimmed, and does not appeal to most

[1] "Law as a Cultural Study," in the American Law School Review, Fall, 1917, p. 335.

students, who become rigid common-law lawyers on the day they enter law school, sharing with their elders at the bar an unwarranted admiration for judges as compared with legislators and administrators."[1] Much of this admiration for judges and disregard of legislators results from the fact that "students habitually think of themselves as advocates-to-be, and not as participants in the legislative process, much less as persons whose views on legislative issues, on public policy, have any importance."[2]

For the very reason that students so easily and quickly become common law lawyers, a few teachers of public law have strongly recommended that the importance of statutory law should be stressed early in the curriculum. The Columbia School of Law has been one of the institutions to put this suggestion into practice. Beginning with 1928 a required first-year course in legislation was offered to acquaint prospective lawyers with statutory law contemporaneously with common law. Professor Noel T. Dowling, for one, thought it necessary to start early with legislation and to follow with courses in constitutional and in administrative law. He taught the course in legislation until it was merged into a course in legal method in 1944. He then taught the legislative part of that course until 1946. Some years ago when the University of Virginia introduced legislation as a first-year course in its law school, Professor Dowling collaborated as a visiting professor with Dean Ribble in giving the course for a semester. The materials used had been prepared expressly as an early introduction to statutory law by Harry W. Jones, then a visiting lecturer at the Columbia School of Law.

A considerable number of schools have followed the recent practice of Columbia by introducing a first-year course in legal method. Dowling, Patterson, and Powell's Materials for Legal Method, which includes some attention to the interpretation of statutes and the use of legislative materials, is generally used. However, the majority of the law schools probably do not yet

[1] Riesman, David, Jr., "Law and Social Science: A Report on Michael and Wechsler's Classbook on Criminal Law and Administration," in Yale Law Journal, February, 1941, p. 649.
[2] Ibid., p. 650.

have a course in legislation, as such, whether designed for the first, second, or third year. In 1940–1941 before the war had temporarily robbed the schools of many teachers, the Directory of Teachers in Member Schools of the Association of American Law Schools classified only thirty-six law instructors as having taught legislation from one to ten years and four, more than ten years.[1] No fewer than 109 teachers of constitutional law were listed.[2] Although large reliance cannot be placed upon the accuracy of these figures, it may safely be concluded that the number of instructors prepared to teach legislation was distressingly small. The experience and the interest gained by many law professors who served the federal government during the war is now beginning to be apparent, and the schools of the future are likely to give far larger attention to training in legislation.

As in the case of administrative law, it must not be assumed that the absence of a specific course indicates lack of reference to statutory materials. In recent years such materials have increasingly been introduced in the specialized courses. This could scarcely fail to occur when legislation has progressively supplanted judge-made law in many areas. Whether the interpolations are as yet sufficiently numerous and adequately stressed is extremely doubtful.[3] It is evident, however, that this device of interpolation is indispensable. No course in legislation should be expected to deal with specific statutes, no matter how important,

[1] West Publishing Co., St. Paul, p. 226.

[2] *Ibid.*, pp. 211–212.

[3] One of the most surprising proofs of the importance of statutory law, and one which is greatly encouraging law instructors to focus more attention upon it, is the growing attention given by judges to statutes and the legislative process. Some courts have come to look upon statutes as commands from legislatures which they must accept, whether they approve or not. Such courts rarely pronounce a statute unconstitutional, unless it conflicts with explicit constitutional provisions such as the guaranty of freedom of speech in the First Amendment to the federal Constitution, or requirements as to titles and other detailed matters in state constitutions. But statutes are also being used by judges for affirmative purposes. This is particularly true in tort cases, where penal statutes are regarded as establishing tests for negligence, and in contract cases, where agreements which run counter to policies expressed in penal statutes may be denied enforcement. Thus statutes may help judges to define conduct to which "the reasonable man" will supposedly conform. Again statutes are sometimes considered as principles to be employed in reasoning by analogy in common law actions, or as suggesting a development of policy which may give direction to the court's thinking.

unless used for illustrative purposes. Statutes become meaningful only when presented in the context of the specialized subject under discussion. Other functions are reserved for courses in legislation.

Many schools, nevertheless, have taken it for granted that they have fulfilled their obligations by thus making statutory material a part of the established courses. The University of Chicago Law School, for example, long reasoned that there is no more justification for offering a course in legislation as such than there is for offering a course in administrative law. It maintained that there should be correlated in every course whatever is essential from the common law, statutory law, administrative law, and comparative law. When asked where the nature, scope, and function of legislation should be examined, it answered, "in a course in jurisprudence." Recently, however, the School has become interested in various research questions which tend to emphasize the realities of the legislative process for the very reason that an answer to some of these questions is to be found only in statutory enactment. In the autumn of 1947, moreover, it expects to introduce a seminar in legislation and drafting problems, particularly problems arising from the outmoded Illinois Constitution.

Most teachers of legislation would not agree that the use of statutory material in standard courses is sufficient. Professor Willard Hurst, who has brought marked ability to the formulation and teaching of courses in legislation at the University of Wisconsin, states their attitude thus:

Complete incorporation is an insufficient ideal and one not shortly to be realized. Even when full credit is given, there remains the essential need for helping the student form a working philosophy of the proper relation between law-maker and law-applier. And this job cannot be done adequately without an attempt to convey some practical sense of what constitutes good advocacy, in addition to presenting statutory materials in the matrix of the facts of community life from which statute law comes. The whole task is too critical and too large to be squeezed into the crowded confines of existing courses.[1]

[1] "The Content of Courses in Legislation," in University of Chicago Law Review, February, 1941, p. 287.

Since courses in legislation are relatively young and published teaching materials were almost nonexistent prior to 1934, every instructor has been largely free "to do about as he wanted to." It is now essential to see what he wanted to do. In 1934 Dean Roscoe Pound published Outline of a Course on Legislation, a pamphlet of fifty-nine pages printed by the Harvard University Press. The principal topics indicate the scope of the outline: history of legislation, agencies of legislation, content of legislation, preparation for legislation, province and subject matter of legislation, drafting of laws and modes of regulation, means of making laws effective, mechanics of enactment, interpretation of laws, operation of statutes, amendment, abrogation and repeal, relation of the traditional law to legislation. Under extensive subtopics relating to each of the above are numerous bibliographical references. The Outline presents a detailed plan for a broad scholarly course in legislation for advanced students that would require much reading from source materials, including judicial opinions.

Whether this Outline has ever been utilized largely by any teacher of legislation except Professor Horace Read of the University of Minnesota, who assisted Dean Pound in its preparation while a research fellow at Harvard, is not known. At least, he has said that from working on it he gained much of the orientation that he afterward utilized in his course at Minnesota to which further reference will be made.

Two years later Dr. Joseph P. Chamberlain published Legislative Processes: National and State,[1] an invaluable textbook broadly concerned with the law-making function of Congress and state legislatures. Although extensively used by students of political science, its use in law schools has been slight for at least three reasons. In spite of the fact that law-trained men participate in some or all of the steps involved in the preparation, introduction, and enactment of almost every statute, whether federal or state, teachers of legislation have generally been more concerned with training for advocacy than in fitting attorneys to participate

[1] D. Appleton-Century Co., New York, 1936.

efficiently and creatively in the legislative process. Where any attention was given to this process—until recently— it was often thought that the student could gain basic information by private reading of a book such as Dr. Chamberlain's, without utilizing classroom time for discussion. This attitude runs counter to that of experts in legislation, who view the legislative process as intricate enough to require the closest study. Finally, the book was a text written in a simple, straightforward manner. Its illusive simplicity, however, was rooted in Dr. Chamberlain's profound knowledge of the subject. For half a century the law schools had been so absorbed in the use of case materials that they had lost all perspective about the place and the function of the textbook in legal education. Even now when the need for some textual material has become patent, it is utilized most sparingly and in the form of introductory chapters, explanatory paragraphs interpolated between cases, numerous footnotes, and law-review articles.

Thomas I. Parkinson's Cases and Materials on Legislation[1] circumvented the difficulties encountered by Legislative Processes. It was a collection of source materials comparable in form and organization to the customary casebook, but including much information besides judicial opinions. Particularly through insertion of the brief "documentary history of a statute" from the time of its inception until it has been signed by the President, the book throws some light on the legislative process. However, it was designed primarily as a basis for discussion of the problems which the formulation of legislation and its enforcement present to the lawyer in private rather than in public practice.

After ten years of experience in the teaching of legislation and also in legislative counseling and statutory drafting, Professor Frank E. Horack of Indiana University Law School published, in 1940, his Cases and Materials on Legislation.[2] This volume is now extensively utilized in those schools that offer a course in legislation, generally to second or third-year but sometimes—as at Indiana—to first-year students. It was the purpose of this book,

[1] Copyright by Parkinson, New York, 1936. Privately printed.
[2] Callaghan and Co., Chicago.

said Horack, to provide the prospective lawyer, in a day when law of statutory origin has become so important, with those materials which he must use, whether as legislator, legislative counsel, lobbyist, or attorney. Thus Horack's aim was somewhat broader than that of Parkinson.

He interpreted the achievement of his goal as requiring a more systematic and detailed examination of the legislative process. Nearly half of his volume was devoted to this subject. His first chapter of 150 pages considered the very important question of how legislative policy is formulated. In his second equally long chapter on legislative organization and procedure, he attempted to present a picture, not of an empty arena but of legislative combat as it occurs from the time a bill is introduced until it has been passed or has failed to pass over a Presidential veto. His final chapter on the legislative process described how legislative action is influenced, and what steps have been taken to regulate that influencing process. The second part of the volume, entitled Statutes as the Culmination of the Legislative Process, considered the interpretation of statutes by the courts, a subject certainly of great importance but one that had provided, because of its usefulness to advocates, the predominant content of many earlier courses in legislation.

Horack undoubtedly believes that his casebook prepares the prospective advocate as well, or better, than other teaching materials which omit any considerable discussion of the legislative process in order to concentrate their entire attention upon the highly evolved doctrines of the separation of powers, the constitutionality of statutes, and particularly the interpretation of statutes. What is more, its usefulness as training for lawyers acting in other capacities is conspicuous. From an occasional school that has recently decided to place greatly increased emphasis upon the legislative process, however, the criticism comes that the book fails to treat that process in nearly enough detail.

Besides the basic question asked by all teachers of legislation of how courses in the subject can be introduced generally into law schools, no other question is of such paramount importance as that of what should be the content of the courses offered. Training of the future advocate cannot be ignored, particularly if his role is interpreted to include both adequate representation of the client's interest and assistance to the court in the use of statutory materials. But it must be remembered that only a small proportion of attorneys will have the opportunity to appear before the appellate courts, and that many more lawyers will earn their living, in whole or in part, through office counseling, and through engaging in the legislative process as legislators, legislative counselors, or legislative draftsmen. In an era when statutes are becoming an ever larger source of rights and duties, the attorney needs to know how to use the statute book with facility if he is to advise private clients well. The public interest requires, moreover, that efficiency in the legislative branch of government be increased not only through procedural reforms but through the use of more and better technical and advisory skills, particularly in legislative draftsmanship and counseling. Hence it would appear that law-school courses should deal both with the interpretation of statutes and with the function of, and the skills requisite for, the legislative process. These courses, furthermore, should be considered equally important for men entering either private practice or public service.

Three principal methods of dealing with this problem of content are now apparent. In the least developed, one course in legislation is offered to advanced students. The course is enlarged and enriched, as is Horack's casebook, by analysis of the legislative process. The instructor hopes that his colleagues will include statutory materials widely in their courses, and that students will elect administrative law as well as constitutional law, and one or more of the specialized public law subjects such as labor law or trade regulation. There is, however, no carefully planned and integrated curriculum in which the essentials of statutory law and legislation are assigned so definite a place that neither the teacher nor the student can readily sidestep them.

Under the second method, as referred to in connection with the earlier plan at the Columbia School of Law, a course in legislation is offered in the first year for the dual purpose of emphasizing the importance of statutory law and of laying a basic foundation for a sequence of public law courses that would include constitutional law, administrative law, the several specialized public law subjects, and possibly a second course in legislation. Professor Harry W. Jones, who is a strong advocate of the desirability of this method, maintains that such an "introductory course in legislation should be designed as an initial survey of the evolution of purposive public policy and of the problems inherent in the application of a legislative policy to the infinite variety of situations of fact which particular controversies may involve."[1] Although the instructor makes a vigorous effort to establish a base for subsequent work in public law, the process of integration of statutes and the emphasis given to legislation throughout the curriculum tend to remain fortuitous.

Thanks to the marked interest in public law of Lloyd K. Garrison then dean of the Law School, the vigilance of Willard Hurst, and the flexibility of the curriculum committee, the University of Wisconsin achieved considerable success with this method prior to the war. A four-hour, one-semester orientation course known as law in society was required of first-year students. The Wisconsin workmen's compensation act was selected by Mr. Hurst as the framework on which the course was constructed.[2] After a discussion of the earliest English and American judicial cases creating the fellow servant doctrine, attention was concentrated on the experience in Wisconsin in turning from the common law to employers' liability legislation, and from that to the compensation act. Materials were not confined to statutes and cases, but included excerpts from briefs of counsel and from legislative, executive, and administrative records, portions of party platforms, and of the minutes of proceedings of leading pressure groups such as the state federation of labor, together with personal accounts of the background of the compensation

---

[1] Cases and Other Materials on Legislation. Unpublished edition, 1940, p. iv.

[2] Hurst, Willard, "The Content of Courses in Legislation," in University of Chicago Law Review, February, 1941, pp. 291–294.

act by persons prominent in its enactment. Assigned readings of treatises and law-review articles discussed general juristic problems implicit in the material on industrial accidents: the nature of conflicts of interest, the litigious process as a method of lawmaking in the adjustment of conflicts, limitations of ignorance and economic bias in the judicial process, concepts of judicial responsibility toward statute law, the continuity of legislative policy, and the background of the "rule" of strict construction of statutes. The great advantages of this course were: first, concentration upon the evolution of legal efforts to meet a particular community problem placed the legislative process in living comparison with judicial and administrative activity. There was scope in such a course especially for detailed comparison of litigious and legislative law-making. Second, focusing upon the unfolding of a single problem gave the time and space necessary to a convincing re-creation of the life and movement behind fundamental legislation.

Subsequent to this introductory course, Wisconsin offered not only the public law courses mentioned above but also municipal corporations, patents, public utilities, and taxation. In addition, Mr. Hurst gave a three-hour semester course in legislation designed to train second or third-year students in advocacy, in the use of statutes in counseling, and in an understanding of the statutory matrix into which new legislative acts would have to be fitted. Around the concept of the intention of the legislature as a theme, he built the problems of the use of extrinsic evidence of legislative intent, of doctrines of strict and liberal construction, and of the use of statutes by analogy in tort and contract litigation. Questions of statutory interpretation were prefaced by an exploration of the proper handling of constitutional issues under the "presumption of constitutionality," and the factual emphasis developed through this doctrine in recent years by the Supreme Court. Thus students were made aware of the need for placing any legislative act within its factual context, and of the importance of policy-making involved in the interpretative process.

The third method of teaching statutes and the legislative process is a further, but exceedingly important, extension of the second. Legislation is again offered at the beginning of the curriculum, and numerous advanced courses in public law are available. But it is realized that what is also needed is the integration of a new emphasis throughout the whole law training. As Hurst has written, "The justification for that effort runs so deep into the law school's responsibilities for education in the philosophy and craftsmanship of the profession, that it cannot be denied in the reformation of the curriculum to meet the needs of our society."[1] Hence where schools are moving in the direction of utilizing this third method, the entire course of study is being more largely re-oriented toward the implications of public law, and toward making prospective lawyers realize that public policy is inextricably woven into private law. Training, therefore, is being introduced for those tasks of legislative draftsmanship and counseling which are likely to confront attorneys, whether they be in government service or in private practice.

An attempt to utilize this third method, extending probably well beyond that of any other school, has recently been undertaken at the College of Law of the University of Nebraska.[2] Dean Beutel, who was associated with several federal agencies during the war and was also chairman of the In-Service Training Joint Committee for federal lawyers, became even more convinced than formerly that legal education must undergo extensive revision if it were to keep pace with law as actually practiced today by lawyers.

The new curriculum at Nebraska, therefore, is based on the assumption that the future lawyer will spend a large part of his time in dealing with problems of the body politic. It recognizes

[1] "The Content of Courses in Legislation," in University of Chicago Law Review, February, 1941, p. 295.

[2] It may be noted that the increased and largely new faculty of the University of Pennsylvania is now engaged in a comprehensive reconsideration of legal education at that institution. The fact that Dean Earl G. Harrison and most of his faculty have had significant experience in government service, as well as private practice, should result in an appreciation of the public function of law and the civic responsibility of the lawyer which promises well for the future.

public law as an integral and fundamental part of the legal system and of the lawyer's practice. Hence, a surprising amount of public law has been introduced, both as essential parts of other courses and as specific courses.[1] Students, moreover, will be obliged to study much of this public law. All courses listed in the first year, most of those of the second year, and at least one of the two laboratories will be required of everyone. In the third and fourth · years the student can scarcely escape the election of some public law. Because the number of courses offered has been sharply reduced over old types of curricula through the process of elimination and of reassembling materials in larger teaching units, it will be almost impossible for him to fill his schedule, as has been done in many law schools, with electives in the common law.

In the first year at Nebraska, two-semester courses not only in legislation but in constitutional law are presented as "practical fundamentals in modern life." Even the course entitled introduction to law includes preparation in that generally neglected field of how to find and use public law materials. In the second year a two-semester course is offered in administrative law, and one-semester, alternating courses in labor law and government regulation of business are scheduled. The law of commercial transactions—generally appearing in most school bulletins under such titles as sales, negotiable instruments, commercial and investment paper—is treated by Dean Beutel as a one-year course the title of which, interpretation of uniform commercial statutes, indicates the emphasis placed upon statutory development.

In the third year a course in social legislation has been introduced which is concerned with those federal and state statutes that are attempts to remedy social maladjustments. Two alternating courses, new to law schools but of marked significance if government is viewed as America's "largest industry," have been planned. The one on problems of federal government organization will analyze the various types of legal patterns involved in the organization of government bureaus; the interrelationship of

[1] See not only the Bulletin of the University of Nebraska College of Law, 1946–1947, but also Frederick K. Beutel's The New Curriculum at the University of Nebraska College of Law, reprinted from the June, 1946, Nebraska Law Review.

government organization; means of control of government corporations and other government agencies; solutions of problems
of friction between government agencies, and between these agencies and private organizations. The alternating course is on
government contracts. It proposes to examine the law applicable
to government contracts, whether federal, state, or local; compare the contract forms of various government agencies; consider
means of enforcement; and view the function of the Court of
Claims and the Comptroller General's Office. In the fourth year
which is required of all students entering the College of Law
after only two years of academic work, a course in taxation will
be given, and also an advanced course in property which will supposedly include some consideration of zoning and land planning.

Besides greatly sharpening the emphasis upon the theory of
public law, Dean Beutel concluded that technical practice work
over and beyond what is now offered by most schools is essential,
and that instruction in the art of procedure and drafting of instruments can best be conducted by the clinical method. Hence
he provided two laboratories, the Practice Laboratory and the
Legislative Laboratory, one of which will be a prerequisite for
the LL.B. degree in the three-year curriculum and both of which
will be required of students in the four-year course of study. The
Practice Laboratory is concerned with training for private practice, and for advocacy both before the lower and the appellate
courts, under conditions as nearly resembling those of a law
office and court as possible. In addition to preparation and argument of briefs, much attention is to be given to the drawing of the
various types of legal documents which constitutes the major work
of many attorneys, especially of those who practice in the smaller
communities. The significance of this Practice Laboratory cannot
be gainsaid. It is, however, the Legislative Laboratory which is
pertinent to the present discussion. Before examining plans for
this clinical training, a brief digression is important.

In spite of the fact that nearly all legislative drafting, whether
for the Congress, state assemblies, or municipal councils, is done
by law-trained persons, the opinion is widely prevalent that often

it is badly done. Drafting exact enough to cover all exigencies is certainly not a possibility, and hence interpretation of statutes will remain a necessity. But much of the uncertainty of statutory law, much of the difficulty of administering it, and much of the time spent by the courts in construing it, apparently arises from drafting which could have been appreciably better. Preparation for this very important function would seem, therefore, to devolve squarely upon the law school. Yet legal education has given less attention to it even than to courses in legislation.

Many instructors have dismissed the desirability of such preparation on the ground that training in so specific a technique is not the province of a *professional* institution. This point of view completely ignores the broader aspects of training inherent in the drafting process. Jack B. Tate, general counsel for the Social Security Administration, maintains that work in drafting, accompanied by class criticism, should provide the finest possible opportunity for the rigorous group thinking that is essential to effective public administration.[1] From his long association with the Legislative Drafting Research Fund of Columbia University, Professor Dowling has asserted to the writer that law-school preparation in the subject gives a precision of thought and of writing that is not only ideal for subsequent drafting of legislative bills but for enabling the private practitioner to synthesize points of view and to work out administrative policies that may be of great value to a wide variety of corporate bodies. Finally, Dean Vanderbilt states: "Between legislative drafting and statutory construction lie all the complicated questions of public policy and legislative technique that go into the making of our statutes. When one considers the grand total of the output of our legislative bodies and its significance both to society and to the individual, one cannot but conclude that it is unsafe to continue to ignore these fundamental topics of bill drafting, legislative procedure and statutory construction."[2]

[1] "Training for Government Service," in American Law School Review, April, 1942, p. 1305.

[2] "Procedure as the Core of Undergraduate Law Study," in Association of American Law Schools Handbook, 1943, p. 43.

Some small attempt was made to remedy this situation prior to Pearl Harbor. Individual instructors occasionally assigned the drafting of statutes as exercises, or even called upon a few students for assistance in obtaining data needed for the drafting of a bill they had been asked to prepare. Law reviews sometimes published recommendations for new legislation, including a "model bill" which students had drafted at least in part. But such training was fortuitous. It depended largely upon the pleasure of the particular professor; it was not the result of carefully formulated educational policy.

At Columbia formalized means for offering training were potentially available but little exploited. The Legislative Drafting Research Fund, established as early as 1911 and located in the law-school building, had had considerable influence upon legislative drafting in this country. It had acted as draftsman and adviser to congressional and legislative committees or commissions, to departments of federal and state governments, and to important private organizations that wished to promote specific legislative proposals. It had also been instrumental in establishing a federal drafting bureau.

Here was the perfect laboratory, so it would have seemed, where students could have been given clinical instruction. Yet the School of Law made no concerted effort to use the Fund largely. Its past and present attitude is reflected in the current Bulletin of Information that devotes only six lines of print to one of Columbia's distinctive institutions, without even naming the staff which includes the distinguished Professors Chamberlain and Dowling.[1] It states little more than that "special opportunities are offered to advanced students who desire to study legislative methods or to carry on research work in connection with the study of administration and legislation." As a matter of fact, two or three second- and third-year students have generally been taken annually into the Fund as assistants. So excellent has been the training provided these men, that many of them have subsequently occupied positions of legislative counsel. But for the

[1] September 7, 1946, p. 25.

body of law students the Fund has never served as a legislative laboratory, although Professor Chamberlain has expressed the desire that its function should be thus expanded.

Although economic resources have been considerably fewer at the University of Minnesota, the experience has been more fruitful. In the enlarged and enriched curriculum which Dean Fraser had introduced both for the purpose of more adequately training attorneys and of improving the law, provision had been made for a course in legislation. Professor Read joined the faculty in 1934 as instructor, and set out to design a course which would attempt to serve the dual goal envisaged by Dean Fraser. So far as training in purely professional technique is concerned, the course seeks to enable the lawyer to handle statutes in the solution of cases, and to draft bills for his clients with some degree of expertness and an appreciation of the complex and manifold problems often involved. It also seeks to help the lawyer fulfill his duties as a citizen in a democracy and as a possible legislator.

The course combines theory and practice. The Selected Legal Materials on Legislation,[1] assembled by Read for class use in mimeographed form, considers some of the topics already mentioned in other legislation courses, such as statutory interpretation and the attitude with which courts approach statutes. Much of the course, however, is more sharply focused upon the task of the draftsman and counselor. The form and language of all parts of a statute are studied. So are the functions which legislation has performed in the moulding of social, economic, and political institutions; the relative values of the various means devised to make laws effective; the question of what can and cannot be accomplished by legislation; the role played by pressure groups in influencing the legislative process. Chamberlain's Legislative Processes, National and State, is required collateral reading.

Simultaneously with these classroom discussions, Read attempts to give his students some real understanding of formula-

---

[1] At present Read and John W. MacDonald, professor at Cornell Law School, are collaborating in the preparation of materials on legislation, to be published by the Foundation Press. These materials, when available, will replace the mimeographed ones now used at Minnesota.

tion of legislative policy and the actual functioning of the legislative process through requiring that they do certain exercises, including the drafting of a bill. An analytical study is made of the statutes enacted during the last session of the state legislature. In examining a particular act assigned him, the student is expected to answer specific questions that Read has arranged under the topics: substance of the act, its statutory history, its legislative history, its derivation, its constitutionality, its history subsequent to enactment. A short paper embodying research is also required on some topic, such as certain aspects of special legislation in Minnesota; the stultifying effect of legislative precedent in the development of various types of social legislation; or the approach of a particular judge to the problem of statutory interpretation as reflected in his opinions.

Prior to the drafting of a bill, the student is given a questionnaire designed to enable him to determine whether or not there should be a new law for dealing with the particular problem, and, if so, what its scope and effect should and probably would be. The questions he must attempt to answer are as follows:

1. What is the subject matter of the proposed new law, i.e., with exactly what phases of human affairs, economic, social, or political is the proposed law concerned?

2. What reliable data, literature, expert opinion, and advice on the present problem in its economic, social, and political aspects are available? What is their cumulated effect?

3. What is the present Minnesota law on the subject?

4. What is the broad objective of the proposed new law?

5. What are the specific fact situations for which the present law is alleged to provide an inadequate or undesirable solution?

6. Does the alleged defect actually exist?

7. If so, is the situation unique to Minnesota, or has the same or a similar defect in the law been dealt with by the legislature of any other state or country?

8. If another state or country has dealt with such a defect, what statutory remedy did it devise?

9. What has been the experience of such other state or country in applying its statute judicially and administratively? Have any

theoretical and practical difficulties been encountered? If so, what means have been taken to overcome them?

10. Have the above-mentioned statutes of other states or countries been judicially or administratively construed?

11. Have the governmental officers charged with the administration of such statutes any criticism or suggestion for improving them?

12. Has the legislature of Minnesota ever considered or enacted legislation in any phase of human affairs essentially related to the subject now under consideration? If so, what has been its general policy? Would any Minnesota statutes be in *pari materia* with the proposed new law? If so, how would they interplay? Adapt and answer questions 8 to 11 to any Minnesota statutes included in question 12.

13. What specific solution do you recommend to remedy the defect you are now considering?

14. Does your solution involve either legislative administration or law-making in the sense of laying down rules of general application?

15. If the latter, what is the immediate and specific object or purpose of the new law that you propose?

16. What are the likely economic, social, and political results and implications of your proposed solution?

17. What are the various sanctions and other devices available for use in obtaining the objects of your proposed law?

18. With particular and not exhaustive reference to question 17, does the subject matter of your proposed law indicate that it will be self-executory, or must administrative machinery be utilized?

19. What modifying effect, express or implied, will your new law have on presently existing law, both common and statutory?

20. Is there any question concerning the constitutionality of your proposed law: under the federal constitution; under the Minnesota constitution?

21. In the light of careful appraisal of your answers to the foregoing questions, do you recommend the enactment of a new law? If so, draft the necessary bill.

Bar associations and various organized business interests frequently submit requests to the Law School for the preparation of bills. Thus students have an opportunity to concern themselves with the drafting of statutes which, although relatively simple, will actually be submitted to the state legislature. Prior to the war, the legislature itself asked for assistance during the period when it was in session, and a group of selected students was assigned, part-time, to act under supervision as a legislative drafting bureau.

Although such careful, detailed training cannot be given as the Columbia Fund furnishes annually to two or three chosen men, Professor Read has been able to guarantee that a considerable proportion of the Minnesota students will leave the School reasonably competent to deal with the less complicated aspects of the legislative process. An elective tutorial, moreover, is offered to fourth-year students who have passed the course in legislation with a grade of B or better. Some three or four men annually avail themselves of this opportunity to obtain a greater degree of expertness.

For a course as broad in scope as Read's to attain a considerable degree of success, two assets are requisite: time and a budget adequate to permit individualized instruction. Both the textual subject matter and training in the techniques of drafting are of sufficient importance to warrant that they be taught either as two courses or that two semesters be devoted to them. Because of Dean Fraser's conviction of the importance of this work, Read has been exceptionally fortunate in his time allotment. He not only has at his disposal sixty classroom hours distributed over an academic year, but he is able to require a considerable block of the student's time for outside preparation of practical work. No other course in the School, except practice and procedure, is so favored.

To achieve substantial results, moreover, drafting requires highly individualized instruction. Even if the goal be that of broad orientation of the prospective attorney to the legislative process, rather than preparation of the specialist in draftmanship as at Columbia, it is doubtful whether a teacher, unassisted, can give adequate attention to more than a dozen students. Hence instruction in drafting tends to be expensive. Read has met the situation as best he could by pressing the students in his tutorial into action. Shortly, however, paid teaching assistants will be made available.

The distressing financial situation encountered generally by legal education will be discussed later. Therefore, one need only remark here that no *large* advances can be made by most schools in instituting individualized programs, whether in drafting or in other areas, until professional law training is awarded financial consideration more nearly comparable to that for training in some of the other professions.

The lack of an adequate budget, however, is no valid excuse for omitting the subject of draftsmanship. Methods are available whereby students can be provided with some degree of competency. Read utilizes one method under relatively propitious circumstances. In a letter to the writer Hurst has suggested another, designed for schools which are as yet reluctant to devote so much as a semester exclusively to legislative draftsmanship. Statutory drafting would be made part of a substantial four-hour course in the drafting of selected types of legal documents. If a problem in statutory drafting were assigned as one of three designated problems, the student would gain appreciable insight and skill, and many a school might be more readily receptive to such training.

Through the Legislative Laboratory at Nebraska, Dean Beutel has devised a third solution which seems exceptionally promising within the financial limitations imposed upon his institution. It seeks to make the function of, and experience in, draftsmanship an integral part of a much broader examination of the purpose and means of achieving and administering socially desirable legislation. The year-long workshop proposes to analyze the principles of legislative drafting which emerge from a critical evaluation of selected recent and pending legislation; to collect economic and sociological data requisite to the preparation of specified statutes; to investigate certain social problems which might lend themselves to solution through legislative enactment; to consider what types of government agency and what methods of administration and enforcement are best suited to achieve social objectives. Drafting bills designed to achieve such objectives will be required. Also required will be the writing of legal memoranda in support of the validity of proposed legislation, and the preparation of reports for submission to legislative bodies.

Because of the fact that the University of Nebraska is situated in Lincoln, the same opportunity will probably be available as at the University of Minnesota for students to assist in the drafting of bills to be submitted to the legislature. Examination and preparation of legislation, however, will extend beyond that actually under consideration at the capitol. It will include training in problems such as the codification of existing law now being carried on by the Commissioners on Uniform State Laws; reorganization of government machinery through legislation for the purpose of increasing administrative efficiency; definition of areas where legislation is outworn, or nonexistent but badly needed.

When the writer recalls the conversation she once had with Dean Harno who extemporaneously outlined one problem after another in Illinois from oil fields to the school system, in connection with which legal research leading to new or improved legislation is requisite, she concludes that the difficulty of the Nebraska Legislative Laboratory will not be one of finding areas in which to work. It will rather be that of selecting areas which first will provide the maximum as training for future lawyers, and second will permit the University to contribute to the development of the state and nation.

TEACHING METHODS

If the curriculum is to be enriched on behalf of giving prospective lawyers a wider competence for dealing with the complex problems of our contemporary culture, more than reorganized and new teaching materials are requisite. Teaching methods must undergo extensive alteration. But these alterations can profitably be introduced only after careful general consideration of how legal education is to achieve its broadened purpose. Otherwise they will be random experiments interpolated here and there within the curriculum. As such, they will remain experiments that cast no large influence over the law school, or they will die—like so many excellent undertakings in legal education —because the intellectual climate in which they struggled to exist finally suffocated them.

In "Education for Law Teachers," Professor Henry Weihofen has performed an initial, significant service to the law-school world by pointing to theories and methods inductively established by educational psychology that might aid in determining how law teaching can be made more effective.[1] Instructors of law had so long identified themselves with the function of the practicing attorney rather than that of the educator that they had been almost totally unaware of the potential contribution of specialists in education to the solution of their problem.

Weihofen begins his article with references to psychological theories of motivation. He recapitulates the conclusion of scores of scientific studies of motivation in the sentence, "It is intense effort that educates." Without a drive to learn, no learning occurs, regardless of how long one is exposed to the material. Conversely, some strong incentive will cause one to learn with amazing facility, even under the most adverse conditions. How can the theory of incentive, Weihofen inquires, be utilized so that the law student will retain enthusiasm and zeal in the second and third years, after the exhilaration of the case method and of entering a professional school has worn thin? He finds one answer in the studies of incentives at Yale University which demonstrated the importance of making clear to students the *purpose* of academic work and its relation to their central objective. Weihofen concludes that a course in real property which begins with an examination of feudal rules of tenure, and waits until later to develop the significance of these rules (if any) in modern law, flagrantly disregards the significance of *purpose*.

[1] In Columbia Law Review, May, 1943, pp. 423–448.

On the other hand, even advanced students who find themselves in a seminar such as Professor Carey's in contemporary
public aspects of real property, work so assiduously—as has
already been seen—that the instructor becomes disturbed lest
they have no time left for preparation of other courses. The purpose of what they are doing appears entirely clear to them; they
are struggling with the problems of their own age and environment. They have the feeling, not of preparing stereotyped exercises for an "academic" institution, but of actually participating
in the life and work of the world. They are willing, moreover, to
study and use materials from preceding generations or centuries
if it can be demonstrated that those materials will give them
added insight into the on-going problems with which they are
dealing.

In *purpose*, therefore, lies an important clue to what is prerequisite for effectiveness in any teaching method. Three comprehensive methods have thus far appeared—case method, problem method, and clinical method—which are competent, if
skillfully and not excessively used, to provide the incentive
needed. Of these, only the first and two segments of the third
have been extensively utilized by law schools generally or even
by individual schools on any carefully planned and organized basis.

Case Method. One of the chief reasons for the great success
achieved by the case method has been the sense it has given
students of examining "real" situations. To the degree that it has
not succeeded more completely, failure may be attributed to the
fact that predominantly it has been the only teaching method
used, and that many instructors have employed it in a routine
and unimaginative way. Just as the best play on Broadway needs
to be restudied at frequent intervals, so the case method, after
more than a half-century of hard wear, is today in need of critical
overhauling. Its teachers are equally in need of a "refresher
course" in how to use it, and how to refrain from over-using and
abusing it. From a process of renovation the case method would
emerge as a still indispensable and even more effective instrumentality.

Problem Method. The Columbia seminar in governmental administration, outlined earlier, is an excellent illustration of the use of the problem method. Emphasis has been shifted from teaching students law, which has been the primary purpose of the case method, to teaching them to be lawyers. The problems formulated demonstrate the degree to which assignments can be made to resemble those on which government attorneys and opposing counsel work, and yet be designed exclusively to serve educational ends. Much of the potential value of the problem method lies in its adaptability to reproducing the atmosphere of situations with which lawyers actually find themselves confronted, but situations which are graded to correspond to the student's intellectual background, skill, and judgment, and from which those elements of repetitiousness and irrelevancy that characterize every law office have been deleted. The problem method is an answer to Professor Cavers' criticism, "The basic trouble is that we've gone instrumentalist in our law while we've remained conceptualist in our teaching."[1]

According to Cavers, who has been one of the most ardent spokesmen for the problem method, no fewer than five distinct advantages might be expected to result from its utilization.[2] First, students would learn law by using it. Second, they would come to *understand* law by putting it to use. Third, the skill that would be acquired as they gained in understanding would be no inconsiderable by-product. Fourth, an incentive would be provided which would drive them intellectually and make them like being driven. Finally, a solution might be found for that difficult pedagogical question of how to present the economic or social aspects of legal problems without reducing students to reading, learning, and repeating what various writers have had to say in treatises and monographs.

Considerable recognition has long been given to the value of the problem method. Many references have been made to it in

[1] "In Advocacy of the Problem Method," in Columbia Law Review, May, 1943, p. 454.
[2] *Ibid.*, pp. 455–456.

professional meetings and in print.[1] Much has been accomplished by individual teachers who have used it incidentally in their case-method courses. A smaller number have experimented with it more formally, either in connection with conventional courses or with new seminars. Thus, prior to the war, Weihofen taught the course in constitutional law at the University of Colorado exclusively by the problem method. The problems were mimeographed. Under each, appeared a list of relevant cases and other references which students were expected to examine as they attempted to solve the particular problem. Cavers taught conflict of laws in much the same manner at Duke. Charles W. Carnahan, of Washington University School of Law, published a casebook on Conflict of Laws which included many problems expressly to permit simultaneous use of the two methods.

The problem method has met with small acceptance, however, by the majority of the faculty in schools where suggestions have been made to extend its use beyond that of a mere supplement to the case method, and to utilize it as one of the major techniques for instruction. This results in part from the new and often taxing demands which it makes upon the teacher. Few prepared problems, to say nothing of problem books, are available. Hence, the instructor must undergo the time-consuming task of formulating his own problems. But formulation requires knowledge of a subject that is both broad and very specific, and the type of mind that is given to construction of problems. Obviously law instructors who are called upon to teach subjects in which they are not specialists, can scarcely be expected to have the knowledge requisite for use of this method. Often inadequate as is the assistance provided them by the casebook, it is an almost indispensable tool. Many persons, moreover, show marked ability in analyzing difficult problems, but demonstrate lesser ability in constructing problems from the vast array of legal and social data that lie scattered about them.

[1] As illustration, see the excellent report of the Committee on Teaching and Examination Methods of which Professor Frank R. Strong was chairman, that appeared in the Handbook of the Association of American Law Schools, 1942, pp.86–90.

Finally, the problem method presupposes—for maximum efficiency—small classes, individualized instruction, and ample library facilities. These are luxuries which many schools find it hard to provide because of financial stringency. Neither this nor the other difficulties, however, are generally insurmountable, and hence can scarcely be used to absolve at least those schools with the larger teaching staffs and budgets from engaging in this method. As the economically more fortunate institutions succeed in perfecting it, the results can be made available to other schools.

In extensive preliminary planning at Duke University prior to the war and in the article already referred to, Cavers attempted to devise a logical and relatively simple way for utilizing the problem method, quite separate from the case method.[1] He wanted to make it the principal teaching instrument of the second year, and possibly of third-year seminars. He suggested that a school select a field of law that has grown up around a central core of familiar, related transactions, such as commercial transactions, land transactions, estates, or business associations. It could then develop a sequence of the transactions presenting problems, and teach the law of the field, or so much of it as needs teaching, by trying to solve those problems. The problems might sometimes be strung on the thread of a succession of imagined dealings. For example, much of what is now taught by the case method under vendor and purchaser, conveyancing, and mortgages could be developed around the acquisition of a tract of farm land, its subdivision for a suburban development, the sales of the lots and their financing, and the ultimate foreclosure. Such a problem course might be confined to the consideration of only those matters that conventionally have been treated in the casebook courses. But it would also provide opportunity to examine, in addition, questions of land use and credit policy that have been largely ignored.

Cavers assumed that a substantial part of the student's time during the second year would be devoted to one such course.

[1] "In Advocacy of the Problem Method," in Columbia Law Review, May, 1943, pp. 456–461.

For teaching purposes the class would be divided into sections of not more than fifteen students. Since an instructor could adequately supervise one or at most two sections, many schools would have to arrange for the services of several instructors. Blocks of hours, such as five afternoons a week from one-thirty to five-thirty o'clock, would be set aside for the course. Class sessions would depend, in frequency and length, upon the specific needs of the subject material and the students. During by far the largest part of this time, however, students would work on the particular problems assigned them. The instructor would not only be always available for consultation, but recourse to him would be encouraged. Practicing lawyers might be called upon for advice concerning problems similar to those with which they constantly deal. If public law subjects were treated by the problem method, social scientists and administrators might equally well be asked to perform a similar service.

Roughly one problem a week would be assigned, according to Cavers' plan. It would be subdivided so that individual students, or groups of two or three, might work on small parts of it. At the first session in a given week a discussion of the facts presented in that week's assignment would probably be profitable. A preliminary awareness of the questions of law and policy, private or public, lurking in these facts should be developed. Further facts might be wanted. An examination of their relevance would often be illuminating in itself. So, too, might be some consideration of how the needed information could be obtained by an attorney. Individual tasks would then be distributed.

These tasks should be sufficiently limited as not to require protracted research. Frequently they might relate to matters on which the law is supposed to be reasonably well settled. Preferably the problem should be laid in a specific jurisdiction. Thus the student would get the feel of the law of a single state, "wherein the case law of other states plays a part subordinate to the indigenous product and wherein statutes may be maltreated but cannot be ignored."[1]

[1] *Ibid.*, p. 457.

When the group reassembled, the ambit of discussion would not have to be restricted by the precise limits of the problem. The problem would, however, provide a point of reference, even if attention were directed to some matter of broad jurisprudential significance or to some economic consequence of the established legal pattern. The instructor would be wise, in Cavers' opinion, to avoid the report technique which generally reduces a seminar to a lecture course conducted by students who are ill-qualified lecturers. In order to provide a common store of knowledge adequate to support group discussion, one of two methods might be used. The subdivisions of the major problem might be so closely interlaced that one student (or group of students) would gain some grasp, through his own research, of the law relating to his fellows' problems. The second method would be to provide a background of law pertinent to the week's assignment for all to share. This might be done by lecture, or by assigning certain leading cases or textual material relating to the subject. Some or all of these same methods might be employed to cover certain aspects of the subject not falling within the scope of the problems, yet too important to ignore.

Research in the law books would not be the only kind of work demanded. Problems should be so devised as to require students to determine the courses of action indicated for their hypothetical clients and to prepare any necessary legal instruments. Research, case study, counseling, and drafting would be intermingled in much the same way, if not in the same proportions, as in actual law practice.

Clinical Method. This is a third teaching device to which considerable attention is currently being directed. Nearly fifteen years ago Judge Jerome Frank became its most enthusiastic sponsor with his publication of "Why Not a Clinical Lawyer-School?"[1] Since then the number of disciples has slowly but steadily grown. Some persons would probably view this method as too nearly like that of the problem method to justify placing it in a separate category. The matter is one of small importance.

[1] In University of Pennsylvania Law Review, June, 1933, pp. 907–923.

What is important is the fact that several teaching techniques, which may conveniently be grouped under the word "clinical," have been tried in the past and still others are coming into use, that have marked significance for diversifying instruction in legal education and hence increasing its stimulus and possible effectiveness.

The first two of these techniques have had a long and very successful record in law schools generally. They are the moot court and the law review. The moot court provides a limited amount of usually excellent and required "practical" training for advocacy. Students are assigned appellate or trial-court cases. They investigate the law, prepare briefs, and argue the cases orally in a setting which closely approximates that of a courtroom. Frequently visiting judges preside over the "court."

An interesting variation on the moot court was recently tried with success at Yale where an attempt was initiated to give students clinical work in negotiation and arbitration as well as in litigation before appellate courts.[1] Actual cases, obtained from the files of the American Arbitration Association and elsewhere, were assigned to students in the roles of clients, witnesses, and attorneys. Conferences between clients and attorneys, and negotiations between two sets of attorneys were undertaken. Even when the negotiations proved successful, it was assumed, for the purpose of the next step, that no agreement had been reached and that the case would proceed to arbitration. At this stage, experienced arbitrators made their services available upon request. Throughout the entire process, the proceedings were informal, dignified, and realistic.

The law review, whose editorial board is composed of some fifteen second- and third-year students with the highest scholastic records, furnishes almost unparalleled incentive for undertaking legal research and for learning how to write. So successful has it been that Cavers has even argued that its success overlies that of the case method.[2] Students engaged in law-review work rapidly

[1] James, Fleming, Jr., "An Arbitration Laboratory in Law School," in Arbitration Journal, Spring, 1947, pp. 79–83.

[2] "In Advocacy of the Problem Method," in Columbia Law Review, May, 1943, pp. 450–451.

develop analytical keenness, resourcefulness, articulateness, and capacity to penetrate below the surface of problems. They then bring their enlarged intellectual maturity to the case courses. Hence what many teachers attribute to the effectiveness of the case method should instead be attributed, Cavers believes, to the law-review problem method.

Unfortunately this excellent technique has been limited to what Howard C. Westwood, a practicing attorney, has designated sa the intellectual aristocracy. The very students most in need of help in learning to write, to diagnose and solve problems, and to develop critical skills in selecting and using pertinent doctrine and data are cut off from this instrumentality. Many schools, moreover, provide no substitute. Westwood has therefore advocated that "the law review should become the law school." In an article thus entitled,[1] he argues that writing should begin in the last quarter of the first year by requiring that students prepare two or three case notes in connection with regular courses. In the second and third years, formal classes should be cut by at least 50 per cent in order that time might be provided for law-review work, "the really important education and training." Under this plan the substantive law would be reduced to a few large lecture courses dealing broadly with only very important subjects. The moot court and the legal clinic would be continued for variety, practice in oral argument, and practical experience.

Every student, in Westwood's opinion, should be required to participate in law-review activities. Teams of second- and third-year students should be formed in the number needed to include the entire student body. The first team would be selected and would function exactly as at present. The second team would be composed of some fifteen students in the second highest scholarship rank, the third of students in the third highest rank, and so on. The law school should expect the first and second groups to edit their reviews with almost no faculty participation. Beyond that point, however, faculty assistance should begin and should extend in ever-increasing amounts to each successive group.

[1] In Virginia Law Review, September, 1945, pp. 913–919.

Criticism, revision, and guidance provided to the less able or diligent students should, in fact, become a major responsibility of law instructors, overshadowing formal teaching and the preparation of casebooks.

Mr. Westwood's discussion suffers from the same shortcoming as that of other authors who are so extremely interested in one teaching method that they exaggerate its utility. Nevertheless, his article reinforces the very important argument that the *kind* of training provided by the law review should be provided to *every* student, and most particularly to the C rather than the A grade student.

This the University of Chicago has attempted to do for a decade. The method used, however, has been the tutorial rather than the law review, which remains the distinguished product of a small selected group of students and of faculty advisers. Every first-year student is required to engage in individual writing and legal research under the guidance of a tutor. Approximately one-half of the student's last year, moreover, is devoted to seminars in which research and writing are unavoidable. This program is probably still unique among American law schools in its use of the tutorial system and its insistence upon training for everyone in these important skills. The School reports that the results have been extremely gratifying.

Legal clinics, most often spoken of as legal aid clinics, are another type of clinical experience that has been cultivated on a restricted scale. Strictly speaking, a legal clinic is a law office operated for teaching purposes. Its clients are generally poor persons who apply for assistance. Students handle their cases, at least in the initial stages, under the supervision of the director. Occasionally the clinical program includes research and technical assistance provided upon request to practicing lawyers or various corporate bodies. Sometimes the legal clinic is part of a law school or under its immediate control. Again it is part of a legal aid society with which a school has made arrangements for instruction.

Although the legal clinic has as yet found a place for itself in very few educational institutions, several law teachers—and most

particularly Professor John S. Bradway of Duke University—are
its ardent proponents. They maintain that it gives the student an
opportunity to synthesize what he has learned in theory in many
different courses; it teaches him how to plan and conduct a campaign in a legal case; it helps him to learn to deal with the human
factors involved in legal proceedings; it provides a test of his de-
pendability, judgment, initiative, and other characteristics.

Many of the schools that are without clinics have expressed
reasons for not undertaking this kind of instruction: some say
that they are not located where they can readily obtain clients;
others feel that they cannot assume the financial and administrative responsibility; still others declare that their curricula are
already overcrowded. Finally, certain schools do not regard
clinical work with poor clients favorably, since they maintain
that their students will enter a very different type of practice, for
which legal aid experience would be of little assistance.

These reasons have some validity, but ways to circumvent the
difficulties undoubtedly could have been found if the schools had
had stronger convictions about the desirability of this kind of
clinical practice. With the extensive unmet needs for the services
of law-trained persons that characterize most of the United
States, each school should be able to obtain legal work, not necessarily confined to the cases of poor persons, which would yield
valuable clinical experience and would incidentally permit the
institution to make some contribution to social development.

A fourth method for providing clinical experience, even less
developed than that of the legal clinic, is apprenticeship training.
Walton Hamilton's experiment in sending a small group of Yale
students to Washington for a semester has already been reviewed.
Prior to the war the University of Wisconsin expected students to
spend two summers in local public and private law offices approved by the School. Fellowships were granted three thoroughly
competent graduate students annually for apprenticeship in the
law offices of the state government. Dean Garrison hoped thereby
to encourage young lawyers to enter the public service. At the
time of Pearl Harbor the University of Cincinnati was experi-

menting with placing students in local law offices for summer apprenticeship training. Recently the Washington College of Law, as noted earlier, has announced the initiation of clinical training in the national capital available to any law school in the country which wishes to send its students there.

Such undertakings have been so small that they would scarcely be worth recording were it not for the fact that they contain vital possibilities. Postwar legal education appears to regard clinical training with growing favor. Many faculty members have come to believe, as the result of the legal work in which they engaged subsequent to 1941, that ways must be found to make teaching more purposeful by relating it closer to the work of the lawyer. Apprenticeship training and also the legal clinic have at least provided suggestive patterns of "situations" in which the student is called upon to act much as he is likely to act in his professional life, and where he can see a problem in its entirety and its dynamic aspects rather than as a grouping of static fragments. It is possible that one or both of these types of clinical experience, perhaps in broader or modified form, may now undergo considerable development. In the process of growth, great care would need to be exercised to guarantee that the clinical training was first and foremost educational. Several professions in the past have encountered grave difficulties because clinical work was inadequately planned or inadequately supervised by the teaching institution, or because the service agency that provided the clinical cases expected the student to do work which was more useful to it than to his educational progress. From such hazardous experiences these professions are only now emerging. What they have learned should be a helpful source of guidance to legal education in instituting a form of training that is potentially of great significance but that cannot be successfully undertaken without much painstaking.

RESEARCH

Throughout this portion of the monograph references to research have casually appeared. It must now be said, as emphatically as possible, that no program of legal education will meet the needs of persons entering the public service or of attorneys who engage in the broader aspects of private law practice, unless very substantial training in research is provided. If policy-making and administration, whether carried on in the official bureau or the private office, are to be truly in the public interest, they must be based on the best facts that can be had and on the most objective interpretations possible, rather than on emotional responses, the "research" contributions of lobbyists, or what persons in responsible positions assume the facts to be.

Carefully designed techniques for obtaining and interpreting facts have been utilized far too little within American government and also within private enterprise. However, the National Resources Planning Board, the Temporary National Economic Committee, the Attorney General's Committee on Administrative Procedure, the Bureau of the Budget, the Division of Tax Research of the Department of the Treasury, the Bureau of Research and Statistics of the Social Security Administration have demonstrated how research can profitably be used by public bodies as a basis for the determination of program and policy.

For the very reason that so much of what he does even to the drafting of relatively simple memoranda eventuates in action, the lawyer pre-eminently needs to know how to find, interpret, and employ facts and theories—social, economic, political, and philosophical, as well as legal. The action he sets in motion, moreover, is frequently not isolated and incidental but is an integral part of an on-going program. Hence every determination, however simple, may have marked consequences for the form and scope of future action.

The law schools have provided excellent preparation in finding, interpreting, and using the common law. We have seen that their success with statutory materials has been less distinguished. Achievement in teaching students to look up or prepare relevant non-legal data and then apply these data to the legal solution of social problems has been negligible in the great majority of law schools. So has achievement in training students to engage in joint undertakings with various other specialists, or to call upon them for advisory assistance. If the thesis of Robert S. Lynd's powerful Knowledge for What? is valid,[1] the adequacy of legal education may come to be judged increasingly by the degree to which it assists the prospective lawyer to learn how to integrate facts and theories drawn from many sources and how to work with specialists of many kinds.

About the training of students in research the law schools have written or have said at their annual conventions relatively little. The distinguished Hohfeld, however, argued the urgent need, in "A Vital School of Jurisprudence and Law," for a graduate institution whose function it would be to train men, not for the practice of law in its traditional sense, but to become "professorial jurists," and "jurists" specifically fitted for legal authorship, for legislative reference and drafting work, for positions in administrative and legislative commissions and executive departments, and for the top leadership of the bar and bench.[2] In such training emphasis upon investigation and research would almost unavoidably be paramount.

If consideration of the student's need for preparation in research has received small formal attention, much more has been written about the desirability of scholarly research that transcends the preparation of casebooks, of correlating social science concepts and facts with legal research, and of establishing institutions where research may be pursued. It is not necessary here to review the content of those exploratory articles and speeches that are primarily concerned with theoretical questions about areas of needed research and methodology. Professor Roscoe Pound's impressive address, "The Opportunities for Developing Research in the Field of Jurisprudence,"[3] or Frankfurter, Llewellyn, and Sunderland's "The Conditions for and the

---

[1] Princeton University Press, 1939.

[2] In Fundamental Legal Conceptions as Applied in Judicial Reasoning and Other Legal Essays, by Wesley Newcomb Hohfeld, edited by Walter Wheeler Cook. Yale University Press, 1934, pp. 360–363.

[3] In Journal of Proceedings and Addresses of the Thirty-Third Annual Conference of the Association of American Universities, 1931, pp. 119–134.

Aims and Methods of Legal Research,"[1] are illustrative of the more thoughtful of such literature.

About plans for the creation of research institutions, however, something more needs to be said. During the second half of the twenties and the decade of the thirties, a number of law-school men permitted themselves to visualize centers, generally established under the control of their particular schools, which would be primarily devoted to research but which in some instances would have additional aims. A few of these men actually made written plans for the creation of such centers and undertook the promotion of their plans. Dean Smith was one. He became so convinced that knowledge obtained through research must be made the basis of action looking toward social change that he ardently sought to establish a research center at Columbia University. There he hoped that law-trained men would co-ordinate and synthesize pertinent data and theories advanced both by lawyers and social scientists, in an effort to solve some of the baffling economic and social problems of our era.

Illustrative of another attempt to provide for extensive organized research was the plan drawn some years later by Dean Harno and Professor W. E. Britton of the University of Illinois. They wished to see created at the University a center which would combine a legal research bureau, a graduate school designed to synthesize law and the social sciences in a program leading to the Ph.D. degree in law, and a course in training for the public service. The distinctive feature of this plan was the insistence that the legal research bureau should focus attention upon continuing examination of Illinois law and its administration. After adequate studies had been made, reports would be written designed for legislative, executive, or administrative consideration. Thus the bureau would serve as an unofficial agency for the improvement of law and administration in the state.[2]

[1] In American Law School Review, March, 1930, pp. 663–681.

[2] In the specialized field of law enforcement, Professor Alexander M. Kidd of the School of Jurisprudence at the University of California did considerable preliminary arranging for the creation of an institute of criminology. Although the institute was planned to begin modestly, it would ultimately combine, were funds available, *Footnote continued on page 243.*

Only one of the sizable plans drawn was actually translated into institutional form: Walter Wheeler Cook's blueprint for a university school of jurisprudence which would be devoted to the study of law as a social institution. Cook argued that American courts of last resort render nearly 25,000 decisions yearly, while legislative bodies enact vast numbers of statutes. These laws produce important effects on the political, economic, and social life of the nation. Yet no agencies exist whose specific duty it is to determine *what* are the effects. Hence, he insisted that the exclusive function of at least one, non-professional school should be that of ascertaining how our legal system actually functions, what the defects are, how improvements can be achieved. For this purpose the Institute for the Study of Law was opened in 1928 at Johns Hopkins University. Cook, as director, was assisted by two outstanding law professors, Herman Oliphant and Hessel E. Yntema, and by the well-known economist, Leon C. Marshall. The institution began under propitious circumstances. A few years later gifts and grants for its maintenance were not obtainable, and it was forced to close.

As the result, legal education entered the postwar era with not so much as one research center in operation. A half-dozen schools have had and continue to have modest funds for research at their disposal. Generally, however, these funds have been distributed, without systematic plan, to subsidize relatively small, individual pieces of research. Frequently the research has been done by law teachers with little participation by social scientists and other specialists. It is obvious that the entire question of the function, purpose, and financing of research needs to be reconsidered.[1]

Footnote continued from page 242.

teaching, service, research, laboratories, and a museum. Kidd proposed that it draw its teaching and research staff from men with distinguished experience in law enforcement and criminal scientific investigation; from law teachers concerned with criminal law and its administration; from criminologists, psychologists, and psychiatrists; and from persons experienced in pertinent social investigation.

[1] During the past two decades a considerable number of the most able minds in the law-school world have been occupied with the restatement of the common law, which the American Law Institute has sponsored and the Carnegie Corporation has financed. Valuable as is the restatement, it has been to some degree responsible for draining both interest and energy into one field of research at the expense of other fields probably even more in need of cultivation.

Why did the earlier plans fail to elicit larger academic and community interest and financial support? Were they perhaps *too* broad in scope, or not sufficiently specific? Were they sometimes drawn without prolonged discussions with social scientists or other needed specialists, and with university administrators and the interested laity? Were they possibly too explicit about the lawyer's place in the research program and not explicit enough about the responsibility to be assumed by other important personnel? Had the funds been obtained, were there enough law-trained men with sufficient preparation in more than common law research to prepare working blueprints, participate in, and administer such important undertakings?

Realistic answers to such questions should be of basic help in planning for the future of research. But there are other questions of even greater immediate importance in their relation to professional education. Should the projected programs have been more closely integrated with the teaching function of the law school? Most of the persons responsible for making the plans obviously viewed research as an instrumentality for assisting the bar, bench, and public in their essential task of using law for socially desirable and often affirmative ends. Did these persons equally take into consideration the imperative need of all students for training in research; the value of research as a teaching method; and the importance of that kind of research which would yield data and theories useful for enriching specific law-school courses or for determining what the content of the curriculum should be? Did they attempt to discover whether it was possible to mark out areas of research which would contribute guidance to those outside the law-school walls, and yet would simultaneously forward the education of students?

None would gainsay the fact that every possible encouragement should be given to the establishment of graduate research centers if it be certain that they will minister most effectively to the social welfare. Such encouragement, however, must not be permitted to obscure the importance of research training for undergraduate students. In many of the discussions and plans that characterized the late twenties and the thirties, law students and the under-graduate law school as a teaching institution seem to have been largely lost to view. Opportunity would have been provided a few exceptional students, but, as in the case of the law review, the intellectual aristocracy would have benefited at the expense of the great majority. Yet two facts appear inescapable. First, the training of students is the primary task of legal education. Second, as already said, any school that sends a prospective lawyer out to engage in legal work as law is practiced today without providing him with research skill has not met one of its most elementary responsibilities.

Hence any immediate plans for research probably need to be drawn in terms of the undergraduate school and its students, and not of the graduate institution. As these plans are translated into program and as they evolve and enlarge, they are almost certain to indicate what next steps should and can be taken. Not only will the student profit from this reorientation; research itself is likely to rest on a more substantial foundation if it grows out from, but remains attached to, the heart of the undergraduate school instead of being established in a center. The disconcerting truth is gradually being borne in on us that "centers," by virtue of their considerable detachment from a parent, frequently do not remain centers of vitality but gradually become centers of isolation.

From the point of view of giving the student more training in research than he has previously had, several current developments in legal education are distinctly promising. Seminars are likely to become increasingly popular. Their growth will un-doubtedly be accompanied by emphasis upon student investiga-tion. Legislative drafting may find a recognized place for itself within the curriculum. If so, it can furnish distinctive occasion for training in research. Should the problem and clinical methods be made established forms of instruction, they would provide excellent opportunity for pertinent research. Through the tutorial system, research could easily be encouraged.

Although all of these developments are as yet in initial stages, they have demonstrated their potential usefulness in providing a way whereby search, examination, and correlation of other than judicial opinions can be readily achieved. Moreover, as greater flexibility develops in selecting the content of curricula and teaching methods, research can itself be made an instrumentality not only for providing the student with a much needed technique but for enhancing the effectiveness of many courses. Already the law schools at the University of Nebraska and the University of Chicago have made formal plans to utilize research for the training of students in an essential skill, as a recognized method of instruction, and as a way of obtaining new materials needed in specific courses or outside the law school.

Research thus tied to the classroom and the clinical laboratory in a reciprocal process of giving and taking may prove significantly vital. But soundness as well as vitality is requisite. Hence research designed to serve current practical needs must lead out to the stimulation of more "fundamental research" on which it can draw. Large productive efforts in viewing the interrelatedness of various aspects of social or economic problems, and in framing basic working principles are essential. Without them, the school engaged in the more immediate research task is likely to find that its "solution" of a problem is scarcely a solution at all, because it has failed to consider the entire matrix within which the specific problem is embedded, or because it has bottomed its research on unproved assumptions that are later discovered fallacious.

IMPLEMENTATION OF PROPOSED CHANGES

For any considerable expansion of the intellectual horizon of legal education, at least three things are prerequisite: larger financial resources, teaching staffs, and research and clinical facilities; an over-all Plan for each school; and a more affirmative attitude toward the task of law and government.

Society has long assumed that the needs of a law school are a building, a few instructors of professorial rank, and a small, specialized library. So unacquainted with legal education has the public been that it would probably take for granted that only enlarged enrollments would require appreciable increase in staff or facilities. As long as instruction was confined to the textbook and its successor, the casebook, a school could manage to exist not too badly if given the minimum essentials. Classes were almost inevitably much too large, contact between professor and student too formal, and reliance upon the classbook too great. Nevertheless, the situation was not intolerable and was not emphatically protested either by the several deans or by the Association of American Law Schools. This was the standard provision which was made—and is still made in the vast majority of schools—for legal education. Its only virtues have been that the professorial salaries have been very good as compared with others in the university, except those in the medical school, and the number of teaching hours has been small in relation to hours in the academic college. Hence some opportunity has been provided for writing, research, and advisory functions outside the school.

The twenty-three institutions visited by the writer between 1939 and 1941 were among the financially most fortunate law schools of the country. Yet, many of them had budgets of less than $100,000, and those with budgets of more than $200,000 could perhaps have been counted on the fingers of one hand. Enrollments ranged from slightly fewer than 100 in two schools to nearly 1,400 in one, but the median was approximately 250. The professional staff, including the librarian, sometimes an assistant librarian, and often a few part-time instructors, averaged about fifteen. The somewhat larger income of the schools at present has not appreciably improved the situation because of the excessive rise in costs and in student registration. The schools, moreover, expect drastic reductions in fees once the great flood of veterans has been graduated.

To attempt to provide professional education for some 250 students of the kind that has been envisaged in this monograph cannot be done with double the budget now available to most of these twenty-three schools. The training that has been contem-

plated here requires library facilities rich in social science and
non-legal materials of many kinds, as well as in public law materials that most schools at present possess only in limited amounts.
Even though the university library were to be utilized far more
extensively than in the past, it could but partially meet this need.
The training, furthermore, requires the equipping and staffing
of a clinical laboratory, and perhaps a legal [aid] clinic in
addition. Even though research were oriented around the student
and legal education and were more modest than that expected
of a "center," considerable funds for professional staff, supplies,
research materials, field trips, counsel, publication, and secretarial assistance would be requisite.

An enriched curriculum needs money in reasonable amounts
for engaging the services of occasional lecturers and consultants,
and for permitting both faculty and students to make essential
trips whether for clinical observation, apprenticeship training,
or intellectual stimulus. Of very real importance in any broadened course of study is the bringing of persons—particularly non-
lawyers—from the university or elsewhere for an afternoon, a
semester, or a year, and the sending of faculty and students to
examine, if not to participate in, the work of the lawyer as counselor, mediator, negotiator, draftsman, advocate, judge, government attorney, and administrator. Equally important is it for
faculty and students to see examples of corporate endeavor,
whether the TVA or the Texas oil industry, that pose economic,
social, and political questions illustrative of those with which
lawyers have to wrestle. Soundly conducted observational trips
and properly designed moving pictures would do more than
months of reading to make the realities of the lawyer's task
within the physical and cultural setting of America "come alive."
The process of legal education is constantly retarded for the very
reason that students, and also faculty, have not had sufficiently
broad life experience on which to build. Anyone who doubts the
validity of that statement, should ask Professor Karl N. Llewellyn
what he gained from his first trip to the TVA and what the implications were for him as a law teacher.

Above everything, the regular salaried staff of the school must be drastically enlarged if legal education is to move forward in perspective and accomplishment. Individualized instruction in writing, drafting, research, the solving of theoretical problems, and the handling of actual cases demands the services of many persons. Preferably these persons should be of widely varying ages and kinds of experience if the best possible balance of vitality, diversity of interest and point of view, and seasoned judgment is to be maintained. Besides the teaching and research staffs, other personnel are equally requisite. Students need expert guidance and counseling not merely in matters of curriculum but in relating themselves to the "purpose" of the law school and of law practice. Such guidance no busy dean's office can provide and no committee of instructors should be expected to offer. Finally any law school that embarks on an expanded type of education must have adequate library, clerical, and secretarial personnel available at all times. Perhaps nothing reveals so instantly to the visitor the distressing paucity of funds as do the library staffs of perhaps three persons and the two or three secretaries, all wretchedly paid, who constitute the entire auxiliary service of the majority of law schools. Even in the most fortunate institutions where the librarian, generally a lawyer, draws a professorial salary and where more numerous and competent library assistants and secretaries are available, few instructors are able to call for stenographic or research aid whenever needed.

About such needs society has almost no knowledge, and universities themselves are most inadequately informed. A university president was recently complaining bitterly that further equipment for electrical laboratories alone would cost his institution $90,000. If the equipment were available for purchase, however, it would be bought immediately. Science and medicine have had phenomenal success in educating persons outside those fields to an understanding that the professional education of scientists and physicians, if good, is expensive, and, if not good, may be positively dangerous to the public. The trend of history, and the very fact that the laity can see, if not evaluate the importance of, the

physical equipment used in such teaching institutions have contributed much to the layman's education. But let no one think
that science and medicine have not made long and vigilant efforts
to further this educational process.

The law schools, individually or collectively, have undertaken
no such a program of education, partly because they have not
clarified their own thinking about what the curriculum should be
and hence what funds would be needed. Therefore, when deans
have pressed for small increments to their budget, policy-making
officials have tended to view them as persons representing a
partisan interest, whose requests should be scrutinized with great
care. Although this monograph is not the appropriate place for
any extended statement about the financing of legal education,
the writer wishes to interpolate the outline of one interview with
an administrator in a great state university whose function was
comparable in nature to that of the federal director of the Bureau
of the Budget. The interview casts a revealing light upon the
educational problem with which law schools (and the legal
profession) are faced.

At the time of the writer's visit, the administrator was greatly
worried about his university's medical school. It had not ranked
so high as had been hoped in the examination made by the Council on Medical Education and Hospitals of the American Medical
Association. Although it was already receiving annually some
eight times as much as was the law school, the university could
see no way of raising it to the relative position desired among the
then 66 degree-conferring medical schools of the country without
increasing its budget by approximately 50 per cent.

The writer questioned whether even this large increase would
accomplish what was wished. So vast have been the improvements in medical education since 1910 that the number of distinguished institutions is today relatively large and competition
among them is very keen. Why did the university feel the need
"to place" in the first ten medical schools? With training so effectively controlled by the Council on Medical Education, was the
university not able to provide society with some guarantee of a

reasonable degree of proficiency short of saying that it ranked near the very top? Was the university attempting to raise all of its other divisions to a level as high as that of the medical school? If not, was the allocation to medical education being made at their expense? What objective tests were used to determine how funds *should* be distributed? Was the law-school budget reasonably adequate to meet current needs? Did the law school contemplate changes in the curriculum which would make greatly enlarged demands on the exchequer? If so, could they be accommodated and yet permit the medical school its increased allowance?

It must be clearly understood that the writer was not arguing against the adequate financing of medical education. She has some understanding of how necessarily expensive is the operation of teaching laboratories, hospitals, and clinics. Moreover, she greatly respects that profession which has stated its case so clearly and incisively that the response of the university world and of the public is magnanimous. What she wanted to know was whether legal education—not as it has been largely conducted but as it might function were training focused squarely upon aiding the prospective lawyer better to fulfill a social obligation of great complexity and immeasurable consequences—could hope to compete for attention with medical education when allocation of funds was being made. The administrator's answer was unmistakable in its implication: he personally had long thought law as important, perhaps even more important, than medicine, but he would never have expected that a "disinterested" person would tell him the same thing or would plead for an increase in appropriations for legal education.

At the earliest possible moment a thorough, completely objective study of the existent financial situation in legal education ought to be made. Such a study is within the province of the Association of American Law Schools or the Section of Legal Education and Admissions to the Bar of the American Bar Association. Whatever its sponsorship, it should have the support and co-operation of both bodies. The study should be immediately followed by an educational program designed to make known, not only to the entire bar and bench but to all interested laity, exactly what is being paid for legal education, what can be provided for that sum, and what is requisite for a type of professional education that will fit men with the maximum of efficiency for the essential functions not only of legal craftsman but of policy-maker and administrator.

University officials need to be faced promptly with this challenge—a challenge which no individual dean can reasonably or appropriately make. It is a safe assumption that more adequate financing of legal education would not be done at the expense at least of the scientific and medical schools. Their voices are too strong to permit such an occurrence. If the university treasury could not bear the increased demand upon it, additional funds would have to be sought from public and private sources. This is a rich and potentially generous country. But no considerable contributions can be expected either through taxation or gifts until society has been instructed in what is needed and why. Should the university, law school, or bar association not feel competent to undertake the task of interpretation and request for funds, specialists are available who have successfully raised large sums for purposes far less important and sometimes even less easy to explain to the public.

Of almost as much importance to the future of legal education as an adequate budget and staff is a working Plan, which has been democratically formulated through the joint efforts of the faculty and to which at least a majority of the faculty subscribes. No law school can move ahead rapidly or with some singleness of purpose until it has a blueprint that charts its aims and synthesizes proposals and experiments for achieving those aims.

Whenever large, productive, and co-ordinated activity has appeared within a law school, it has generally stemmed from the conference table where the teaching staff spent many arduous days in attempting to communicate their ideas to each other, in reconciling conflicts, and in drafting the consensus of the group.

The vitality achieved at Columbia and Yale before 1930 and at
Chicago a few years later can be attributed in no small measure
to prolonged efforts to view legal education as a unified process
whose purpose was the preparation of lawyers to function within
a social, rather than a more strictly legal, environment.

Such efforts greatly transcend those usually made by the curriculum committee with which most schools are provided. Sometimes a school is able to call upon the ability and devotion of a
Paul R. Hays, who as chairman of a committee on curriculum
was willing to struggle during the later years of the war to foresee
how postwar education at Columbia might be improved. Usually,
however, these committees are occupied with examination of
fragments of law training or with necessary but routine matters.
Rarely does a Plan emerge.

Sometimes a carefully drawn, broad-gauged Plan has issued
from the office of the dean. One such Plan was considered almost
radical when instituted nearly twenty years ago. It still furnishes
a curriculum well in advance of that of most schools. Another,
recently formulated, is of exceptional significance in its emphasis
upon public law and government functions. Although these Plans
are extremely valuable in themselves, they probably should not
be used as a pattern in methodology by other schools. For the
very reason that the dean is willing to assume the responsibility,
the several instructors tend to feel that they may be excused from
participation in the planning process. They execute the Plan with
enthusiasm, but they do not gain the experience or the broader
interest that comes from being a party to the process. Creative
ideas concerning the philosophy and implementation of legal
education begin and are likely to end in the dean's office.

In the vast majority even of the schools visited there is as yet
nothing that can be designated as a Plan, spelled with a capital
letter. Important changes in the curriculum have been made by
reducing the number of small courses offered, enriching the
teaching materials, and adding new courses. But these changes
have been adaptations, little by little, to current situations. Most
often they have resulted from the imagination and initiative of

the individual instructor who succeeded in winning a vote of confidence in his undertaking from faculty colleagues. They are not based upon an over-all examination of the function of the particular school and a prepared work sheet of methods for translating function into curriculum.

If a school is to grow both initially and continuously, the Plan must be conceived of, not as something finished, but as a first scene in a never finished act. It must be flexible enough to permit changes, interpolations, deletions, and reorientation, as experience indicates. Were it allowed to become static, it would be worse than none, for even individual attempts which have proved richly helpful in the past might be stifled.

Once a working Plan has been drawn, the law school should find its position greatly strengthened not only within its own walls but in its relations with the university administration, the bar, and the public. At present there are schools that cannot make an impressive request for sponsorship or for additional funds, except to offset higher costs. They have no other proposal to present than that for the continuation of their present limited curriculum. The university is likely to think that sufficient provision is already being made for such continuation; the imagination of the bar and the public is not stirred. But let the school have a blueprint of what it earnestly seeks to do and let it transform enough of that blueprint into an actual demonstration of its intention and ability, and it will then be in a position to make effective representation to those who can contribute funds, advisory assistance, and prestige.

In a century that has moved so far in the direction of planning, legal education cannot afford to neglect this instrumentality for advancing its inner growth and for rallying external support.

Finally, one of the most significant ways whereby the law school can effect true enlargement and enrichment of legal education is through a more affirmative attitude toward law itself, toward government, toward the lawyer's role in government, and toward the law-school's responsibility for training the lawyer to play that role.

Law has been viewed by society, and even to a considerable degree by the law schools, chiefly as a form of social control which imposes limitations upon what would otherwise be "free" activity. Progress is generally assumed to have been achieved by alterations in economic, social, and cultural institutions. Thus the concept of law has been largely negative: negative in its emphasis upon prohibitions, and negative in its not being included among the primary means for social change. But governments everywhere in the United States have been continuously moving, with differing degrees of conviction and effectiveness, in the direction of planning to meet social needs, whether for education, health and other social services, or for preserving and utilizing our natural resources. Every plan which a government has transformed into operating program has been achieved through the instrumentality of law.

Therefore, any philosophy of law which is cognizant of reality must, to quote a pertinent statement by Professor Fuchs, "recognize the function of law as the servant of social needs and emphasize the distinctive contribution of law to meeting those needs. Only a legal profession conscious of both can combine in suitable proportion humility, self-respect, and insistence upon the values of efficiency, liberty, and justice under governmental processes." Only a law school which stresses the affirmative purpose of law, Fuchs might have added, can give the student that springboard for creative action that not only is craved by youth but is indispensable to our national life.

Even more negative has been the attitude of the law-school world toward government and its purposeful role. Dean Green once wrote that in "about 1930 we finally came to realize that government could no longer be regarded as a flaccid sort of an evil, but that government is society's instrumentality through which the processes of law are made to work for the social and economic good of the whole group."[1] Unquestionably awareness of the importance and power of this instrumentality has broad-

[1] The Annual Report of the Dean of the School of Law, Northwestern University, 1939, p. 4.

ened and deepened. Perception increased throughout the 1930's and was enlarged during the war years by the occasion provided many teachers to participate in government.

Some residue nevertheless remains of the earlier view of government "as a flaccid sort of evil" or worse. But what is more disturbing, for the professional education of students, is the larger lack of positive interest in, and concern about, that stupendous agency which at once keeps the nation from falling overnight into absolute confusion, and which guarantees to its citizens an extraordinarily wide variety of benefits. Recognition of "government as society's instrumentality" may exist, but unless recognition is translated into affirmative action, it avails little. The time is more than ripe for every law school to make formal provision that *all* students be provided with objective and detailed analysis of the strengths and weaknesses of government, of its relative virtues and vices as compared with other large-scale industry, and of the extent to which it achieves or fails to achieve designated purposes.

In the estimation of the late Joseph B. Eastman and Harold D. Smith, whose opinions can scarcely be disregarded, government would come off surprisingly well in such an analysis. Two decades ago when Eastman was speaking to the National Association of Railroad and Utilities Commissioners, he remarked that most taxpayers, including many who ought to be better informed have a wholly inadequate idea of what they are getting for their money.[1] The tendency is to regard taxes as a debit without any offsetting credit. "Now my observation of the public service . . . is that with all the defects of that service, and there are many of them and some scandals just as there are in private business, the true story of its accomplishments would disclose an astonishing and magnificent net balance on the credit side." After recounting the many public services from education to parks that we take almost for granted, Eastman made the following observation: "If an advertising agency of the caliber of that which serves the

---

[1] "The Public Service," in National Association of Railroad and Utilities Commissioners Proceedings of the Thirty-Eighth Annual Convention, 1927, pp. 46–47.

Bell telephone system were given the job of exploiting the accomplishments of the scientists and engineers of the Federal government in the fields of agricultural research, irrigation, forestry, standards, the geological survey and the like, I believe that agency would be bewildered by the multitude and magnitude of its opportunity."

Eighteen years later Harold D. Smith, out of his exceptional experience as director of the pivotal Bureau of the Budget, wrote these sentences[1]:

The war tested the skills of both public and private management as they had never been tested before. Everyone is familiar with the success of private management in meeting the demands made upon it. Governmental management certainly has met the challenge equally well, far more ably than many people would believe. Perhaps in government we had farther to go to begin with, but a strong case can be made that in recent years government has progressed more rapidly in management than has business. Already business can profit greatly from the experience of government in this field. Private managers do not often recognize this important fact. However, if government continues its present rate of progress, business before long will realize it can learn from government many valuable lessons in large-scale management.

One reason for this is that the vastness of governmental undertakings provides a ground for experimentation in all sorts of management techniques. Government is so huge and so complex that the problems it presents to management are different in both size and nature from those confronting private management. In effect, government provides a tremendous laboratory in which many variables can and must be tested to a degree impossible in private industry.

In the face of the accusations of inefficiency customarily heaped upon the federal government, Smith's testament of affirmation is so unexpected and breath-taking that it recalls the unabashed enthusiasm of J. B. Priestley's essay on the Grand Canyon. Priestley ended that essay, one will remember, by declaring that every morning of his life every official of the federal government ought to draw himself up and with great pride but equally great humility remind himself, "*I* am on the staff of the Grand Canyon."

[1] The Management of Your Government. Published by Whittlesey House, copyright, 1945, by McGraw-Hill Book Co., New York, pp. 25–26.

If the law schools were to point to government as the guardian of many a kind of Grand Canyon on whose staff the lawyer could be proud to be found, and were then to bend their best efforts to preparing men and women for that guardianship and its further strengthening, not even the greater financial remuneration of the Wall Streets of America would put government at a disadvantage in recruiting personnel of outstanding competence and excellent professional training.

The story is told that Wendell Willkie began his long negotiations with David Lilienthal over the Commonwealth and Southern Corporation, which ended in mutual respect and friendship, with a feeling of distrust. Why should Lilienthal be concerned with the TVA when he could earn twenty times as much in private practice? Why did he seem interested only in public service? The answer—whose truth Willkie later made applicable to himself—was simply that Lilienthal had been given one of the most important jobs, in its implications for this country and scores of other countries, that had ever been entrusted to an American.

A great opportunity and a similarly great responsibility still lie ahead for legal education. They are the task of implanting conviction in faculty and students, both of whom have been conditioned by the opinion of a nation that has never entirely grown to repose abiding faith in its government, that government *is* important; that through no other means, perhaps, may the lawyer so largely determine his own future and that of all of us.